VOGUE® KNITTING
AMERICAN COLLECTION

VOGUE KNITTING

AMERICAN COLLECTION

Edited by Trisha Malcolm

THE BUTTERICK® PUBLISHING COMPANY
NEW YORK

B

THE BUTTERICK® PUBLISHING COMPANY
161 Avenue of the Americas
New York, New York 10013

Editor-in-Chief
Trisha Malcolm

Editor
Annemarie McNamara

Art Director
Christine Lipert

Associate Art Director
Chi Ling Moy

Designer
Lee Ryder

Managing Editor
Jean Guirguis

Copy Editor
Suzie Elliott

Editorial Coordinator
Kathleen Kelly

Yarn Editor
Teva Durham
Veronica Manno

Technical Editor
Jacquelyn Smyth

Contributing Editors
Lila Chin
Carla Scott
Charlotte Parry

Photo Archivist
Sherry Onna Handlin

Production Managers
Lillian Esposito
Winnie Hinish

Technical Advisor
David Joinnides

Executive Vice President and Publisher, Butterick® Company, Inc
Art Joinnides

President and CEO, Butterick® Company, Inc
Jay H. Stein

1 3 5 7 9 10 8 6 4 2

Library of Congress Cataloging-in-Publication Data
Vogue Knitting: American Collection / Edited by Trisha Malcolm
p.   cm.

ISBN: 1-57389-020-0.
1. Knitting–United States–Patterns. II. Title: American Collection
TT819.U6 V64 2000   00-040365
746.43'20432-dc21   CIP

Introduction

Over the years, *Vogue® Knitting* magazine has had the opportunity to work with many of the most recognized talents in American hand-knit design. While some of these designers had already made their mark in the knitting and yarn industry, others were relatively unknown before their work arrived on our magazine pages. Since then, our editors and readers have been able to chart the burgeoning careers of these gifted craftswomen. Issue after issue, year after year, we've benefited from their expertise and learned how to put that special quality into our own knitting.

This collection is a celebration of these fabulous designers. Michele Rose, Kristin Nicholas, Norah Gaughan, Mari Lynn Patrick, Pam Allen, Nicky Epstein, Deborah Newton, Lily Chin—all great designers and great women who deserve to be singled out and recognized for their enormous contribution to the field of knitting.

And while each designer has pursued her craft in a very individual way, the end result is always the same: top-notch fashion and unbeatable technical style. It was enlightening to learn from them how their individual patterns were conceived and developed—in fact, many of the techniques employed by today's knitters were unheard of before these designers applied their wisdom and wit to this time-honored craft. Thus it is fitting that the book concludes with a chapter devoted to Elizabeth Zimmermann, the woman who revolutionized knitting in the 20th century, and her daughter, Meg Swansen, who's taking it into the 21st.

Creating a book devoted to women so passionate about their craft was inspiring. Our editors worked closely with each designer, going back over almost two decades of publications to find the best of their work. Our entire staff joined in on the project, eager to take this book from dream to reality. While our technical editors got busy preparing the patterns, our yarn editors were hard at work making sure all of the yarns were up to date. We also dug up the original film, just to make sure we had the very best photographs to illustrate the projects featured.

Whether it's the sublime fit, the masterful detail, or the polished styling, the work of these designers stands apart and is why we gave them the title of Master Knitters of the '90s. Now you can learn their secrets and discover how to achieve the professional quality and designer look their work embodies. Of course, these are by no means all of the great designers featured in *Vogue® Knitting*—a heart-felt "thank-you" to all the designers who have given so much of themselves to this craft we so dearly love.

For the first time ever, the works of America's most talented designers together in one stunning volume.

Table of Contents

● Introduction 5

● Before You Begin 8
  Yarn Selection
  Gauge
  Reading Patterns
  Following Charts
  Knitting Terms and Abbreviations
  Needle Chart

● Pam Allen 10
  Mother & Daughter Cherry Cardigans 12
  Crazy Quilt Jacket 18
  Ribbed Pullover 22
  Child's Cardigan 25

● Lily Chin 28
  Reversible Rib Shawl 30
  Colorful Caps 32
  Embroidered Cardigan 34
  Mohair Aran 38
  Draped Pullover 41

● Nicky Epstein 44
  Tapestry Afghan & Hat 46
  Diamond Aran 50
  Paper-Doll Sweater 54
  Chenille Leaf Pullover 57

● Norah Gaughan 60
  Cabled Vest 62
  A-Line Tunic 65
  Ribbed Cardigan 69
  Dragonfly Pullover 72

● Kristin Nicholas 76
  His-and-Hers Pullovers 78

  Leaf Pullover 84
  Classic Guernsey 87
  Embroidered Pillow 90

● Deborah Newton 92
  Pleated Pullover with Bows 94
  Cashmere Pullover 97
  Shawl-Collared Cardigan 100
  Pink Pullover 103
  Gauntlet Gloves & Hat 106

● Mari Lynn Patrick 110
  Summer Tunic 112
  Summer Dress 115
  Tailored Jacket 118
  Wrapped Pullover 121
  Cashmere Shawl 124

● Michele Rose 126
  Fair Isle Pullover & Cap 128
  Western Jacket 132
  Patchwork Cardigan 135
  Fair Isle Pullover 138

● Meg Swansen &
  Elizabeth Zimmermann 142
  First American Aran 144
  Twisted-Stitch Cap 147
  The Moebius Ring 150
  The Tomten Jacket 152
  Garter-Stitch Blanket 154
  Best Baby Sweater 156

● Resources 158

● Acknowledgements 160

Before You Begin

This book was designed as an anthology of patterns. For more precise technical explanation, refer to Vogue Knitting—The Ultimate Knitting Book *(New York: Pantheon Books). See page 159 to order.*

YARN SELECTION

Some of the yarns, or colors, used in the original designer patterns are no longer available. We have provided substitute yarns readily available in the U.S. and Canada at the time of printing. The Resources on page 158 lists addresses of yarn distributors—contact them for the name of a retailer in your area or for mail-order information.

If you wish to substitute a yarn, check the gauge carefully to ensure the finished garment will knit to the correct measurements. To facilitate yarn substitution, *Vogue Knitting* grades yarn by the standard stitch gauge obtained in stockinette stitch. There is a grading number in the Materials section of each pattern. Look for a substitute yarn that falls into the same category—the suggested gauge on the ball band should be comparable to that on the Yarn Symbols Chart (right).

After successfully gauge-swatching in a substitute yarn, you'll need to determine yarn requirements. First, find the total length of the original yarn in the pattern (multiply number of balls by yards/meters per ball). Divide this figure by the new yards/meters per ball (listed on the ball band). Round up to the next whole number. The answer is the number of balls required.

GAUGE

To ensure a successful project, always knit a gauge swatch before beginning. Normally, gauge is measured over a four-inch (10cm) square. Using the needles and yarn suggested, cast on enough stitches to knit a square at least this size. Gauge is usually given in stockinette stitch, but if the pattern calls for a specific stitch, work this stitch for the swatch. Measure stitches carefully with a ruler or gauge tool. If the swatch is smaller than the stated gauge (more stitches per inch/cm), try larger needles. If it is larger (fewer stitches per inch/cm), use smaller needles. Before proceeding, experiment with needle size until the gauge exactly matches the one given.

If a pattern calls for knitting in the round, it may tighten the gauge, so if the gauge was measured on a flat swatch, take another reading after beginning the project.

READING PATTERNS

Each pattern is rated for technical ability.

YARN SYMBOLS

The following numbers 1-6 represent a range of stitch gauges. Note that these numbers correspond to the standard gauge in stockinette stitch.

1 FINE WEIGHT
(29-32 stitches per 4"/10cm)
Includes baby and fingering yarns, and some of the heavier crochet cottons.

2 LIGHTWEIGHT
(25-28 stitches per 4"/10cm)
Includes sport yarn, sock yarn, UK 4-ply and lightweight DK yarns.

3 MEDIUM WEIGHT
(21-24 stitches per 4"/10cm)
Includes DK and worsted, the most commonly used knitting yarns.

4 MEDIUM-HEAVY WEIGHT
(17-20 stitches per 4"/10cm)
Also called heavy worsted or Aran.

5 BULKY WEIGHT
(13-16 stitches per 4"/10cm)
Also called chunky. Includes heavier Icelandic yarns.

6 EXTRA-BULKY WEIGHT
(9-12 stitches per 4"/10cm)
The heaviest yarns available.

Choose a pattern that fits within your experience range. Read all instructions thoroughly before starting to knit a gauge swatch and again before beginning a project. Familiarize yourself with all abbreviations (see Knitting Terms and Abbreviations, opposite). Refer to the *Vogue Knitting* book for clear explanations of any stitches or techniques you may not be familiar with.

Generally, patterns are written in several sizes. The smallest appears first, and figures for larger sizes are given in parentheses. Where only one figure appears, it applies to all sizes. Highlight numbers pertaining to your size before beginning.

Knitted measurements are the dimensions of the garment after all the pieces have been sewn together. Usually, three measurements are given: finished chest; finished length; and sleeve width at upper arm. The finished chest measurement is the width around the entire sweater at the underarm. For cardigans, the width is determined with the front bands buttoned. Finished length is measured from the highest point of the shoulder to the bottom of the ribbing. Sleeve width is measured at the upper arm, after all increases have been worked and before any cap shaping takes place.

Schematics are a valuable tool for determining size selection and proper fit. Schematics are scale drawings showing the dimensions of the finished knitted pieces.

Work figures given inside brackets the number of times stated afterward. Directions immediately following an asterisk are to be repeated the given number of times. If the instructions call for working even, work in the same pattern stitch without increasing or decreasing.

KNITTING TERMS AND ABBREVIATIONS

approx approximately

beg begin(ning)

bind off Used to finish an edge and keep stitches from unraveling. Lift the first stitch over the second, the second over the third, etc. (UK: cast off)

cast on A foundation row of stitches placed on the needle in order to begin knitting.

CC contrast color

ch chain(s)

cm centimeter(s)

cont continue(ing)

dc double crochet (UK: tr-treble)

dec decrease(ing)—Reduce the stitches in a row (knit 2 together).

dpn double-pointed needle(s)

foll follow(s)(ing)

g gram(s)

garter stitch Knit every row. Circular knitting: knit one round, then purl one round.

hdc half-double crochet (UK: htr-half treble)

inc increase(ing)—Add stitches in a row (knit into the front and back of a stitch).

k knit

k2tog knit 2 stitches together

lp(s) loops(s)

LH left hand

m meter(s)

M1 make one stitch—With the needle tip, lift the strand between the last stitch worked and next stitch on the left-hand needle and knit into the back of it. One stitch has been added.

MC main color

mm millimeter(s)

oz ounce(s)

p purl

p2tog purl 2 stitches together

pat pattern

pick up and knit (purl) Knit (or purl) into the loops along an edge.

pm place markers—Place or attach a loop of contrast yarn or purchased stitch marker as indicated.

psso pass slip stitch over

rem remain(s)(ing)

rep repeat

rev St st reverse Stockinette stitch—Purl right-side rows, knit wrong-side rows. Circular knitting: purl all rounds. (UK: reverse stocking stitch)

rnd(s) round(s)

RH right hand

RS right side(s)

sc single crochet (UK: dc - double crochet)

sk skip

SKP Slip 1, knit 1, pass slip stitch over knit 1

sl slip—An unworked stitch made by passing a stitch from the left-hand to the right-hand needle as if to purl.

sl st slip stitch (UK: single crochet)

ssk slip, slip, knit—Slip next 2 stitches knitwise, one at a time, to right-hand needle. Insert tip of left-hand needle into fronts of these stitches from left to right. Knit them together. One stitch has been decreased.

st(s) stitch(es)

St st Stockinette stitch—Knit right-side rows, purl wrong-side rows. Circular knitting: knit all rounds. (UK: stocking stitch)

tbl through back of loop

tog together

WS wrong side(s)

wyif with yarn in front

wyib with yarn in back

work even Continue in pattern without increasing or decreasing. (UK: work straight)

yd yard(s)

yo yarn over—Make a new stitch by wrapping the yarn over the right-hand needle. (UK: yfwd, yon, yrn)

* repeat directions following * as many times as indicated.

[ ] Repeat directions inside brackets as many times as indicated.

FOLLOWING CHARTS

Charts are a convenient way to follow colorwork, lace, cable, and other stitch patterns. *Vogue Knitting* stitch charts utilize the universal language of "symbolcraft." Each symbolcraft symbol represents the stitch as it appears on the right side of the work. For example, the symbol for the knit stitch is a vertical line and the symbol for a purl stitch is a horizontal one. On right-side rows, work the stitches as they appear on the chart—knitting the vertical lines and purling the horizontal ones. When reading wrong-side rows, work the opposite of what is shown; that is, purl the vertical lines and knit the horizontal ones.

Each square on a chart represents one stitch and each horizontal row of squares equals a row or round. When knitting back and forth on straight needles, right-side rows (RS) are read right to left, wrong-side rows (WS) are read from left to right, bottom to top. When knitting in rounds on circular needles, read charts from right to left on every round, repeating any stitch and row repeats as directed in the pattern. Posting a self-adhesive note under the working row is an easy way to keep track on a chart.

Sometimes, only a single repeat of the pattern is charted. Heavy lines drawn through the entire chart indicate a repeat. The lines are the equivalent of an asterisk (*) or brackets [] used in written instructions.

KNITTING NEEDLES

US	METRIC	UK
0	2mm	14
1	2.25mm	13
	2.5mm	
2	2.75mm	12
	3mm	11
3	3.25mm	10
4	3.5mm	
5	3.75mm	9
	4mm	8
6		
7	4.5mm	7
8	5mm	6
9	5mm	5
10	6mm	4
10½	6.5mm	3
	7mm	2
	7.5mm	1
11	8mm	0
13	9mm	00
15	10mm	000

Pam Allen

Pam Allen remembers well the first time she submitted designs to *Vogue Knitting*. "They all came back," she admits, "but one came with a little note attached from the editor, Nancy Thomas, saying, 'We really liked this one. It came really close to being a final. Keep up the good work.' In fact, I have that letter around here. Just to have some acknowledgement that something had gotten that close was so encouraging, because *Vogue Knitting* is like the pinnacle, if you can make it in *Vogue Knitting* you've made it. So I kept trying and trying, and finally they bought a little girl's sweater." That was the start of a long and fruitful working relationship between magazine and designer that exists to this day.

Surprisingly, Pam Allen did not set out to become a knitwear designer. In fact, after earning her master's degree in linguistics, Pam envisioned herself traveling the world teaching English. But her natural creative talent and interest in fashion and textiles kept drawing her back to knitting, a skill she first learned as a child growing up in Chicago. She believes one of her grandmothers taught her to knit, but she doesn't really recall clearly anymore. "As long as I can remember, I liked to make things," she explains. "For many years sewing is what I did. I always liked knits, but it wasn't until high school that I began seriously knitting." She recalls that back then, fashion magazines like *Mademoiselle* and *Glamour* published knitting patterns. "So I started knitting with the idea of

making something that would look a little trendy," she says.

Pam never studied design formally, but instead developed her skills on the job. Taking a break from college, she worked briefly as a seamstress, then opened her own boutique, called Mariposa, in 1970. After several years of working around the clock supporting her own business, Pam decided to return to school and earned first a bachelor's degree in French, then a master's degree in linguisitcs. It was during an academic year in Paris that her interest in knitting was reignited. She began to knit bountifully, drawing inspiration from the beautiful yarns and exquisite fashions found in the French capital.

After graduation, Pam began selling her sweaters at a local crafts cooperative. As her work gained popularity, she decided to further her knowledge of the craft by attending The National Needlework Association trade show in New York City. It was there that Pam's first big career break came. "I went to this trade show in New York, a yarn show," she recalls, "and as I was leaving to go back to the airport, I got into a cab with this lady who turned out to be Norma O'Leary, then fashion and crafts editor at *Family Circle*. When I told her what I did, she said, "Why don't you send me some of those little children's sweaters?" So I did. I sent three sweaters and she bought the designs for each one."

After her first patterns were published, Pam discovered

> "I think
> for anyone
> who knits,
> there's just
> something in
> the actual act
> of doing it
> that's very
> satisfying."

that she could make more money designing and publishing sweaters than selling them retail. "So I asked myself, well, there are all these other publications, who designs for those magazines? Somebody must!" she says. "I began querying these different magazines and I sent a design I particularly liked to *Vogue Knitting*. It must have been 1983. The editor I spoke with said, "We really don't work that way, but we do hold presentations where we introduce all the ideas and themes we're working on. Why don't you come?" So, once again, I flew down to New York for that one day."

The Crazy Quilt Cardigan, pictured on page 18, was one of the first adult designs chosen by the *Vogue Knitting* editors. "I was thrilled that they picked that," she says. "The theme was the Wild West and pioneers, and my grandmother was a real Missourian, a real Ozark lady. She did a lot of quilting, a lot of rag-rug making, and I think my appreciation of that kind of thing really came from her. So there was a sentimental aspect. I also like the idea of recycling things into another medium, going from one to another." Pam also enjoyed working collaboratively with the magazine editors. "The woman I worked with at *Vogue Knitting* was really helpful," she recalls. "We'd talk about different embroidery stitches and what I was doing." She remembers the editors suggesting a different shape for the cardigan, and she admits being pleased

with the result. "That's one of the nice things about working for a magazine," she says. "Sometimes it is frustrating when they change things, but most of the time I'm happy to compromise, and I learn sometimes by doing something differently."

Unlike many professional designers, Pam doesn't farm out her projects to other knitters. Instead, she prefers to knit each garment herself, developing and shaping her designs as they are being created. "I come up with a basic plan," she explains, "but I never really stick to it. I always change it some way or another, which is one of the reasons I don't have other people knit for me. I'm a terrible perfectionist." She acknowledges, though, that such a high degree of perfectionism limits the volume she can generate. And after years of hard work, Pam has reached a point in her career when she no longer designs on pure speculation, preferring instead to have editors call with a specific request.

An avid reader and devoted mom, Pam lives with her children in the picturesque coastal town of Camden, Maine. Much as she views knitting as an evolutionary process, Pam is reluctant to set a fixed plan for her own future. While she still enjoys contributing to publications like *Vogue Knitting*, she would like to explore other creative paths away from the demands of editors and yarn companies. What is assured, though, is that wherever Pam goes and whatever she does, success will certainly follow.

Something special for you and the little girl in your life! Cheery cherries are scattered over these sweet, retro-style cardigans. The matching sweaters are cropped short with set-in sleeves and rounded necklines. Shown in woman's size Small and child's size 6. The Mother & Daughter Cherry Cardigans first appeared in the Spring/Summer '95 issue of *Vogue Knitting*.

Mother & Daughter Cherry Cardigans

FOR INTERMEDIATE KNITTERS

SIZES
Woman's Version: To fit size X-Small (Small, Medium, Large).
Child's Version: To fit size 2 (4, 6, 8) or 21 (23, 25, 27)"/53 (58, 63, 68)cm chest. Directions are for smallest size with larger sizes in parentheses. If there is only one figure, it applies to all sizes.

KNITTED MEASUREMENTS
Woman's Version:
● Bust at underarm (buttoned) 36 (39, 42, 45)"/91.5 (99, 106.5, 114)cm.
● Length 17 (18, 19½, 21)"/43 (45.5, 49.5, 53)cm.
● Sleeve width at upper arm 16 (16, 17, 18)"/40.5 (40.5, 43, 45.5)cm.

Child's Version:
● Chest at underarm (buttoned) 26 (29, 32, 33½)"/66 (73.5, 81, 85)cm.
● Length 11½ (12¼, 12½, 13½)"/29 (31, 32, 34.5)cm.
● Sleeve width at upper arm 11 (12, 12, 13)"/28 (30.5, 30.5, 33)cm.

MATERIALS
Woman's Version:
● 5 (6, 7, 8) 1¾oz/50g skeins (each approx 127yd/115m) of Lang/Berroco, Inc. *Fiorina* (cotton 4) in #1508 beige (MC)
● Five ½"/13mm buttons
Child's Version:
● 3 (3, 4, 5) 1¾oz/50g skeins of Lang/Berroco, Inc. *Fiorina* in #1508 beige (MC)
● Five ⅜"/10mm buttons
Both Versions:
● 1 skein each in #1560 red (A), #1517 dark green (B), #1547 light green (C), #1524 grey (D), #1565 coral (E) and #1568 brown (F)
● One pair each sizes 2 and 5 (2.75 and 3.75mm) needles OR SIZE TO OBTAIN GAUGE
● Stitch markers and tapestry needle
Note
Two of the original colors used for this sweater are no longer available. Comparable color substitutions have been made, which are available at the time of printing.

GAUGE
25 sts and 32 rows to 4"/10cm over St st using size 5 (3.75mm) needles. FOR PERFECT FIT, TAKE TIME TO CHECK GAUGE.

Notes
1 When working child's sweater, work only complete motifs.
2 Work all sts outside charts in St st with MC.
3 Small colors can be knit in or worked in duplicate st on completed pieces.

WOMAN'S VERSION

BACK
With smaller needles and MC, cast on 111 (117, 123, 129) sts.
Rib row 1 (RS) *K1, p1; rep from * end k1.
Rib row 2 P1, *k1, p1; rep from * to end. Rep rows 1 and 2 for ¾"/2cm. Change to larger needles.
Beg body chart: Row 1 (RS) With MC, k1 (4, 7, 10), place marker (pm), work body chart over 109 sts, pm, k1 (4, 7, 10). Cont in pat through chart row 58 (66, 74, 82)—piece measures approx 8 (9, 10, 11)"/20.5 (23, 25.5, 28)cm from beg.

Armhole shaping
Cont in pats, bind off 6 sts at beg of next 2 rows, 2 sts at beg of next 2 rows, dec 1 st each side every other row twice—91 (97, 103, 109) sts. (Note: If necessary for your size, cont in St st with MC only once chart is complete.) Cont in pats until armhole measures 8 (8, 8½, 9)"/20.5 (20.5, 21.5, 23)cm.

Shoulder shaping
Bind off 6 (7, 7, 8) sts at beg of next 6 rows, then bind off 7 (6, 7, 6) sts at beg of next 2 rows. Bind off rem 41 (43, 47, 49) sts.

LEFT FRONT
With smaller needles and MC, cast on 55 (61, 67, 73) sts. Work rib as for back, end with a WS row. Change to larger needles.
Beg body chart: Row 1 (RS) With MC, k3 (9, 15, 21) sts, pm, work chart over 52 sts. Cont in pats as established until piece measures same length as back to armhole.

Armhole shaping
Cont in pats, bind off 6 sts at beg of next row, 2 sts from armhole edge once, then dec 1 st at armhole edge

every other row twice—45 (51, 57, 63) sts. Cont in pats until piece measures 15 (16, 17½, 19)"/38 (40.5, 44.5, 48)cm from beg, end with a RS row.

Neck and shoulder shaping

Next row (WS) Cont in pats, bind off 8 (10, 12, 12) sts (neck edge), work to end. Cont to bind off at neck edge, 4 (4, 5, 6) sts once, 3 (3, 4, 6) sts once, 2 (3, 4, 5) sts once, then dec 1 st at neck edge 3 (4, 4, 4) times, AT SAME TIME, when same length as back to shoulder, shape shoulder as for back.

RIGHT FRONT

Work as for left front, beg with st 56, work chart over 54 sts, k1 (7, 13, 19). Cont in pats as established, reversing all shaping.

SLEEVES

With smaller needles and MC, cast on 50 (50, 52, 54) sts. Work rib as for back, inc 1 st on last WS row—51 (51, 53, 55) sts. Change to larger needles.

Beg sleeve chart: Row 1 (RS) With MC, k2 (2, 3, 4), pm, work chart over 47 sts, k2 (2, 3, 4). Cont in pats, inc 1 st each side (working inc sts into chart pat or St st with MC) every 4th row 10 (10, 12, 14) times, every 6th row 15 times—101 (101, 107, 113) sts. Cont in pats until piece measures 18 (18, 18½, 19)"/45.5 (45.5, 47, 48)cm from beg.

Cap shaping

Bind off 6 sts at beg of next 2 rows, 4 sts at beg of next 6 rows, 3 sts at beg of next 6 rows, 2 sts at beg of next 4 rows, 4 sts at beg of next 2 rows, 5 sts at beg of next 2 rows—21 (21, 27, 33) sts.

Next row (RS) Ssk, bind off to last 2 sts, k2tog, bind off last st.

FINISHING

Block pieces. Sew shoulder seams.

Neckband

With RS facing, smaller needle and MC, pick up and k109 (117, 125, 133) sts around neck edge.

Next row (WS) *P1, k1; rep from *, end p1. Rib for ¾"/2cm. Bind off in rib.

Left front band

With RS facing, smaller needle and MC, beg at left front neck edge, pick up and k108 (118, 128, 140) sts along center front.

Next row (WS) P2, *k1, p1; rep from *, end p2. Cont in rib as for neckband. Bind off in rib. Place markers for 5 buttons, the first ½"/1.5cm from lower edge, the last ½"/1.5cm from neck edge and 3 others evenly between.

Right front band

Work 2 rows rib as for left band.

Row 3 (buttonhole row) (WS) *Rib to first marker, p2tog, yo twice; rep from * to end. Complete as for left band. Set in sleeves. Sew side and sleeve seams. Sew on buttons.

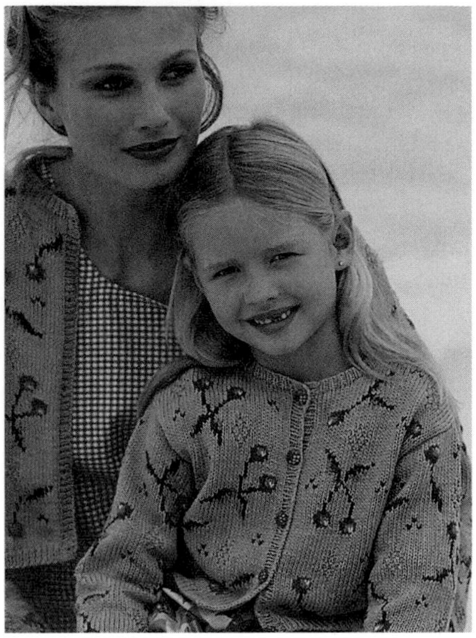

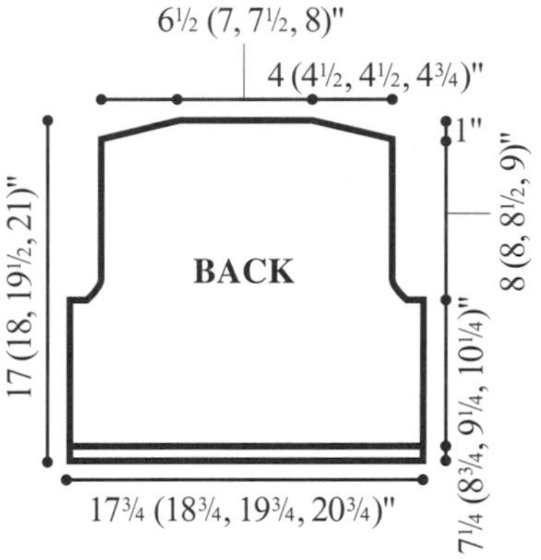
6½ (7, 7½, 8)"
4 (4½, 4½, 4¾)"
1"
8 (8, 8½, 9)"
17 (18, 19½, 21)"
BACK
7¼ (8¾, 9¼, 10¼)"
17¾ (18¾, 19¾, 20¾)"

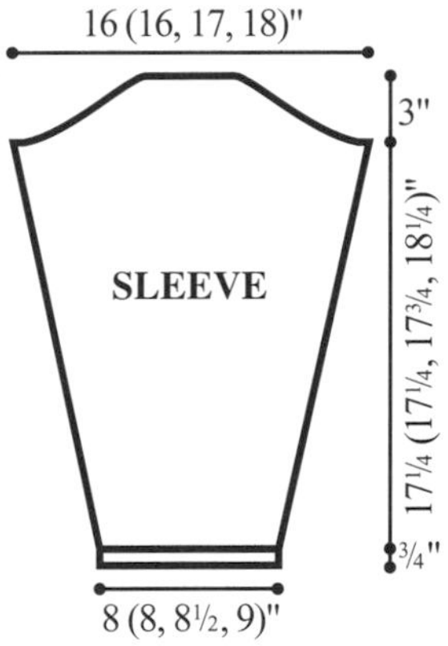
16 (16, 17, 18)"
3"
SLEEVE
17¼ (17¼, 17¾, 18¼)"
¾"
8 (8, 8½, 9)"

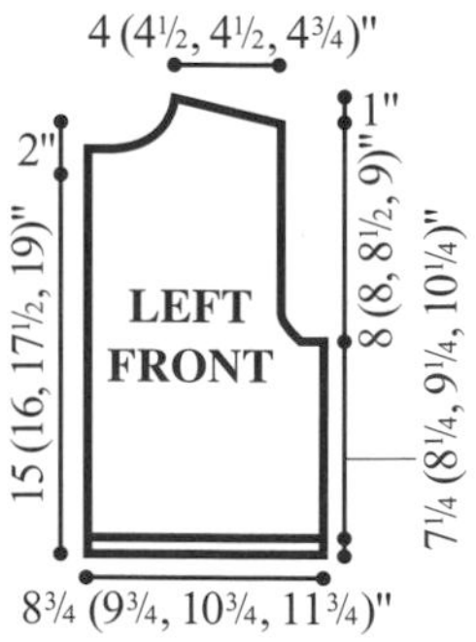
4 (4½, 4½, 4¾)"
2"
1"
8 (8, 8½, 9)"
15 (16, 17½, 19)"
LEFT
FRONT
7¼ (8¼, 9¼, 10¼)"
8¾ (9¾, 10¾, 11¾)"

CHILD'S VERSION

BACK

With smaller needles and MC, cast on 87 (93, 99, 107) sts. Work rib for ¾"/2cm as for woman's version. Change to larger needles. Beg and end as indicated, work through chart row 36 (38, 40, 44)—piece measures approx 5¼ (5½, 5¾, 6¼)"/13.5 (14, 14.5, 16)cm from beg.

Armhole shaping

Cont in chart pat, bind off 5 sts at beg of next 2 rows, 3 sts at beg of next 2 rows, dec 1 st each side every other row 3 times—65 (71, 77, 85) sts. Work through chart row 80 (86, 88, 96)—armhole measures approx 5½ (6, 6, 6½)"/14 (15, 15, 16.5)cm.

Shoulder shaping

Bind off 7 (7, 7, 8) sts at beg of next 2 rows, then bind off 6 (7, 8, 9) sts at beg of next 4 rows. Bind off rem 27 (29, 31, 33) sts.

LEFT FRONT

With smaller needles and MC, cast on 36 (42, 48, 50) sts. Work rib as for back, end with a WS row. Change to larger needles.

Beg body chart: Row 1 (RS) Beg with st 16 (10, 4, 2), work to st 52. Cont in chart as indicated, work until same length as back to armhole.

Armhole shaping

Cont in chart pat, bind off 5 sts at beg of next row, 2 (2, 3, 3) sts from armhole edge once, then dec 1 st at armhole edge every other row 2 (2, 3, 3) times—27 (33, 37, 39) sts. Cont in chart pat through row 71 (77, 81, 87).

Neck and shoulder shaping

Next row (WS) Cont in pat, bind off 3 (4, 6, 6) sts (neck edge), work to end. Cont to bind off at neck edge, 2 (3, 3, 3) sts twice, then dec 1 st every other row 1 (2, 2, 1), AT SAME TIME, when same length as back to shoulder, shape shoulder as for back.

RIGHT FRONT

Work as for left front, beg with st 56 of chart, and reversing all shaping.

SLEEVES

With smaller needles and MC, cast on 40 (42, 44, 46) sts. Work rib as for back, inc 1 st on last WS row—41 (43, 45, 47) sts. Change to larger needles.

Beg sleeve chart: Row 1 (RS) Beg with st 4 (3, 2, 1) work sleeve chart, end with st 44 (45, 46, 47). Cont in chart pat, inc 1 st each side every 4th row 5 (9, 5, 8) times, every 6th row 9 (7, 10, 9) times—69 (75, 75, 81) sts. Work through row 78 (82, 86, 90)—piece measures approx 10½ (11, 11½, 12)"/26.5 (28, 29, 30.5)cm from beg.

Cap shaping

Bind off 2 (3, 3, 4) sts at beg of next 2 rows, 2 sts at beg of next 6 rows, 4 sts at beg of next 8 rows—21 (25, 25, 29) sts.
Next row (RS) Ssk, bind off to last 2 sts, k2tog, bind off last st.

FINISHING

Block pieces. Sew shoulder seams.

Neckband

With RS facing, smaller needle and MC, pick up and k71 (75, 79, 83) sts around neck edge. Work as for woman's version.

Left front band

With RS facing, smaller needle and MC, beg at left front neck edge, pick up and k68 (72, 74, 80) sts along center front. Work as for woman's version.

Right front band

Pick up and rib for 2 rows as for left band. Complete as for woman's version.

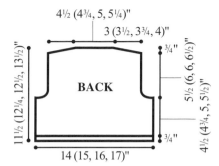

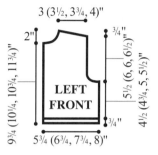

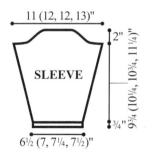

Body Chart

Sleeve Chart

Stitch Key

- ☐ Beige (MC)
- △ Red (A)
- ⊤ Dark green (B)
- ⊠ Coral (E)
- ∨ Light green (C)
- ⊏ Grey (D)
- ▭ P on RS, k on WS with MC
- ◺ Brown (F)

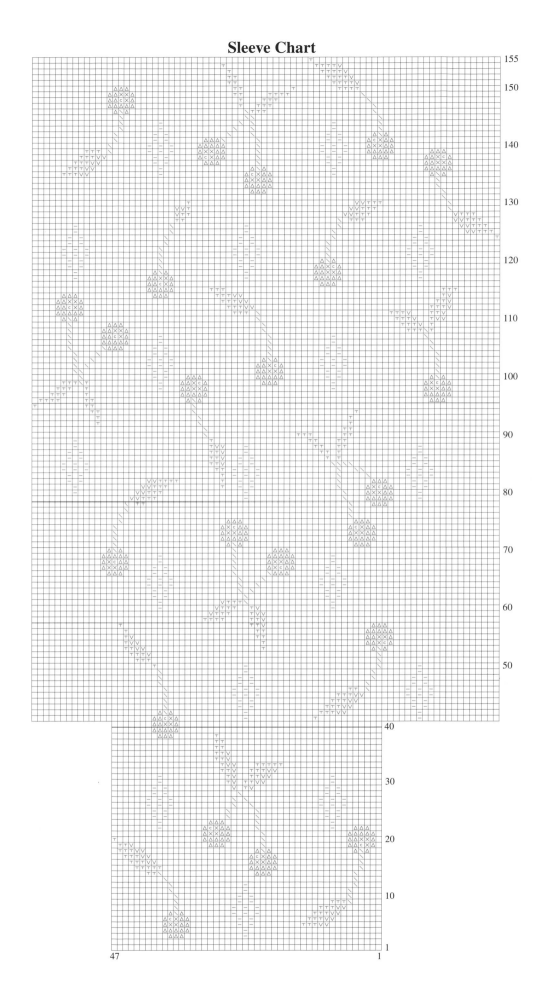

Pam Allen's Crazy Quilt jacket takes inspiration from the opulent quilted bed-covers of the Victorian era. The kimono-style jacket features drop shoulders, seed stitch, I-cord bands, and applied embroidery. The patchwork design leaves room for improvisation and personalized touches. The Crazy Quilt Jacket first appeared in the Fall '92 issue of *Vogue Knitting*.

Crazy Quilt Jacket

FOR EXPERIENCED KNITTERS

SIZES
To fit Small (Medium, Large). Directions are for smallest size with larger sizes in parentheses. If there is only one figure, it applies to all sizes.

KNITTED MEASUREMENTS
- Bust at underarm (buttoned) 43½ (45¾, 48½)"/110.5 (116, 123)cm.
- Length 22¾"/58cm.
- Sleeve width at upper arm 19 (20, 21)"/48.5 (51, 53.5)cm.

MATERIALS
- 6 1¾oz/50g balls (each approx 110yd/100m) of Reynolds/JCA *Paterna Handknitting Yarn* (wool 4) in #50 black (A)
- 4 balls in #710 blue (B)
- 3 balls each in #815 brick red (C), #439 gold (D) and #106 grey (E)
- 2 8yd/7.4m skeins each of *Paternayan Persian Yarn* in #434 taupe, #405 beige, #473 light taupe, #511 steel blue, #513 medium blue, #922 light mauve, #484 rose beige, #742 light gold, #731 mustard, #642 olive and #602 green
- One pair each sizes 6 and 7 (4 and 4.5mm) needles OR SIZE TO OBTAIN GAUGE
- Bobbins
- Two 1"/25mm buttons

Note
Two of the original colors used for this sweater are no longer available. Comparable color substitutions have been made, which are available at the time of printing.

GAUGE
20 sts and 28 rows to 4"/10cm over St st using size 7 (4.5mm) needles. FOR PERFECT FIT, TAKE TIME TO CHECK GAUGE.

STITCH GLOSSARY
Seed Stitch (over even # of sts)
Row 1 *K1, p1, rep from *.
Row 2 (WS) Knit the p sts and purl the k sts. Rep last row for seed st.

Notes
1 Use a separate bobbin for each block of color. When changing colors, twist yarns on WS to prevent holes.
2 Some of the traditional embroidery stitches used are: Fern st, Rosette Motif, Butterfly Chain, Sheaf, Feather, Double Feather, Fly, Overlapped Fly, Double Row Fly, Herringbone, Breton, Feathered Chain, Spine Chain, Blanket, Open Cretan, Wheatear and Detached Wheatear. Refer to an embroidery stitch book for these and other stitches.

BACK
With smaller needles cast on 19 (22, 25) sts with B, 32 sts with E, 23 sts with C, 34 (37, 40) sts with B using the cable cast-on method as foll: Cast on 2 sts using the knitting-on cast-on. *Insert the RH needle between the two sts on the LH needle. Wrap the yarn around the RH needle as if to knit and pull the yarn through to make a new st. Place the new st on the LH needle from the front of the loop. Rep from *—108 (114, 120) sts. Matching colors as established, work 2 rows of garter st (1 ridge on RS). Change to larger needles and St st.

Row 1 (WS) Beg and ending as indicated and reading chart from left to right, work chart through row 148.

Shoulder shaping
Bind off 12 (13, 14) sts at beg of next 4 rows, then 11 (12, 13) sts at beg of next 2 rows. Bind off rem 38 sts for back neck.

LEFT FRONT
With smaller needles and cable cast-on, cast on 9 sts with C, 34 (37, 40) sts with B—43 (46, 49) sts. Matching colors as established, work 2 rows of garter st (1 ridge on RS). Change to larger needles and St st.
Row 1 (WS) Beg and ending as indicated and reading chart from left to right, work chart until piece measures 8"/20.5cm from beg, end with a WS row.

Neck and shoulder shaping
Next row (RS) Work to last 3 sts, work full-fashioned dec as foll: k2tog, k1. Cont in chart, AT SAME TIME, work full-fashioned decs every 12th row 7 times more—35 (38, 41) sts. Cont to work in chart pat until same length as back to shoulder. Work shoulder shaping at side edge as for back.

RIGHT FRONT
With smaller needles and cable cast-on, cast on 19 (22, 25) sts with B, 24 sts with E—43 (46, 49) sts. Matching colors, work 2 rows of garter st (1 ridge on RS). Change to larger needles and St st.
Row 1 (WS) Beg and ending as indicated and reading chart from left to right, work right front to correspond to

sts with C, 9 (11, 13) sts with B—58 (62, 66) sts. Matching colors, work 2 rows of garter st (1 ridge on RS). Change to larger needles and St st. Beg and ending as indicated and reading chart from left to right, work chart, AT SAME TIME, inc 1 st each side (working incs into chart pat) every 6th row 19 times—96 (100, 104) sts. Work even until piece measures 17 (18, 18)"/43 (45.5, 45.5)cm from beg. Bind off.

FINISHING
Block pieces. Work embroidery along color changes and in color blocks as desired on each piece. Sew shoulder seams.

Collar and I-cord edge
With larger needles and A, cast on 25 sts.
Row 1 (RS) Work 22 sts in seed st, k3.
Row 2 (WS) Sl 3, work 22 sts in seed st. Cont to rep rows 1 and 2 until piece measures 8"/20.5cm from beg, end with a WS row.

left front, reversing shaping and working full-fashioned decs as foll: K1, ssk, work to end of row.

SLEEVES
With smaller needles and cable cast-on, cast on 26 (28, 30) sts with E, 23

Button loop
Next row (RS) Work in seed st for 22 sts; working on last 3 sts only, *k3, slip same 3 sts back to LH needle; rep from * for 10 times.
Next row (WS) Sl 3, work 22 sts in seed st. Cont to work rows 1 and 2 until piece measures 45"/114.5cm from beg, end with a WS row. Work button loop as before. Cont to work until piece measures 53"/134.5cm from beg. Bind off. Sew seed st edge around fronts and neck edge, easing to fit. Sew 1 button opposite button loop outside on left front at collar edge. Sew 2nd button inside right front at collar edge. Place markers 9½ (10, 10½)"/24 (25.5, 26.5)cm down from shoulders on front and back for armholes. Sew top of sleeves between markers. Sew side and sleeve seams.

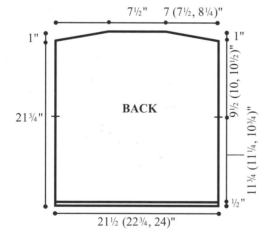

BACK

7½"   7 (7½, 8¼)"
1"   1"
9½ (10, 10½)"
21¾"
11¾ (11¼, 10¾)"
½"
21½ (22¾, 24)"

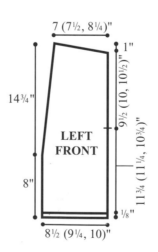

LEFT FRONT

7 (7½, 8¼)"
1"
9½ (10, 10½)"
14¾"
8"
11¾ (11¼, 10¾)"
⅛"
8½ (9¼, 10)"

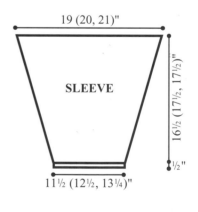

SLEEVE

19 (20, 21)"
16½ (17½, 17½)"
½"
11½ (12½, 13¼)"

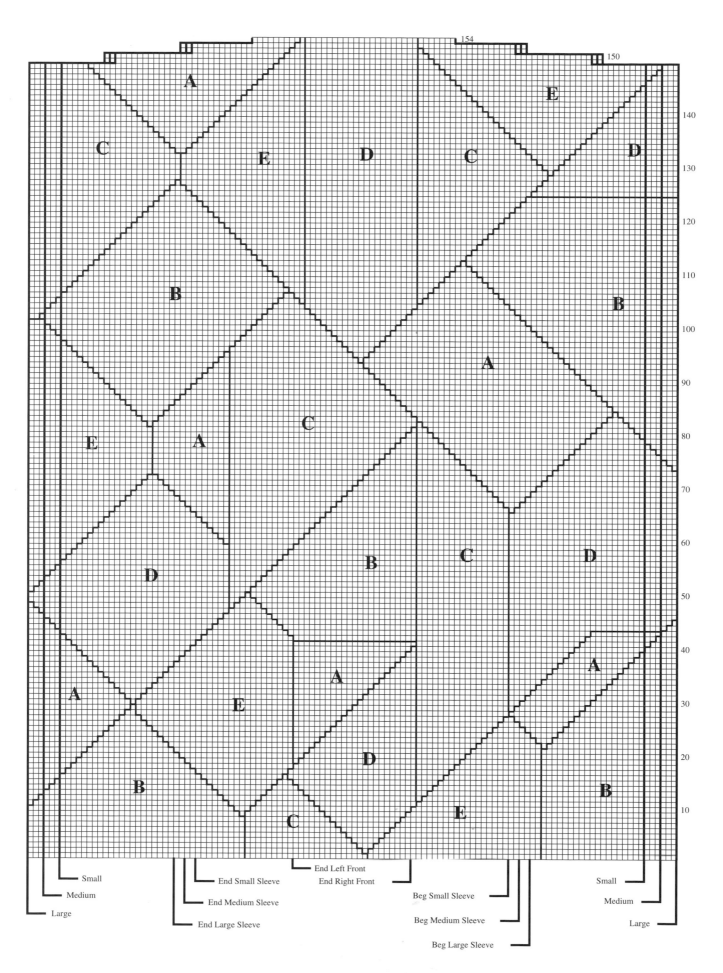

154

150

A

E

C

E

D

C

D

140

130

B

B

120

110

100

A

90

E

A

C

80

70

D

B

C

D

60

50

A

E

40

A

E

30

D

20

B

B

10

C

E

Small

Medium

Large

End Small Sleeve

End Medium Sleeve

End Large Sleeve

End Left Front

End Right Front

Beg Small Sleeve

Beg Medium Sleeve

Beg Large Sleeve

Small

Medium

Large

Tuxedo styling gives this roomy, ribbed pullover a casual elegance that always looks right. The sweater is oversized with angled armholes, side slits, and a round neck edged with single crochet. Shown in size Medium. The Ribbed Pullover first appeared in the Spring/Summer '94 issue of *Vogue Knitting*.

Ribbed Pullover

FOR INTERMEDIATE KNITTERS

SIZES
To fit Small (Medium, Large). Directions are for smallest size with larger sizes in parentheses. If there is only one figure, it applies to all sizes.

KNITTED MEASUREMENTS
- Bust at underarm (buttoned) 40 (42½, 45½)"/101.5 (108, 115.5)cm.
- Length 25 (26, 27)"/63.5 (66, 68.5)cm.
- Sleeve width at upper arm 17 (18, 19)"/43 (46, 48)cm.

MATERIALS
Original Yarn
- 9 (10, 11) 3½oz/100g balls (each approx 187yd/170m) of Wendy/Berroco, Inc. *Wendy 100% Cotton* (cotton 4) in #1113 ecru
Substitute Yarn
- 15 (16, 18) 1¾oz/50g balls (each approx 118yd/109m) of Naturally/S.R. Kertzer, Ltd. *Cotton Connection DK No. 5* (cotton/wool/linen 4) in #05 ecru
- One pair size 5 (3.75mm) needles OR SIZE TO OBTAIN GAUGE
- Size C/2 (2.5mm) crochet hook
- Seven ½"/1.5cm buttons
- Cable needle (cn) stitch markers
- Stitch markers and holders

Note
The original yarn used for this sweater is no longer available. A comparable substitution has been made, which is available at the time of printing. Check gauge of substitute yarns very carefully before beginning.

GAUGE
28 sts and 29 rows to 4"/10cm over k2, p3 rib slightly stretched using size 5 (3.75mm) needles. FOR PERFECT FIT, TAKE TIME TO CHECK GAUGE.

STITCH GLOSSARY
3-st Front Purl Cross Sl 2 sts to cn, hold to *front* of work, p1, k2 from cn.
3-st Back Purl Cross Sl 1 st to cn, hold to *back* of work, k2, p1 from cn.
4-st Front Cable Sl 2 sts to cn, hold to *front* of work, k2, k2 from cn.
4-st Back Cable Sl 2 sts to cn, hold to *back* of work, k2, k2 from cn.
5-st Front Cable Sl 2 sts to cn, hold to *front* of work, sl next st to 2nd cn, hold to back, k2, k1 from 2nd cn, k2 from first cn.
5-st Back Cable Sl 3 sts to cn, hold to *back* of work, k2, sl 1 st from cn to LH needle and knit it, k2 from cn.

BACK
Cast on 139 (149, 159) sts.
Row 1 (RS) K3, [p3, k2] 26 (28, 30) times, end p3, k3.
Row 2 P3, k3, [p2, k3] 26 (28, 30) times, end p3. Rep rows 1 and 2 until piece measures 4"/10cm from beg, inc 1 st each side on last RS row and end with a WS row 141 (151, 161) sts.
Next row (RS) P2, k2 [p3, k2] 26 (28, 30) times, end p3, k2, p2.
Next row K the knit sts and p the purl sts. Rep last 2 rows until piece measures 16½ (17, 17½)"/42 (43.5, 44.5)cm from beg, end with a WS row.

Armhole shaping
Next row K2tog, work to last 2 sts, ssk—139 (149, 159) sts. Cont to dec 1 st each side every other row 5 times—129 (139, 149) sts. Work even until armhole measures 8½ (9, 9½)"/21.5 (23, 24.5)cm. Bind off all sts.

FRONT
Work as for back until piece measures 10½ (11, 11½)"/27 (28, 29.5)cm from beg, end with a WS row.
Next row (RS) Work 32 (37, 42) sts in rib pat, p77 sts, work to end.
Beg tuxedo bib: Next row (WS) Work 32 (37, 42) sts in pat, place marker (pm) p2, k1, p6, k1, [p2, k3] 3 times, p2, k1, p6, k1, p2, k3, p2, inc 1—75 (80, 85) sts. Place rem 67 (72, 77) sts on holder.

Right front
Beg charts: Row 1 (RS) Sl 1 knitwise, k2, p3, k2, pm, work 10 sts of chart #1 over next 8 sts, pm, work 17 sts of chart #3, pm, work 10 sts of chart #1 over next 8 sts, pm, k2, work in pat to end—79 (84, 89) sts. Work through row 6 of charts #1 and #3.
Next (buttonhole) row Work 4 sts, yo, p2tog, work in pats to end. Work through row 22 of chart #1, then cont

to rep row 3-22. Work through row 24 of chart #3, then cont to rep rows 1-24, AT SAME TIME, rep buttonhole row every 14th row for a total of 7 buttonholes. When piece measures same as back to underarm, shape armhole as for back—73 (78, 83) sts. When armhole measures 7"/18cm, end with a WS row.

Neck shaping

Next row (RS) Bind off 10 sts in pat, ssk, bind off 3 sts, k2tog, bind off 2 sts, work to end—56 (61, 66) sts. Cont to bind off at neck edge 5 sts once, 3 sts once, 2 sts once, then dec 1 st every other row 2 (2, 4) times. When piece measures same as back, bind off rem 44 (49, 52) sts.

Left front

Next row (RS) Work 67 (72, 77) sts from holder and cast on 7 sts—74 (79, 84) sts.
Next row (WS) K8, p6, k1, [p2, k3] 3 times, p2, k1, p6, k1, p2, work to end.
Next row (RS) Work 32 (37, 42) sts in rib as established, pm, k2, pm, work 10 sts of chart #1 over next 8 sts, pm, work 17 sts of chart #2, pm, work 10 sts of chart #1 over next 8 sts, pm, p5, pm, k2—78 (83, 88) sts. Cont in pats as established, working 2 sts at center front edge before first marker in garter st and next 5 sts in rev St st. When piece measures same as back to armhole, shape armhole as for back—72 (77, 82) sts. When piece measures same as back to neck, end with a RS row.

Neck shaping

Next row (WS) Bind off 9 sts in pat, p2tog, bind off 3 sts, p2tog tbl, bind off 2 sts, work to end—56 (61, 66) sts. Cont to bind off at neck edge 5 sts once, 3 sts once, 2 sts once, then dec 1 st every other row 2 (2, 4) times—44 (49, 52) sts. When armhole measures same as back, bind off rem sts.

SLEEVES

(Note: Use chart #2 for left sleeve and chart #3 for right sleeve. For ease in

finishing, mark each sleeve after completion.) Cast on 55 sts.

Row 1 (RS) K2, p2, [k2, p3] 9 times, end k2, p2, k2. Placing markers after first 9 sts and before last 9 sts, work 3 rows even in rib pat as set.

Next (inc) row (RS) K2, m1, work to last 2 sts, m1, k2.

Next row [P2, k3] 11 times, end p2. Work pats and incs simultaneously as foll: keep first and last 2 sts in St st, work inc row (working inc sts into k2, p3 rib pat) every other row 5 (11, 16) times, every 4th row 26 (24, 22) times, AT SAME TIME, when piece measures 4½"/11.5cm from beg, end with a WS row.

Next row (RS) Work to first marker, p37, work to end.

Next (preparation) row (WS) Work to marker, p2, k2, p4, k2, [p2, k3] 3 times, p2, k2, p4, k2, p2, work to end.

Beg pats: Next row (RS) Work to marker, k2, p2, pm, k2, m1, k2, pm, p2, pm, work 17 sts of chart #3 (for right sleeve) or chart #2 (for left sleeve), pm, p2, pm, k2, m1, k2, pm, p2, k2, work to end.

Next row K the knit sts and p the purl sts.

Next row Work to 2nd marker, work 5-st front cable, work to 6th marker, work 5-st back cable, work to end. Cont to work through row 24 of chart #2 or #3, then cont to rep rows 1-24, AT SAME TIME, work 5-st front and back cables every 4th row. When sleeve measures 17 (17½, 18)"/43.5 (44.5, 46)cm from beg and there are 117 (125, 131) sts, end with a WS row.

Cap shaping
Dec 1 st each side every other row 6 times. Bind off rem sts.

FINISHING
Block pieces lightly. Sew shoulder seams. Set in sleeves, sewing each sleeve to appropriate side. Sew side seams beg 4"/10cm from lower edge for slit openings. Sew sleeve seams. With RS facing and hook, beg at right front neck and work 1 row sc evenly around neck edge. Sew on buttons.

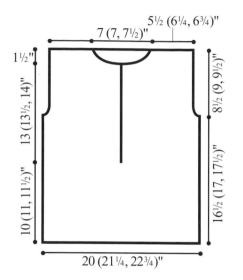

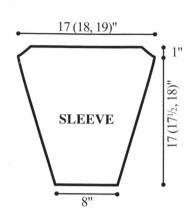

SLEEVE

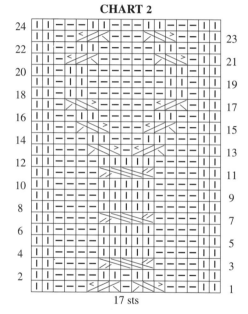

Stitch Key

| | k on RS, p on WS

— p on RS, k on WS

M1

3-st Front Purl Cross

3-st Back Purl Cross

4-st Front Cable

4-st Back Cable

5-st Front Purl Cross

5-st Back Purl Cross

CHART 2

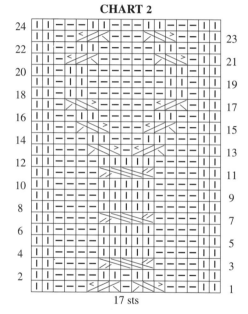

17 sts

CHART 1

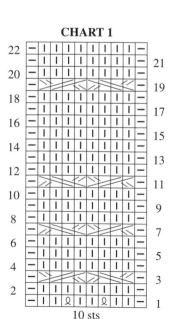

10 sts

CHART 3

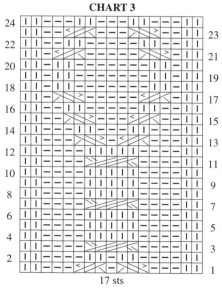

17 sts

Child's
Cardigan

Here's a summer charmer with timeless appeal! Pointelle panels
and scalloped lace edging are the focal point of this adorable
little girl's cardigan. The Child's Cardigan first appeared in the
Spring/Summer '91 issue of *Vogue Knitting*.

Child's Cardigan

SIZES

To fit 2 (4, 6, 8) years or 21(23, 25, 27)"/53 (58, 63, 68)cm chest. Directions are for smallest size with larger sizes in parentheses. If there is only one figure, it applies to all sizes.

KNITTED MEASUREMENTS

● Chest at underarm (buttoned) 22 (24½, 26¾, 29¼)"/56 (62, 68, 74.5)cm.
● Length 12 (13, 14, 15)"/30.5 (32.5, 35, 37.5)cm.
● Sleeve width at upper arm 11 (12, 13, 14)"/27 (30, 32, 35)cm.

MATERIALS

● 4 (5, 5, 6) 1oz/50g balls (each approx 116yd/106m) of Patons® Cotton D.K. (cotton 3) in #3680 white
● One pair each sizes 2 and 5 (2.75 and 3.75mm) needles OR SIZE TO OBTAIN GAUGE
● Five ⅜"/10mm buttons
● Stitch holders and cable needle (cn)

GAUGE

23 sts and 32 rows to 4"/10cm over lace chart pat using size 5 (3.75mm) needles. FOR PERFECT FIT, TAKE TIME TO CHECK GAUGE.

Note

Body of sweater is worked in one piece to the underarm.

STITCH GLOSSARY

Cross Dec Sl 1 to cn and hold to *back*, sl 1, return first st to LH needle, k2tog, psso.

BODY

With larger needles, cast on 125 (139, 153, 167) sts.

Beg scallop pat: Row 1 (RS) Work first 13 sts, then work 14-st rep 7 (8, 9, 10) times, work to end of chart. Work through row 9 of chart—125 (139, 153, 167) sts. P next row on WS.

Beg lace pat: Row 1 (RS) Work first 4 sts of chart, work 14-st rep 8 (9, 10, 11) times, work last 9 sts of chart. Cont in pat as established until piece measures 6½ (7, 7½, 8)"/16.5 (17.5, 19, 20)cm from beg.

Divide for fronts and back

Next row (RS) Work 29 (33, 36, 39) sts, k2tog and place sts on holder (right front), k2tog, work next 59 (65, 73, 81) sts, k2tog (back), placing rem 31 (35, 38, 41) sts on holder (left front). Cont on back sts only dec 1 st each side every row 2 (2, 3, 3) times more, then 1 st every other row 3 times—51 (57, 63, 71) sts. Cont in pats until armhole measures 5½ (6, 6½, 7)"/13.5 (15, 16, 17.5)cm. Bind off.

RIGHT FRONT

Beg with a WS row, work sts from right front holder and cont shaping at armhole edge only as for back—25 (29, 31, 34) sts. Work even until armhole measures 3½ (4, 4½, 5)"/8.5 (10, 11.5, 12.5)cm, end with a WS row.

Neck shaping

Next row (RS) Bind off 5 (5, 5, 6) sts (neck edge), work to end. Cont to bind off from neck edge 3 sts once, 2 sts once, dec 1 st every other row 3 (4, 4, 5) times. Work even until same length as back. Bind off rem 12 (15, 17, 18) sts for shoulder.

LEFT FRONT

Work to correspond to right front, reversing shaping.

SLEEVES

With smaller needles, cast on 37 (37, 40, 40) sts. Work in k1, p1 rib for ¾"/2cm. Change to larger needles.

Beg lace pat: Row 1 (RS) K0 (0, 2, 2), beg as indicated on chart, work to end of rep, then work 14-st rep twice, k0 (0, 1, 1). Cont in pat as established, inc 1 st each side (working inc sts into pat) every 4th row 0 (11, 7, 12) times, every 6th row 13 (0, 10, 8) times, every 8th row 0 (5, 0, 0) times—63 (69, 74, 80) sts. Work even until piece measures 11 (12, 12¼, 13¼)"/27.5 (30, 31, 33.5)cm from beg.

Cap shaping

Dec 1 st each side every row 3 (3, 4, 4) times, then every other row 3 times. Bind off 51 (57, 60, 66) sts.

FINISHING
Block pieces. Sew shoulder seams.

Neckband
With RS facing and smaller needles, pick up and k75 (77, 77, 81) sts evenly around neck edge. Work in k1, p1 rib for ½"/1.5cm. Bind off in rib.

Left front band
With RS facing and smaller needles, pick up and k65 (71, 77, 83) sts along straight edge of left front. Work in k1, p1 rib for ½"/1.5cm. Bind off in rib. Place markers along band for 5 buttons, the first one ½"/1.5cm from lower edge, the last one ½"/1.5cm from neck edge and 3 others evenly spaced between.

Right front band
Work to correspond to left front band, working buttonholes opposite markers (k2tog, yo) on row 3. Work in k1, p1 rib until band measures ½"/1.5cm. Bind off in rib. Sew on buttons. Sew top of sleeves to straight edge of armholes, then sew armhole decs of front and back to dec sts of sleeve. Sew sleeve seams.

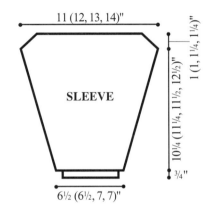

2 (2¾, 3, 3¼)"

4½ (5, 5, 5½)"

2 (2¾, 3, 3¼)"

BACK

LEFT
FRONT

RIGHT
FRONT

BODY

10 (11, 12, 13)"

6½ (7, 7½, 8)"

5½ (6, 6½, 7)"

21½ (24, 26¼, 28¾)"

11 (12, 13, 14)"

1 (1, 1¼, 1¼)"

SLEEVE

10¼ (11¼, 11½, 12½)"

¾"

6½ (6½, 7, 7)"

Stitch Key
I	k on RS, p on WS
–	p on RS, k on WS
O	yarn over
⤸	k2tog on RS
⤹	ssk
▨	no stitch
⤼	sl 1, k2tog, psso
⤽	k3tog
⤾	Cross Dec

LACE PATTERN

6
5
4
3
2
1

— 14-st rep —

Beg sleeve

SCALLOP PATTERN

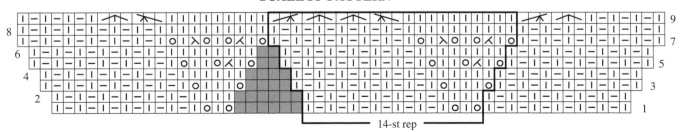

9
8
7
6
5
4
3
2
1

— 14-st rep —

Lily Chin

While trying to break into the fashion field, Lily Chin waited on tables at a popular restaurant in the chic Soho section of New York City. Before coming to work one day, she met with *Vogue Knitting* editors Lola Ehrlich and Nancy Thomas for the very first time. After showing them several of her designs, she hurried to the restaurant to serve the lunchtime crowd. To Lily's surprise, in through the door walked those self same editors who then proceeded to sit in her area. "I waited on them!" she exclaims. "Thankfully, they were apparently having some kind of business lunch and took no notice of me whatsoever."

But it didn't take long for everyone to start noticing Lily Chin. Her first design appeared in *Vogue Knitting* in 1987, and since then her work has shown up everywhere, from runway shows to popular magazines. "It's a big thrill to see supermodels like Cindy Crawford and Naomi Campbell wearing my designs," she shares. In recent years, Lily's work has appeared in several major national publications, including the most recent highlight of her career—a crochet bikini published in the swimsuit issue of *Sports Illustrated*.

Always atune to fashion, Lily grew up around New York's garment industry. Her mother is a Chinese immigrant who worked her way up from seamstress to samplemaker with a major Seventh Avenue manufacturer. Beginning at the tender age of 13, Lily spent her summers working at her mother's firm, helping out with the bookkeeping and other odd jobs, while learning the ins and outs of the "rag trade."

While her mother may have shown her the basics, Lily really taught herself how to knit by reading books on the subject. As a young girl, Lily found knitting and crochet to be a thrifty way of extending her wardrobe. A natural entrepreneur, she started selling her crochet work when still in high school, and soon began working crafts fairs and making accessories for a popular chain of dance stores. She went on to earn a liberal arts degree from Queens College, taking courses in art and film criticism, among others.

With her clothing manufacturing and art background, Lily had no fears entering the unstable field of fashion design. "Knitting is a hybrid of many things," she explains. "It's part art, with the cloth and motifs, and part garment-making. The idea is to translate your vision into knitting. I have an art background, but because of experience in the rag trade, I specialize in garment-making and knitting technique."

Lily's work is characterized as "technique driven." With a husband that is an architectural writer and critic, Lily recognizes architecture as among her creative influences. "It's about structure, building something and letting other people see what's holding it up," she says. "I've never been a fan of plastering a motif on a garment. Knitting is a sculptural medium, you build the fabric as you shape it, versus cloth where you cut out the garment."

Using the Embroidered Cardigan on page 34 as an example, she explains, "Here, the motifs are built into the fabric. The roses themselves are part of the knitting, rather than pasted on after the fact."

One of Lily's greatest technical innovations were reversible cables. "I hope one of my contributions to knitting in general might be the reversible cables," she says. "That is, knit cables that show on both sides." She also likes to play with materials, trying to find a new slant. Discussing the Mohair Aran on page 38, she says: "Most of the time Arans are knit in really smooth yarns. Here, the mohair gives it textural interest."

Coming from New York City with a fashion background, Lily's work has an unmistakable urban edge. "With every piece I try to find something fresh and different. I'm tired of the same old, same old—tired of looking like everyone else," she admits. "I like to make things that reek of personality and uniqueness. I like to put a different spin on it, a little bit of a surprise."

In 1996, Lily began working with fashion designer Isaac Mizrahi. The relationship lasted two and a half years, until the design house closed, giving Lily the opportunity to work on a level she hadn't before. "He was doing the things I was most interested in," she says. "Mass merchandising was more boring and streamlined, it was about designing for machinery...they took out all of the meaty details. With Mizrahi, I was able to do more of what I love. The work was fully-fashioned with fine attention to details." Soon, her

> "With every piece I try to find something fresh and different... I like to put a different spin on it, a little bit of a surprise."

handiwork started showing up in the mass media, not just knitting magazines. "He challenged and pushed me, he helped me hone and refine my skills," she shares. "He made me grow."

Nowadays, Lily travels across the country teaching people how to knit. As one of the top talents in her field, Lily's seminars are in great demand at trade shows, knitting seminars and on cruises. As the knitting world's self-appointed agent provocateur, she enjoys coaxing knitters to rethink their craft and to push beyond the limits of convention. Recently, she staged a "knit-in" to protest a radio ad that referred to knitters as "grannies." A subsequent article appearing in *Time Magazine*, described Lily as a poster child for what knitting is not. The writer went on, "If you think knitting is for grannies, take a look at Lily Chin."

Looking toward the future, Lily anticipates the time when she can knit solely for herself, unfettered by clients' demands and expectations. "My idea of knitting heaven would be to be able to knit things that interest and excite me," she says. "When I work with a manufacturer or magazine, I gear my work for that particular audience. While I pride myself in being able to cater to different audiences, the knitting that's close to my heart is not for a mass level. When I have time on my hands I like to knit what pleases my soul. When I'm not knitting for pay, I'm knitting for me."

Wrap yourself in luxury for an enchanted evening. This reversible ribbed cable shawl is the ultimate indulgence in a super-soft mohair blend. The Reversible Rib Shawl first appeared in the Winter '99/00 issue of *Vogue Knitting*.

Reversible Rib Shawl

FOR INTERMEDIATE KNITTERS

SIZES
One size.

KNITTED MEASUREMENTS
● Approx 22½"/57cm wide by 72"/183cm long

MATERIALS
● 12 1¾oz/50g balls (each approx 192yd/177m) of Filatura Di Crosa/Tahki•Stacy Charles, Inc. *Butterfly* (mohair/acrylic 4) in #400 white
● One pair each sizes 7 and 9 (4.5 and 5.5mm) needles OR SIZE TO OBTAIN GAUGE
● Cable needle (cn)
● Stitch markers

GAUGE
32 sts and 20 rows to 4"/10cm (blocked) over chart pat using size 9 (5.5mm) needles. FOR PERFECT FIT, TAKE TIME TO CHECK GAUGE.

STITCH GLOSSARY
24-st LC Sl 12 sts to cn and hold to *front*, [k2, p2] 3 times, work sts from cn as foll: [k2, p2] 3 times.
24-st RC Sl 12 sts to cn and hold to *back*, [k2, p2] 3 times, work sts from cn as foll: [k2, p2] 3 times.

Note
Use smaller needles for the first and last 7 rows only.

Stitch Key
☐ K on RS, p on WS
⊟ P on RS, k on WS

BACK
With smaller needles, cast on 176 sts.
Beg chart pat
Row 1 (RS) K4, place marker (pm), work sts 1 to 48 of chart 3 times, then sts 1 to 24 once more, pm, k4.
Row 2 Sl 1 wyif, k3, sl marker, work chart pat to last 4 sts, k3, sl 1 wyif. Cont in this way, changing to larger needles after 7 rows have been completed, working first and last 4 sts in garter and sl st pat as established, until piece measures 70½"/179cm from beg. Change to smaller needles and work 7 rows in pat as established. Bind off tightly in rib.

FINISHING
Block lightly.

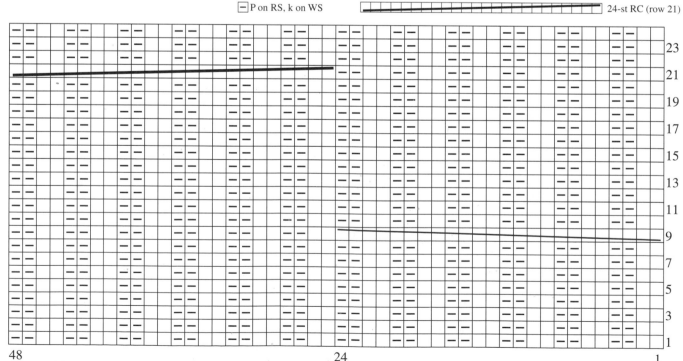

24-st LC (row 9)
24-st RC (row 21)

48   24   1

Striped crowns and textured bias brims give these wool caps a fun and lively look. Lily Chin's inventive dot-and-dash design is shown in three brilliant colorways. The Colorful Caps first appeared in the Fall '91 issue of *Vogue Knitting*.

Colorful Caps

FOR INTERMEDIATE KNITTERS

SIZES
One size fits all.

KNITTED MEASUREMENTS
● Brim circumference 21"/53.5cm.
● Height 7"/18cm.

MATERIALS
All versions:
● 1 .88oz/25g balls (each approx 74yd/67m) of Rowan/Westminster Trading *Lightweight DK* (wool 3) in #084 cream (B)
Version 1:
● 2 balls in #606 dark olive (A)
● 1 ball each in #605 green heather (C), #404 light olive (D) and #405 khaki gold (E)
Version 2:
● 2 balls in #99 eggplant (A)
● 1 ball each in #42 cherry (C), #46 burgundy (D) and #70 dusty rose (E)
Version 3:
● 2 balls in #67 red rust (A)
● 1 ball each in #115 orange (C), #403 light rust (D) and #72 gold (E)
All versions:
● Size 6 (4mm) circular needle, 16"/40cm long
● One set of size 6 (4mm) double-pointed needles (dpn)
● Stitch markers
Note
The original colors may no longer be available. Substitutions will need to be made.

GAUGE
22 sts and 24 rows to 4"/10cm in St st using size 6 (4mm) needles. FOR PERFECT FIT, TAKE TIME TO CHECK GAUGE.

Note
Sl sts as if to purl. Carry colors not in use loosely along WS of work.

STITCH GLOSSARY
Make 1 purl (m1-p) With LH needle, pick up horizontal thread between st just worked and next st, p tbl.

BRIM
With A, cast on 21 sts.
Rows 1 and 3 (WS) P2, p2tog, p15, M1-p, p2.
Row 2 Knit.
Row 4 Drop A and join C; *sl 1 wyib, k3; rep from *, end sl 1. Cont with C only.
Rows 5, 7 and 9 *Sl 1 wyif, k3; rep from *, end sl 1.
Rows 6 and 8 *Sl 1 wyib, p3; rep from *, end sl 1.
Row 10 Cut C and pick up A; *k1, [insert RH needle into back of next st on WS of work 6 rows below (last A row worked), pick up this lp and place on LH needle, k tog with next st] 3 times; rep from *, end k1.
Rows 11-20 Rep rows 1-10 using D for C.
Rows 21-30 Rep rows 1-10 using E for C. Rep rows 1-30 for 6 times more. Rep rows 1 and 2. Bind off. Weave short ends of brim tog to make circle.

CROWN
With RS facing, circular needle and A, pick up and k120 sts evenly spaced along long edge of brim. Join and place marker for beg of rnd. Work in rnds of St st (k every rnd) and switch to dpn when sts allow. Join B.
Rnds 1-3 *With A k4, with B k4; rep from *.
Rnd 4 *With A k4, with B k3, with A k2tog, k3, with B k4, with A k3, with B k2tog, k3; rep from *.

Rows 5-7 *With A k4, with B k3, with A k4, with B k4, with A k3, with B k4; rep from *.
Row 8 *With A k4, with B k2, with A k2tog, k3, with B k4, with A k2, with B k2tog, k3; rep from *.
Rows 9-11 *With A k4, with B k2, with A k4, with B k4, with A k2, with B k4; rep from *.
Row 12 *With A k4, with B k1, with A k2tog, k3, with B k4, with A k1, with B k2tog, k3; rep from *.
Row 13 *With A k4, with B k1, with A k4, with B k4, with A k1, with B k4; rep from *.
Row 14 *With A k4, k2tog, k3, with B k4, k2tog, k3; rep from *.
Row 15 *With A k8, with B k8; rep from *.
Row 16 *With A k3, k2tog, k3, with B k3, k2tog, k3; rep from *.
Row 17 *With A k7, with B k7; rep from *.
Row 18 *With A k2, k2tog, k3, with B k2, k2tog, k3; rep from *.
Row 19 *With A k1, k2tog, k3, with B k1, k2tog, k3; rep from *.
Row 20 *With A k5, with B k5; rep from *.
Row 21 *With A k2tog, k3, with B k2tog, k3; rep from *.
Row 22 *With A k2tog, k2, with B k2tog, k2; rep from *.
Row 23 *With A k3, with B k3; rep from *.
Row 24 *With A k2tog, k1, with B k2tog, k1; rep from *.
Row 25 *With A k2, with B k2; rep from *.
Row 26 *With A k2tog, with B k2tog; rep from *.
Rows 27 and 28 *With A k1, with B k1; rep from *. Cut yarn leaving a 4"/10cm end. Thread end through rem sts to close tip.

Floral motifs give this textured cardigan feminine charm. The borders and cuffs are knitted with eyelets, through which seam binding is threaded to form pretty rosebuds and leaves. The close-fitting cardigan has a mini-shawl collar and set-in sleeves. Shown in size 34. The Embroidered Cardigan first appeared in the Holiday '88 issue of *Vogue Knitting*.

Embroidered Cardigan

FOR EXPERIENCED KNITTERS

SIZES
To fit 32 (34, 36, 38)"/81 (86, 91, 96)cm bust. Directions are for smallest size with larger sizes in parentheses. If there is only one figure, it applies to all sizes.

KNITTED MEASUREMENTS
● Finished bust measurement at underarm (buttoned) 35¾ (37¾, 39, 41)"/88.5 (94.5, 98.5, 102)cm.
● Length 18 (18, 19, 20)"/45.5 (45.5, 47.5, 50.5)cm.
● Sleeve width at upper arm 11¾ (12, 13, 13¾)"/29.5 (30.5, 32, 34)cm.

MATERIALS
● 8 (8, 9, 10) 1¾oz/50g balls (each approx 121yd/110m) of Baruffa/Lane Borgosesia *Maratona*® (wool 4) in #8533 celery
● 1 spool each (each approx 100yd/90m) of Judi and Co. ½" ribbon (rayon 5) in olive green and dusty pink, or seam binding.
● One pair size 6 (4mm) needles OR SIZE TO OBTAIN GAUGE
● Twelve ⅜"/10mm buttons
● Stitch markers and stitch holders
Note
The original ribbon used for this sweater is no longer available. A comparable substitution has been made, which is available at the time of printing.

GAUGE
22 sts and 32 rows to 4"/10cm over textured pat using size 6 (4mm) needles. FOR PERFECT FIT, TAKE TIME TO CHECK GAUGE.

STITCH GLOSSARY
Textured Pat (multiple of 4 sts +1 extra)
Row 1 (WS) Purl.
Row 2 Knit.
Row 3 Purl.
Row 4 K4, *p1, k3; rep from *, end k1.
Rows 5-7 Rep rows 1-3.
Row 8 K2, *p1, k3; rep from *, end last rep k2. Rep rows 1-8 for textured pat.

BACK
Cast on 77 (81, 85, 89) sts. Work in k1, p1 rib for 2"/5cm. Work in textured pat, inc 1 st each side (working inc sts into pat) every 6th row 4 times, every 4th row 6 times—97 (101, 105, 109) sts. Work even in pat until piece measures 9½ (9½, 10, 10½)"/24 (24, 25, 26.5)cm from beg, end with a WS row.

Armhole shaping
Bind off 3 sts at beg of next 2 rows, 2 sts at beg of next 2 rows, dec 1 st each side of next row—85 (89, 93, 97) sts. Work even until armhole measures 7½ (7½, 8, 8½)"/19 (19, 20, 21.5)cm.

Shoulder shaping
Bind off 6 sts at beg of next 8 (6, 4, 2) rows, 7 sts at beg of next 0 (2, 4, 6) rows. Place rem 37 (39, 41, 43) sts on a holder.

LEFT FRONT
Cast on 41 (45, 47, 49) sts.
Row 1 (WS) Sl 2 purlwise, p1, k1, p1, (5-st button band), place marker (pm), rib to end.
Row 2 Rib to marker, sl marker, k1, p1, k3. Rep last 2 rows for 2"/5cm, end with a RS row.

Next row Work 5-st band, work row 1 of textured pat to end. Cont in this way for 2 rows more.
Next row (RS) K4, [p1, k3] 3 (4, 5, 5) times, p1 (1, 0, 1), k1 (1, 0, 1) (row 4 of textured pat), pm, work row 1 of large right flower as foll: cont textured pat over next 7 sts, k2tog, yo, cont textured pat to next marker, end k3 (3, 1, 3), work 5-st band. Cont in this way, working inc sts at side edge (beg of RS rows) as for back, AT SAME TIME, cont textured pat and flowers, sl markers every row, as foll: After 17 rows of right flower have been worked, *work 1 (1, 3, 5) rows in textured pat.
Next row (RS) Work pat to first marker, work large left flower over 18 sts, work 5-st band. Work through chart row 17. Work 1 (1, 3, 5) rows in textured pat.
Next row (RS) Work pat to first marker, work large right flower over 18 sts. Work through chart row 17.* Rep between *'s once, AT SAME TIME, when same length as back to armhole, shape armhole at side edge as for back—45 (49, 51, 53) sts. P 1 row, removing flower marker.
Next row (RS) Work pat to last 15 sts, pm, work med left flower over 8 sts, work to end. Work through chart row 9. P 1 row, removing flower marker.
Next row (RS) Work in pat to last 23 sts, pm, work med right flower over 8 sts, work to end. Work through chart row 9. P 1 row, removing flower marker—piece measures approx 16 (16, 17, 18)"/40.5 (40.5, 42.5, 45.5)cm from beg.

Neck shaping
Notes for working short rows: Sl last st of row before turning as foll:

Before a k st: With yarn in back, sl next st purlwise, bring yarn to front between needles, sl st from RH needle back to LH needle, turn work. To hide the wrap around sl st, work to just before wrapped st, insert RH needle into bottom of wrap and knitwise into st on LH needle and k these 2 tog.

Before a p st: With yarn in front, sl next st purlwise, bring yarn to back between needles, sl st from RH needle back to LH needle, turn work. To hide the wrap around sl st, work to just before wrapped st, insert RH needle from behind into back lp of wrap and sl to LH needle, p2tog.

Next row (RS) Work pat to last 31 sts, pm, work small left flower over 8 sts, work to last 3 sts of buttonband and beg short rows as foll: wrap next st (see short row notes) and turn work, leaving 3 sts unworked.

Next row Work in pat.

Next row Work to 5 sts before end of row, wrap next st, turn, leaving 5 sts unworked.

Next row Work in pat. Cont short rows in this way, working 2 less sts every RS row 3 times more, then working 3 less sts twice, AT SAME TIME, when same length as back to shoulder, work shoulder shaping at underarm edge only as for back. Work 1 row on RS on rem 21 (24, 25, 26) hiding wraps (see short row notes). Place sts on holder. Place markers on buttonband for 12 buttons, first marker ½" from lower edge, the next one ¾" from the first, the next one at the top of the ribbing, the last one at the beg of neck shaping, the other 8 evenly spaced between.

RIGHT FRONT

Work as for left front, reversing shaping, buttonband and neck shaping, and working buttonholes in buttonband opposite markers on RS rows as foll:

Buttonhole row (RS) Work 3 sts of band, yo, k2tog, sl marker, work to end and, AT SAME TIME, working flowers in foll sequence: [large left flower, large right flower] twice, large left flower, med right flower, med left flower, small right flower.

RIGHT SLEEVE

Cast on 39 (41, 43, 45) sts. Work in k1, p1 rib for 2"/5cm. Beg flower pats, textured pat and incs as foll: inc 1 st (working inc sts into textured pat) each side every 8th row 6 (4, 7, 10) times, every 10th row 7 (9, 7, 5) times—65 (67, 71, 75) sts, AT SAME TIME, work pats as foll: Work in textured pat for 3 rows.

Next row Work 12 (13, 14, 15) sts, pm, work med right flower over 8 sts, pm, work to end. Work through chart row 9.

Next row Purl.

Next row Work to first marker, sl marker, work next 7 sts in textured pat, work med left flower over 8 sts, work to end. Work through chart row 9.

Next row Purl.

Next row Work to first marker, work small right flower over 8 sts, work to end. Work through chart row 5. Cont in textured pat until piece measures 17½ (18, 18, 18½)"/44 (45, 45, 46.5)cm from beg, end with a WS row.

Cap shaping

Bind off 3 sts at beg of next 2 rows, 2 sts at beg of next 2 rows, dec 1 st each side every other row 5 times, every 4th row 5 times, every other row 4 times, bind off 2 (2, 2, 3) sts at beg of next 2 rows, 3 (3, 4, 5) sts at beg of next 2 rows, 4 (4, 5, 5) sts at beg of next 2 rows. Bind off rem 9 (11, 11, 11) sts.

LEFT SLEEVE

Work as for right sleeve, working flower charts in the foll sequence: med left flower, med right flower, small left flower.

FINISHING

Block pieces. Sew shoulder seams.

Highneck

Next row (RS) Keeping to pat, work 1 row across 21 (24, 25, 26) sts of right front holder, pm, work back neck sts from holder, dec 4 sts evenly, pm, work next 18 (21, 22, 23) sts from left front, leave rem 3 sts on holder—72 (80, 84, 88) sts. Work short rows as foll: Wrap next st on holder, turn.

Next row Work pat to 2 sts before first marker, k2tog, sl marker, work to next marker, dec 2 sts evenly, sl marker, ssk, work pat to last 5 sts, turn.

Next row Work to last 5 sts, turn.

Next row Work to last 7 sts, dec 4 sts evenly across back neck (between markers), turn.

Next row Work to last 7 sts, turn.

Next row Work to 2 sts before first marker, k2tog, sl marker, ssk, work to 2 sts before next marker, k2tog, sl marker, ssk, work to last 9 sts, turn.

Next row Work to 1 st before first marker, k2tog, remove marker, work to 2 sts before next marker, ssk, remove marker, work to last 9 sts, turn. Cont in this way to work 2 less sts at end of next 2 rows, 3 sts less at end of next 4 rows, 4 sts less at end of next 2 rows—21 sts unworked each end. Work next row to end. Work 1 row on all sts—61 (69, 73, 77) sts.

Ribbing

Work short rows as foll:

Next row Sl 1 knitwise, sl 1 purlwise, k1, p2tog, ssk, *p1, k1; rep from * to last 7 sts, k2tog, p2tog tbl, wrap next st, turn.

Next row Sl 1, rib to last 3 sts, turn.

Next 2 rows Sl 1, rib to last 5 sts, turn.

Next row Rib all sts, closing holes, to last 3 sts, k3tog.

Next row Sl 1, rib to end of row, closing holes, to last 3 sts, p3tog. Sl 1 knitwise, bind off all sts in rib.

Set in sleeves. Sew side and sleeve seams.

RIBBON FLOWERS

Work eyelet letters of chart, beg from WS work and thread as foll:

Large flowers

Thread approx 18"/45.5cm of olive green ribbon and weave through eyelets for stems as foll:

Out through G, in through H;
Out through I,   in through J;
Out through H, in through J;
Out through K, in through L;
Out through J, in through L;
Out through M, in through N;
Out through L, in through N.

Thread approx 18"/45.5cm of mauve ribbon and weave through eyelets for flowers as foll:
Out through A, in through D;
Out through C, in through B;
Out through C, in through D;
Out through B, in through D;
Out through F, in through E;
Out through C, in through G;
Out through B, in through G.

Medium flowers
Thread approx 12"/30.5cm of olive green ribbon and weave through eyelets for stems as foll:
Out through D, in through F;
Out through E, in through F;
Out through G, in through H;
Out through F, in through H.

Thread approx 12"/30.5cm of mauve ribbon and weave through eyelets for flowers as foll:
Out through A, in through D;
Out through C, in through B;
Out through C, in through D;
Out through B, in through D.

Small flowers
Thread approx 12"/30.5cm of olive green ribbon and weave through eyelets for stems as foll:
Out through C, in through D.

Thread approx 12"/30.5cm of mauve ribbon and weave through eyelets for flowers as foll:
Out through B, in through A;
Out through B, in through C;
Out through A, in through C.

Weave loose ends of ribbon into flower or sew into place with needle and thread. Sew on buttons.

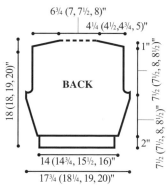

BACK

6¾ (7, 7½, 8)"
4¼ (4½,4¾, 5)"
1"
18 (18, 19, 20)"
7½ (7½, 8, 8½)"
7½ (7½, 8, 8½)"
2"
14 (14¾, 15½, 16)"
17¾ (18¼, 19, 20)"

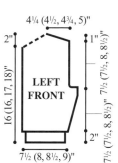

LEFT FRONT

4¼ (4½, 4¾, 5)"
2"
1"
16 (16, 17, 18)"
7½ (7½, 8, 8½)"
7½ (7½, 8, 8½)"
2"
7½ (8, 8½, 9)"
9¼ (10, 10¼, 10¾)"

SLEEVE

11¾ (12, 13, 13¾)"
6"
15½ (16, 16, 16½)"
2"
7 (7½, 8, 8¼)"

Stitch Key
☐ Textured pattern
◯ Yo
⧄ Ssk
⧅ K2tog
⧉ Cast on 2 sts

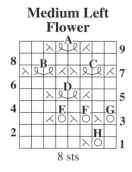

Medium Left Flower
8 sts

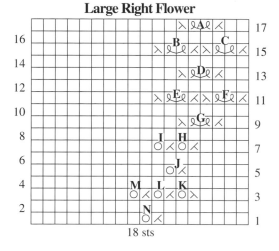

Large Right Flower
18 sts

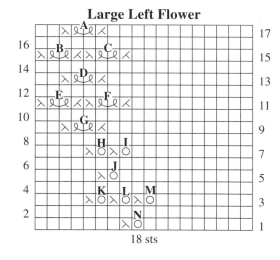

Large Left Flower
18 sts

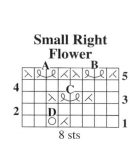

Small Left Flower
8 sts

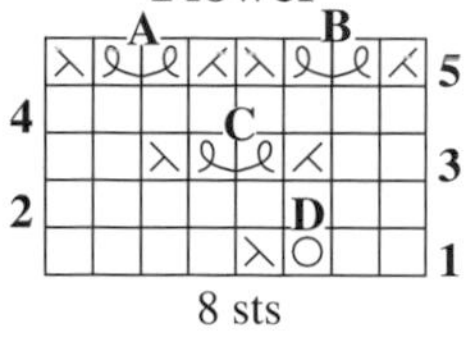

Small Right Flower
8 sts

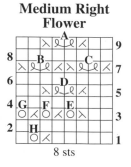

Medium Right Flower
8 sts

This beautiful, plush mohair Aran has an oversized ease ideal for layering. Boasting drop shoulders and a foldover crewneck, the pullover is densely patterned with deep, dimensional stitches for maximum texture. Shown in size Medium. The Mohair Aran first appeared in the Fall '90 issue of *Vogue Knitting*.

Mohair Aran

FOR EXPERIENCED KNITTERS

SIZES
To fit Small (Medium, Large). Directions are for smallest size with larger sizes in parentheses. If there is only one figure, it applies to all sizes.

KNITTED MEASUREMENTS
● Bust at underarm 45 (49, 53)"/113 (123,133)cm.
● Length 28 (29, 29)"/71 (73.5, 73.5)cm.
● Sleeve width at upper arm 20"/50cm.

MATERIALS
Original Yarn
● 16 (17, 18) 1½oz/40g balls (each approx 136yd/123m) of Classic Elite Yarns *Mini Mohair* (mohair/wool/nylon 4) in #8519 pink
Substitute Yarn
● 17 (18, 19) .88oz/25g balls (each approx 268yd/245m) of Filatura di Crosa/Tahki•Stacy Charles, Inc. *Baby Kid Extra* (mohair/nylon 1) in #344 pink
● One pair each sizes 5 and 8 (3.75 and 5mm) needles OR SIZE TO OBTAIN GAUGE
● Cable needle (cn) and stitch markers

Note
Pattern is for sweater only.
The original yarn used for this sweater is no longer available. A comparable substitution has been made, which is available at the time of printing. Check gauge of substitute yarns very carefully before beginning.

GAUGE
● 28 sts to 31½"/9cm and 26 rows to 4"/10cm over chart #1 using 2 strands held tog and size 8 (5mm) needles.
● 12 sts to 1¾"/4.5cm over chart #2 using 2 strands held tog and size 8 (5mm) needles.
● 16 sts to 2¼"/6cm over chart #3 using 2 strands held tog and size 8 (5mm) needles. FOR PERFECT FIT, TAKE TIME TO CHECK GAUGES. (Note: To make gauge swatch, cast on 56 sts. Beg pats: Preparation row (WS) Work 2 sts in garter st, 20 sts chart #1, 2 sts garter st, 12 sts chart #2, 2 sts garter st, 16 sts chart #3, 2 sts garter st. Cont in pats as established for a total of 26 rows. Bind off. Piece measures approx 7½"/19cm wide x 4"/10cm long.)

Notes
1 Use 2 strands held together throughout.
2 First row of all charts is a WS preparation row.

STITCH GLOSSARY
4-st Right Cable Sl 2 sts to cn and hold to *back* of work, k2, k2 from cn.
4-st Left Cable Sl 2 sts to cn and hold to *front* of work, k2, k2 from cn.
8-st Right Cable Sl 4 sts to cn and hold to *back* of work, k4, k4 from cn.
8-st Left Cable Sl 4 sts to cn and hold to *front* of work, k4, k4 from cn.
12-st Left Cable Sl 6 sts to cn and hold to *front* of work, k6, k6 from cn.

Notes
1 Place markers between pats for ease in working.
2 Work first and last st of *every* row in St st for selvage sts. Do not count these sts when measuring pieces.

BACK
With 2 strands held tog and smaller needles, cast on 150 (166, 182) sts. Work in k1, p1 rib for 3"/7.5cm, inc 20 sts evenly across last RS row—170 (186, 202) sts. Change to larger needles.
Beg pats: Preparation row (WS) P1 (selvage st), work 2 sts in garter st, 20 (28, 36) sts in chart #1, *2 sts garter st, 12 sts chart #2, 2 sts garter st, 16 sts chart #3, 2 sts garter st, 12 sts chart #2, 2 sts garter st*, 28 sts chart #1; rep between *'s once, work 20 (28, 36) sts chart #1, 2 sts garter st, p1 (selvage st). Cont in pats as established until piece measures 28 (29, 29)"/71 (73.5, 73.5)cm from beg. Bind off.

FRONT
Work as for back until piece measures 25¼ (26¼, 26¼)"/64 (66.5, 66.5)cm from beg, end with a RS row.

Neck shaping
Next row (WS) K75 (83, 91) sts, join 2nd ball of yarn and bind off 20 sts, work to end. Working both sides at once, bind off from each neck edge 5 sts once, 4 sts once, 3 sts once, 2 sts twice, dec 1 st every other row 3 times—56 (64,72) sts each side. Work even until same length as back. Bind off rem sts each side for shoulders.

SLEEVES
(Note: When there are too few sts to work cable twist, work sts in St st.) With 2 strands held tog and smaller nee-

dles, cast on 66 (70, 70) sts. Work in k1, p1 rib for 2½"/6.5cm, inc 8 sts evenly across last RS row—74 (78, 78) sts. Change to larger needles.

Beg pats: Preparation row (WS) P1 (selvage st), work first 6 (8, 8) sts of chart #3, 2 sts garter st, 12 sts chart #2, 2 sts garter st, 28 sts chart #1, 2 sts garter st, 12 sts chart #2, 2 sts garter st, work last 6 (8, 8) sts of chart #3, p1 (selvage st). Cont in pats as established, inc 1 st each side (working inc sts into pats as foll: next 10 (8, 8) incs in chart #3, 2 sts garter st, 12 sts chart #2, 2 sts garter st, 12 sts chart #1) every other row 28 (20, 20) times, then every 4th row 10 (16, 16) times—150 sts. Work even in pats until piece measures 18¾ (19½, 19½)"/47.5 (49.5, 49.5)cm from beg. Bind off.

FINISHING
Block pieces. Sew right shoulder seam.

Neckband
With RS facing and smaller needle, pick up and k84 sts around neck edge. Work in k1, p1 rib for 2"/5cm, end with a RS row. K next row on WS (turning ridge). Rib for 2"/5cm more. Bind off in rib. Sew left shoulder seam, including neckband. Fold band in half to WS and sew in place. Place markers 10"/25cm down from shoulders on front and back for armholes. Sew top of sleeves between markers. Sew side and sleeve seams.

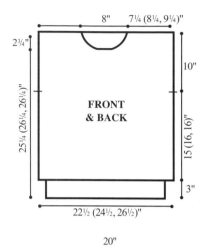

8" 7¼ (8¼, 9¼)"

2¾"

25¼ (26¼, 26¼)"

FRONT
& BACK

10"

15 (16, 16)"

3"

22½ (24½, 26½)"

20"

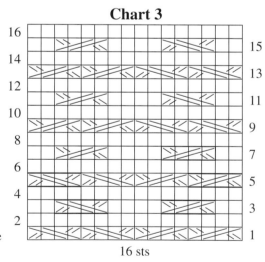

20"

SLEEVE

16¼ (17, 17)"

2½"

9¾ (10, 10)"

Chart 1

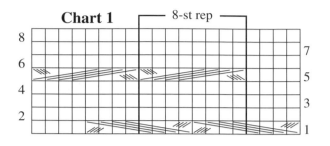

8-st rep

8

6

4

2

7

5

3

1

Chart 2

10

8

6

4

2

9

7

5

3

1

12 sts

Chart 3

16

14

12

10

8

6

4

2

15

13

11

9

7

5

3

1

16 sts

Stitch Key

◹◸◹◸ 4-st Right Cable

◸◹◸◹ 4-st Left Cable

◸◹◹◹◸◹ 8-st Right Cable

◸◹◹◹◸◹ 8-st Left Cable

◹◹◹◹◸◹◸◹ 12-st Left Cable

Draped
Pullover

A graceful twist of sinuous ribbings
shapes this elegant draped pullover.
The surplice sweater is close-fitting with
dolman sleeves and a wrapped waist.
Shown in size 34. The Draped Pullover
first appeared in the Fall '90 issue of
Vogue Knitting.

Draped Pullover

FOR EXPERT KNITTERS

SIZES
To fit 32 (34, 36, 38, 40)"/81 (86, 91, 96, 101)cm bust. Directions are for smallest size with larger sizes in parentheses. If there is only one figure, it applies to all sizes.

KNITTED MEASUREMENTS
● Bust at underarm 34½ (36½, 38½, 40, 42½)"/87 (92, 96, 101, 107)cm.
● Length 23¼ (23¾, 24, 24½, 24½)"/81.5 (82.5, 83.5, 86.5, 86.5)cm.
● Length from center back neck to wrist (without cuff) 26½ (27, 27, 27½, 28)"/67 (68, 68, 69, 70.5)cm.

MATERIALS
Original Yarn
● 16 (17, 19, 20, 22) ¾oz/20g balls (each approx 82yd/75m) of Rowan/Westminster Trading *Edina Ronay Silk and Wool* (silk/wool 2) in #851 camel
Substitute Yarn
● 8 (8, 9, 9, 10) 1¾oz/50g balls (each approx 188yd/170m) of Rowan/Westminster Fibers *True 4-Ply Botany* (wool 2) in #564 beige
● Size 4 (3.5mm) circular needle, 29"/80cm long OR SIZE TO OBTAIN GAUGE
● Stitch markers and holders

GAUGE
26 sts and 34 rows to 4"/10cm over St st using size 4 (3.5mm) needles. FOR PERFECT FIT, TAKE TIME TO CHECK GAUGE.

Notes
1 For ease in working shaping of front pieces, chart or write out pieces for chosen size.
2 To accommodate the large number of sts, work back and forth with circular needle.

STITCH GLOSSARY
Make 1 purl (M1-p) Pick up horizontal thread between st just worked and next st, sl it to LH needle, purl through the back lp.

BACK
With size 4 (3.5mm) needle, cast on 107 (113, 119, 125, 131) sts.
Row 1 (RS) K4, *p3, k3; rep from *, end k1. Working back and forth on circular needle, cont in rib for 1"/2.5cm, end with a WS row. Work in St st for 6 rows.
Next (dec) row (RS) K2, k2tog, k to last 4 sts, ssk, k2. Rep dec row every 6th row 2 (3, 3, 4, 6) times more, every 4th row 6 (6, 6, 5, 2) times—89 (93, 99, 105, 113) sts. Work even until piece measures 8 (8½, 8½, 9, 9)"/20.5 (21.5, 21.5, 23, 23)cm from beg, end with a WS row.
Next (inc) row (RS) K2, m1, k to last 2 sts, m1, k2. Rep inc row every 4th row

1 (0, 0, 0, 0) time, every other row 10 (12, 12, 12, 12) times—113 (119, 125, 131, 139) sts.

Dolman sleeve shaping
Cast on 2 sts at beg of next 2 rows, 3 sts at beg of next 2 rows, 4 sts at beg of next 2 rows, 5 sts at beg of next 2 rows, 6 sts at beg of next 4 rows, 7 sts at beg of next 2 rows—179 (185, 191, 197, 205) sts. Cast on 84 (84, 81, 81, 81) sts at beg of next 2 rows—347 (353, 353, 359, 367) sts. Work even for 36 (36, 38, 38, 38) rows—piece measures approx 4¼ (4¼, 4½, 4½, 4½)"/10.5 (10.5, 11, 11, 11)cm above last cast-on row.

Top of sleeve and shoulder shaping
Next row K154 (157, 157, 160, 164) sts, place marker (pm), k39, pm, k to end. From each sleeve edge, bind off 4 (7, 7, 7, 7) sts 1 (1, 1, 4, 8) times, 6 sts 25 (25, 25, 22, 18) times, AT SAME TIME, when piece measures 22¼ (22¾, 23, 23½, 23½)"/79 (80, 81, 84, 84)cm from beg, work 39 sts between markers in rib to end of piece as foll: P3, *k3, p3; rep from * to marker. When all shoulder bind offs are completed and piece measures approx 23¼ (23¾, 24, 24½, 24½)"/81.5 (82.5, 83.5, 86.5, 86.5)cm from beg, bind off rem 39 sts for back neck.

LEFT AND RIGHT FRONTS
(Note: Work both left and right front at same time using separate balls of yarn.)
Left Front (LF) Cast on 87 (93, 99, 105, 111) sts;
Right Front (RF) With separate ball of yarn, cast on 87 (93, 99, 105, 111) sts.
Row 1 (RS) LF: P4, k3, p3, k4, *p3, k3; rep from *, end k1; **RF**: K4, *p3, k3; rep from * to last 11 sts, then k1, p3, k3, p4. Cont in rib as established for 1"/2.5cm, end with a WS row. (Note: Read next

section carefully before beg to knit. All m1 sts are as to k on RS rows and as to p on WS rows.)

Surplice and side seam shaping
Work surplice shaping as foll:

Row 1 (RS) LF: K12, M1, k2, rib to end; **RF**: Rib to last 14 sts, k2, M1, k12.

Row 2 RF: P12, M1, p3, rib to end; **LF**: Rib to last 15 sts, p3, M1, p12.

Row 3 LF: K12, M1, pm, rib to end; **RF**: Rib to last 12 sts, pm, M1, k12. Cont in this way to inc 1 st (working inc sts into St st) every row before first marker and after 2nd marker 39 (45, 45, 47, 47) times more, AT SAME TIME, at side seam edge (beg of RS rows for LF and end of RS rows for RF) dec 1 st every 4th row 4 (0, 0, 0, 0) times, every other row 13 (23, 23, 23, 25) times, every row 0 (2, 2, 4, 0) times—112 (116, 122, 128, 136) sts and piece measures approx 6 (6½, 6½, 7, 7)"/15.5 (16.5, 16.5, 18, 18)cm from beg.

Crossover waist
Sl first 35 (33, 33, 33, 35) sts in St st of LF and last 35 (33, 33, 33, 35) sts in St st of RF to holders and cont to work on rem 77 (83, 89, 95, 101) sts in rib of each front separately for ½"/1.5cm, end with a WS row.

Dec row (RS) Across each front rib section, dec as foll: K3, *ssk, p1, k2tog, k1; rep from *, end last rep k2 instead of k1—53 (57, 61, 65, 69) sts each side. Work in newly established k3, p1 rib (with k4 at beg and end) for ½"/1.5cm more. Sl these 2 sets of rib sts to holders.

Crossover joining
Next row (RS) K35 (33, 33, 33, 35) sts of LF, pm, then work across RF rib sts as foll: P1, *k3, p1; rep from * to last 4 sts, k4; with separate ball of yarn, hold LF rib sts in front of rib sts just worked and work in established k3, p1 rib to last 4 sts, k3, p1, pm, k35 (33, 33, 33, 35) sts of RF. Work each newly-joined section at same time with separate balls of yarn for 2"/5cm from joining, end with a WS row.

Detach ribs
Sl 35 (33, 33, 33, 35) sts in St st of each front piece to holders, and working across 53 (57, 61, 65, 69) sts in rib of each front separately (beg and end each piece with k4), work for ½"/1.5cm, end with a WS row.

Inc row Across each front rib section, inc as foll: K4, *M1-p, p1, M1-p, k3; rep from *, end k1—77 (83, 89, 95, 101) sts. Work in k3, p3 rib for ½"/1.5cm more. Sl these 2 sets of rib sts to holders.

Rejoining
Next row (RS) Work LF (St st) sts off holder as foll: K2, M1, k to end, then work rib sts from RF piece (what originated as LF rib sts) off holder by k1, pm, then work rib to end; with separate ball of yarn, hold rib sts from LF piece (what originated as RF rib sts) in front of other rib sts just worked and work in rib to last st, pm, k1, and work RF (St st) as foll: k to last 2 sts, M1, k2. Working both sides separately, inc 1 st in this way at side seams of body every 4th row 1 (0, 0, 0, 0) time, every other row 10 (12, 12, 12, 12) times, then cast on for dolman sleeve as for back, AT SAME TIME, cont surplice shaping on next RS row as foll: **LF**: Work to 2 sts before marker, k2tog, work rib over 76 (82, 88, 94, 100) sts; **RF**: Rib to marker, ssk, k to end.

Next row (WS) RF: Work to 2 sts before marker, sl 1, p1, psso, work to end; **LF**: Rib to marker, p2tog, p to end. Cont in this way to dec for surplice shaping every row 40 (38, 36, 33, 31) times more, every other row 19 (14, 11, 9, 9) times, every 4th row 6 (9, 11, 13, 13) times, AT SAME TIME, when sleeve cuff edge measures same as back, bind off from each shoulder edge 4 (7, 7, 7, 7) sts 1 (1, 1, 4, 8) times, 6 sts 15 (15, 15, 12, 8) times and 4 sts once—76 (82, 88, 94, 100) sts of rib rem each side.

Next row (RS) Across each rib section, dec as foll: **LF**: K2, *ssk, p1, k2tog, k1; rep from *, end ssk; **RF**: *K2tog, k1, ssk, p1; rep from *, end k2tog, k2. Bind off rem 51 (55, 59, 63, 67) sts in k3, p1 rib.

FINISHING
Block pieces. Sew top of sleeves and shoulder seams.

Sleeve cuff
Pick up and k 57 (57, 61, 61, 61) sts along cuff edge.

Next row (WS) P2, *k1, p3; rep from *, end k1, p2. Work in k3, p1 rib for 2"/5cm. Bind off in rib. Sew side and underarm sleeve seams. Sew 6"/15cm of V-neck crossover tog to hold closed.

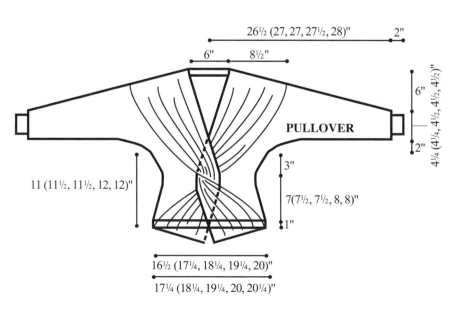

26½ (27, 27, 27½, 28)" 2"

6" 8½"

6"

4¼ (4¼, 4½, 4½, 4½)"

PULLOVER

2"

11 (11½, 11½, 12, 12)"

3"

7(7½, 7½, 8, 8)"

1"

16½ (17¼, 18¼, 19¼, 20)"

17¼ (18¼, 19¼, 20, 20¼)"

Nicky Epstein

In 1979, just for the fun of it, Nicky Epstein entered a sweater in a McCall's Needlework design contest and won. In fact, the editors thought her work was so good that they asked to see more. Nicky quickly whipped up a few more pieces, and sold every one. "I had to reknit them in different yarn, but that's what really started me. They liked everything I brought them," she recalls.

One of the editors Nicky met at McCall's, Lola Ehrlich, went on to work with *Vogue Knitting* magazine. Lola not only recommended Nicky's work to the editors there, she also introduced her to other magazines as well. "Lola Ehrlich was really a big influence, a big part of my success," she remembers. "She encouraged me. I probably would never have approached other magazines, but Lola called *Family Circle*. That's how I got started—my name was just passed around."

First taught by her grand-mother and later by a neigh-borhood friend, Nicky started knitting as a child. She remem-bers knitting clothes for her Barbie dolls, a talent, among others, that Nicky has become known for. After graduating from the Columbus College of Art and Design, Nicky worked first as an art director for a small advertising agency in New York City, then as a fashion stylist for television commercials.

It was after Nicky met and married Howard Epstein, a television advertising executive, that she began to turn her attention increasingly toward knitting. "I had just gotten married and my husband was traveling a lot," Nicky says. "At that time, I was doing styling for television commercials, but it was getting too hard. I was going one place and he was going another. With the knitting, I could take it with me and go with him." It was on one her husband's business trips that Nicky entered the McCall's contest and her career as a handknit designer began.

Nicky recalls the early years of her career fondly. "I used to go the *Vogue Knitting* concept meetings. That's the only connection the designers could have with each

other," she explains. "Vogue was the only one that did that. That's where I met Deborah Newton, Norah Gaughan, a lot of fellow designers. It was really fun. We were really inspired by that. I'd come home and my mind would be racing."

Nicky quickly learned that the only way to stay ahead in the design business was to keep coming up with innovative tech-niques. "When I first started, I did mostly stitchwork, because that's what I knew. But the few times that I did colorwork, I sold everything I put down. That's because not a lot of people were doing it at that time. That was in the early '80s. Then when colorwork started getting more popular, I went into the appliqué work," she continues.

"It's really tough to make a living in this business. In order to keep selling things, I had to reinvent myself by developing different techniques."

To keep her designs up-to-the-minute, Nicky attends fashion shows both here and abroad, tuning herself in to the colors and silhouettes of the season. She also enjoys visiting museums and going to the theater, drawing inspiration from everything from period costumes and medieval tapestries to vintage paper dolls and wrapping papers.

Nicky also teaches knitting workshops, helping new knitters overcome any apprehensions or misgivings they may have about the craft. "I'll do anything to promote knitting," she declares. "I think knitting should be fun. I don't think it should be painful. When I teach, I stress that. There's really no right or wrong way to knit." Her students also benefit from her incredible versatility and acceptance of all things knit. "When I'm teaching, some students will show up with wool, others with acrylic. Both deserve to have good designs accessible to them. So my philosophy is that I'll knit with anything and I'll design with anything."

Recently, Nicky has turned her attention from designing for magazines and yarn companies to writing

"I think knitting should be fun. I don't think it should be painful. When I teach, I stress that. There's really no right or wrong way to knit."

books. She's had three books already published and is now working on her fourth. The books represent many of Nicky's technical contributions, most significantly her unique approach to knitted embellishments, along with her creative flair. In her book, Nicky describes how to attach dimensional appliqués to knitted fabrics, rather than knitting them in. This gives knitters greater design freedom and working ease. "I am really proud of the appliqué knitting book, because it represents twenty years of my work," she says. "It can make something very simple look intricate, as if you spent hours on it, while in fact it is actually very quick and gratifying knitting."

While she hasn't stopped designing for magazines completely, Nicky has been trying to lighten her work load a bit. "I am a little more selective now," she says. "Once in a while I send something out, but mostly the editors call and ask me specifically for something." Still, she doesn't see herself ever not knitting, not designing. "I've been doing this for twenty years," she says. "I can't imagine relaxing and watching television or being in the car without knitting!" And we can't imagine knitting without Nicky Epstein.

Flora and fauna tapestry motifs are richly colored in this masterpiece afghan and whimsical matching hat. The blanket has a framed border and features knit-in grape-motif bobbles and applied embroidery. The Tapestry Afghan & Hat first appeared in the Winter '91/92 issue of *Vogue Knitting*.

Tapestry Afghan & Hat

FOR EXPERIENCED KNITTERS

KNITTED MEASUREMENTS

AFGHAN:
● Width (with borders) 46½"/118cm.
● Length (with borders) 61½"/156cm.

MATERIALS

AFGHAN:
● 17 1¾oz/50g balls (each approx 110yd/100m) of Reynolds *Paterna Handknitting Yarn* (wool 4) in #814 burgundy (MC)
● 1 ball each in #727 grey blue (A), #212 purple (B), #214 light mauve (C), #206 brick (D), #815 rust (E), #808 dark red (F), #954 orange (G), #417 gold orange (H), #150 beige (J), #121 brown (K), #472 medium beige (L), #412 medium brown (M), #439 gold (N), #451 light yellow (P), #548 light green (Q), #908 forest (R), #918 moss green (S), #914 light olive (T), #917 dark olive (U), #616 lilac (W) and #608 dark purple (X) (**Note:** contrasting colors may not use complete balls. For colors A, E, J, and P, you can purchase smaller amounts.)

HAT:
● 3 1¾oz/50g balls (each approx 110yd/100m) of Reynolds *Paterna Handknitting Yarn* (wool 4) in #814 burgundy (MC)
● 1 ball or small amounts each in #727 grey blue (A), #212 purple (B), #214 light mauve (C), #412 medium brown (M), #439 gold (N), #548 light green (Q), #908 forest (R), #914 light olive (T), #917 dark olive (U), #616 lilac (W) and #608 dark purple (X)

BOTH:
● One pair size 7 (4.5mm) needles OR SIZE TO OBTAIN GAUGE
● Bobbins

Note
Some of the original colors used for the afghan and hat are no longer available. Comparable color substitutions have been made, which are available at the time of printing.

GAUGE
19 sts and 26 rows to 4"/10cm over St st and chart pat, using size 7 (4.5mm) needles. TO SAVE TIME, TAKE TIME TO CHECK GAUGE.

Notes
1 Small areas of color on afghan chart can be duplicate st, if desired. Hat chart can be worked in duplicate st, if desired.
2 Use a separate bobbin for each block of color. Do not carry colors along WS side of work.
3 For ease in working, enlarge charts and color in blocks with corresponding colors.

STITCH GLOSSARY
Bobble In next st, k1, p1, k1, p1, k1 all in the same st (5 sts made), turn, p5, turn, k5, turn, p5, turn, k5, pass first, 2nd, 3rd and 4th st over last st made–1 st.

AFGHAN

CENTER PIECE
With MC, cast on 145 sts. Beg with st 1 of afghan chart, work from *right to left* to st 145. Work afghan chart through row 148. Turn chart upside down, working row 147 and beg with st 145, work chart from *right to left* through st 1. Cont to work afghan chart from row 147 through row 1. Bind off.

BORDER
Top and Bottom Borders
With MC, cast on 145 sts. Work top and bottom border chart from right to left to center st, then work from left to right back to beg st. Cont to work chart through row 52, inc 1 st at each side every other row 25 times, as shown on chart—195 sts. P 1 row on RS for turning ridge. With MC only, cont to work in St st, dec 1 st each side every other row until piece measures 1¼"/3cm from turning ridge. Bind off.

Side Borders
With MC, cast on 223 sts. Work side border chart from right to left to center st, then work from left to right back to beg st. Cont to work chart through row 52, inc 1 st at each side every other row 25 times, as shown on chart—273 sts. P 1 row on RS for turning ridge. With MC only, cont to work in St st, dec 1 st each side every other row until piece measures 1¼"/3cm from turning ridge. Bind off.

FINISHING
Block pieces. Sew cast-on edge of borders to center piece. Sew mitered corners. Turn hem to WS at turning ridge and sew in place. Embroider outline st, as indicated on charts, in desired colors.

HAT

SIZE
One size fits all.

BRIM
With MC, cast on 100 sts. Work in St st until piece measures 5¼"/13.5cm from beg, end with a WS row.
Beg bobble chart: Row 1 (RS) With MC, k1, work 14-st rep of bobble chart 7 times, with MC, k1. Work through row 12 of chart. With MC only, work until piece measures 7½"/19cm from beg, end with a RS row. K 1 row for turning ridge. Cont to work in St st until piece measures 4"/10cm from turning ridge, end with a WS row. Work hat chart for 21 rows. With MC only, work even until piece measures 7½"/19cm from turning ridge. Bind off.

CROWN
(Note: Wrap yarn to prevent holes on short rows.) With MC, cast on 17 sts. Beg short rows as foll: *K17, turn, p16, turn, k16, turn, p12, turn, k12, turn, p8, turn, k8, turn, p4, turn, k4, turn, p17. Rep from * 13 times more. Bind off.

FINISHING
Block pieces. Work flowers with C and X, as indicated on chart. Fold brim in half to WS and sew in place. Sew cast-on edge to bound-off edge of crown. Sew crown on brim.

Twisted cord (make two)
Cut 1 piece of yarn 50"/127cm long. Make a knot at each end. Place one end over a doorknob and put a pencil through other end. Turn pencil clockwise until strands are tightly twisted. Keeping strands taut, fold in half. Remove pencil and allow strands to twist onto themselves. Untie ends and re-tie ½"/1.5cm from each end of cord.

Pompoms (make 4)
Cut 2 circular pieces of cardboard each 1"/2.5cm in diameter with ½"/1.5cm hole in center. Then cut a pie-shaped wedge out of each circle. Hold cardboard tog and wrap tightly with

yarn. Clip yarn around circumference of circle. Tie strand of yarn between cardboard. Trim, leaving yarn for attaching. Remove cardboard. Trim pompom. Make two 1"/2.5cm and two 1½"/4cm pompoms. Fold up brim and sew cords to inside. Attach 1 of each size pompom to end of twisted cords.

Chart for Hat

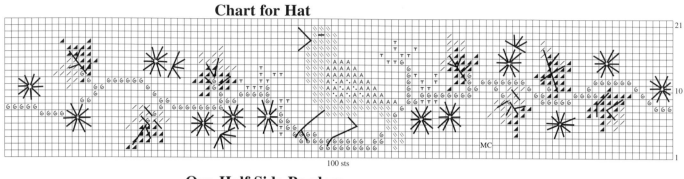

100 sts

One-Half Side Borders

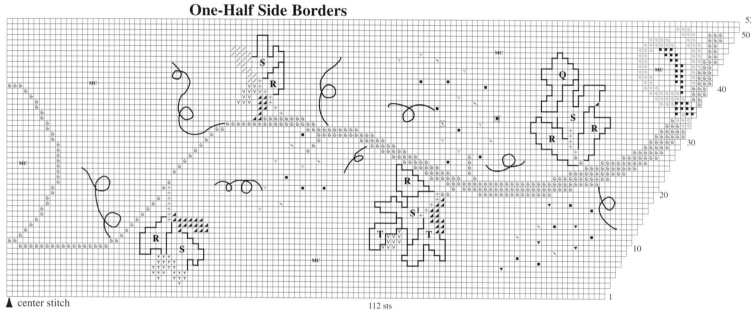

▲ center stitch

112 sts

One-Half Short Borders

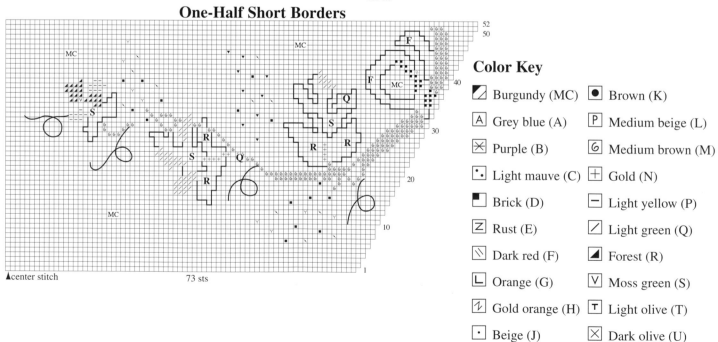

▲center stitch

73 sts

Color Key

Symbol	Color	Symbol	Color
◸	Burgundy (MC)	●	Brown (K)
A	Grey blue (A)	P	Medium beige (L)
⊠	Purple (B)	G	Medium brown (M)
⬝˙	Light mauve (C)	⊞	Gold (N)
◼	Brick (D)	−	Light yellow (P)
Z	Rust (E)	◹	Light green (Q)
◺	Dark red (F)	◣	Forest (R)
L	Orange (G)	V	Moss green (S)
◿	Gold orange (H)	T	Light olive (T)
⬝˙	Beige (J)	⊠	Dark olive (U)

One-Half of Afghan Chart

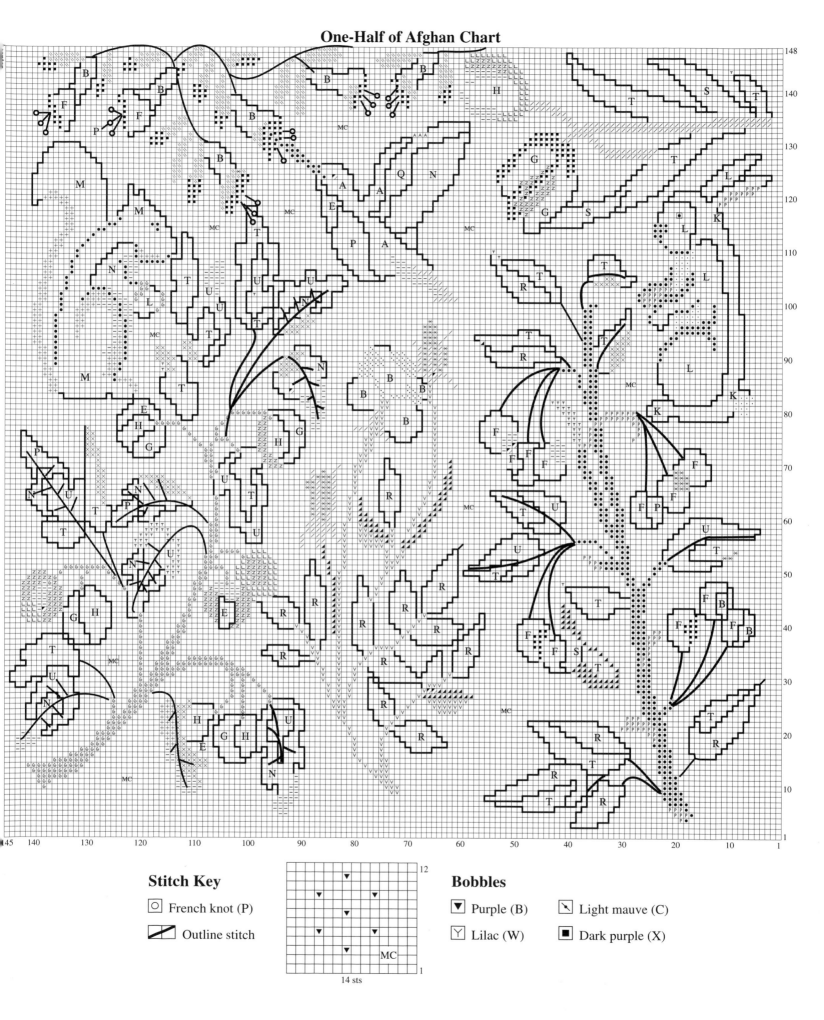

Stitch Key

⊙ French knot (P)

╱ Outline stitch

Bobbles

▼ Purple (B)

Y Lilac (W)

◣ Light mauve (C)

■ Dark purple (X)

14 sts

The soft sheen of a ribbon yarn gives the traditional Aran patterning of this sweater an elegant luster. A fold-back shawl collar, delicate points at the cuffs and fronts, and unique, knit-to-match frog closures add an edge of glamour. Shown in size Medium. The Diamond Aran first appeared in the Winter '98/99 issue of *Vogue Knitting*.

Diamond Aran

FOR EXPERT KNITTERS

SIZES
To fit Small (Medium, Large). Directions are for smallest size with larger sizes in parentheses. If there is only one figure, it applies to all sizes.

KNITTED MEASUREMENTS
● Bust (closed) 32 (36, 40)"/81.5 (91.5,101.5)cm.
● Length (at center back) 18 (18½, 19)"/45.5 (47, 48)cm.
● Upper arm 16 (16½, 17)"/40.5 (42, 43)cm.

MATERIALS
Original Yarn
● 23 (25, 28) 1¾oz/50g balls (each approx 66yd/60m) of Trendsetter Yarns *Piatina* (viscose 4) in #11 champagne
Substitute Yarn
● 21 (23, 26) 1¾oz/50g balls (each approx 147yd/130m) of Trendsetter Yarns *Amazon* (viscose 2) in #11 champagne
● One pair each sizes 6 and 8 (4 and 5mm) needles OR SIZE TO OBTAIN GAUGE
● Size 6 (4mm) circular needle, 16"/40cm long
● Stitch markers and holders
● Two cable needles (cn)
● Size 6 (4mm)
Note
The original yarn used for this sweater is no longer available. A comparable substitution has been made, which is available at the time of printing. Check gauge of substitute yarns very carefully before beginning.

GAUGES
● 22 sts and 36 rows to 4"/10cm over seed st using size 8 (5mm) needles.
● 10 sts to 1"/2.5cm over chart 1 or chart 3 using size 8 (5mm) needles.
● 21 sts to 3¼"/8cm over chart 2 using size 8 (5mm) needles.
FOR PERFECT FIT, TAKE TIME TO CHECK GAUGES.

STITCH GLOSSARY
Seed Stitch
Row 1 (RS) *K1, p1; rep from * to end.
Row 2 K the purl sts and p the knit sts. Rep row 2 for seed st.

Dec 2 Sl 2 tog knitwise, k1, pass 2 slipped sts over k1.
C3R Sl 1 st to cn and hold to *back*, k2, p1 from cn.
C3L Sl 2 sts to cn and hold to *front*, p1, k2 from cn.
C5R Sl 2 sts to cn and hold to *back*, sl next st to 2nd cn and hold to *front*, k2, sl st from front cn to RH needle, k2 from back cn.
C6R Sl 3 sts to cn and hold to *back*, k3, k3 from cn.
C6L Sl 3 sts to cn and hold to *front*, k3, k3 from cn.

Note
Work first and last st of every row in St st for selvage sts. Work all decs and incs inside of these sts.

BACK
With smaller needles, cast on 119 (127, 139) sts. Work in k1, p1 rib for 1½"/4cm.
Preparation row (WS) P2, [k1, p1] 2 (4, 7) times, k1, place marker (pm), p1, *k2, p6, k2, p1, k2, p3, [k1, p1] 4 times,

k1, p3, k2, p1*; rep between *'s twice more, k2, p6, k2, p1, pm, k1, [p1, k1] 2 (4, 7) times, p2. Change to larger needles.
Beg chart pats
Row 1 (RS) K1, work seed st over 6 (10, 16) sts, sl marker, sl 1, work 10 sts of chart 1, beg with row 23, work 21 sts of chart 2, work 10 sts of chart 3, 21 sts of chart 3, 10 sts of chart 1, 21 sts chart 2, 10 sts of chart 3, sl 1, sl marker, work seed st over 6 (10, 16) sts, k1. Cont in pats as established until piece measures 9½"/24cm from beg.

Armhole shaping
Bind off 4 (6, 7) sts at beg of next 2 rows. Dec 1 st each side every 4th row 2 (4, 4) times, every other row 0 (0, 1) times—107 (107, 115) sts. Work even until armhole measures 8½ (9, 9½)"/21.5 (23, 24)cm, end with a WS row. Place sts on a holder.

RIGHT FRONT
With smaller needles, cast on 71 (75, 81) sts.
Row 1 (RS) Rib 33 (35, 38), dec 2, rib 35 (37, 40).
Row 2 K the knit sts and p the purl sts. Rep last 2 rows 4 times more, working 1 less rib st before and after dec 2, ending with a WS row. Change to larger needles.
Next row (RS) Rib 28 (30, 33), dec 2, rib 30 (32, 35)—59 (63, 69) sts.

Beg short rows
Preparation row (WS) P2, [k1, p1] 2 (4, 7) times, k1, pm, p1, k2, p6, k2, p1, k7, p5, k2, turn.
Row 1 (RS) P2, C5R, p2, turn.
Row 2 K2, p5, k3, turn.

Row 3 P3, k2, sl 1, k2, p3, turn.
Row 4 K3, p5, k4, turn.
Row 5 P4, C5R, p4, turn.
Row 6 K4, p5, k5, turn.
Row 7 P5, k2, sl 1, k2, p5, turn.
Row 8 K5, p5, k6, turn.
Row 9 P6, C5R, p6, turn.
Row 10 K6, p2, k1, p2, k7, turn.
Row 11 P6, C3R, k1, C3L, p6, turn.
Row 12 K6, p2, k1, p1, k1, p2, k6, p1, k1, turn.
Row 13 P1, sl 1, p5, C3R, k1, p1, k1, C3L, p5, sl 1, p1, turn.
Row 14 K1, p1, k5, p2, [k1, p1] twice, k1, p2, k5, p1, k2, turn.
Row 15 P2, sl 1, p4, C3R, [k1, p1] twice, k1, C3L, p4, sl 1, p2, turn.
Row 16 K2, p1, k4, p2, [k1, p1] 3 times, k1, p2, k4, p1, k2, p2, turn.
Row 17 K2, p2, sl 1, p3, C3R, [k1, p1] 3 times, k1, C3L, p3, sl 1, p2, k2, turn.
Row 18 P2, k2, p1, k3, p2, [k1, p1] 4 times, k1, p2, k3, p1, k2, p4, turn.
Row 19 K4, p2, sl 1, p2, C3R, [k1, p1] 4 times, k1, C3L, p2, sl 1, p2, k6, p2, sl 1, pm, [k1, p1] 3 (5, 8) times.
Row 20 P2, work seed st to marker, p1, k2, p6, k2, p1, k2, p2, [k1, p1] 5 times, k1, p2, k2, p1, k2, p6, k1, turn.
Row 21 P1, k6, p2, sl 1, p2, k2, [k1, p1] 5 times, k3, p2, sl 1, p2, k6, p2, sl 1, seed st to end.
Row 22 P2, work seed st to marker, p1, k2, p6, k2, p1, k2, p3, [k1, p1] 4 times, k1, p3, k2, p1, k2, p6, k2, p1, k1, turn.
Row 23 K1, sl 1, p2, C6R, p2, sl 1, p2, C3L, [k1, p1] 4 times, k1, C3R, p2, sl 1, p2, C6L, p2, sl 1, seed st to end.
Row 24 P2, seed st to marker, p1, k2, p6, k2, p1, k3, p3, [k1, p1] 3 times, k1, p3, k3, p1, k2, p6, k2, p1, [k1, p1] twice, turn.
Row 25 [P1, k1] twice, sl 1, p2, k6, p2, sl 1, p3, C3L, [k1, p1] 3 times, k1, C3R, p3, sl 1, p2, k6, p2, sl 1, seed st to end.
Row 26 P2, seed st to marker, p1, k2, p6, k2, p1, k4, p3, [k1, p1] twice, k1, p3, k4, p1, k2, p6, k2, p1, [k1, p1] 3 times, k1, turn.
Row 27 [K1, p1] 3 times, k1, sl 1, p2, k6, p2, sl 1, p4, C3L, [k1, p1] twice,

k1, C3R, p4, sl 1, p2, k6, p2, sl 1, seed st to end.
Row 28 P2, seed st to marker, p1, k2, p6, k2, p1, k5, p3, k1, p1, k1, p3, k5, p1, k2, p6, k2, p1, [k1, p1] 4 times, p1. Front shaping is complete. Place marker each side of row. Measure lengths above this marker. Cont in pats as established until same length as back to armhole.

Armhole and neck shaping

Work armhole shaping as for back, AT SAME TIME, dec 1 st at neck edge (beg of RS rows) every other row 10 times, every 4th row 10 times—33 (33, 37) sts. Work even until same length as back to shoulder. Place sts on a holder.

LEFT FRONT

Work to correspond to right front, reversing placement of pats and reversing all shaping.

SLEEVES

With smaller needles, cast on 57 sts.
Row 1 (RS) K1, [p1, k1] 13 times, dec 2, k1, [p1, k1] 13 times.
Row 2 K the knit sts and p the purl sts. Rep last 2 rows 4 times more, working 1 less rib st before and after dec 2, ending with a WS row. Change to larger needles.
Next row (RS) Rib 22, dec 2, rib 22—45 sts.

Beg short rows

Preparation row (WS) P2, k2, p6, k2, p1, k7, p5, k2, turn.
Rows 1-18 Rep short rows 1-18 of right front.
Row 19 K4, p2, sl 1, p2, C3R, [k1, p1] 4 times, k1, C3L, p2, sl 1, p2, k4, turn.
Row 20 P4, k2, p1, k2, p2, [k1, p1] 5 times, k1, p2, k2, p1, k2, p6, turn.
Row 21 C6R, p2, sl 1, p2, k2, [k1, p1] 5 times, k3, p2, sl 1, p2, C6L, p2, turn.
Row 22 K2, p6, k2, p1, k2, p3, [k1, p1] 4 times, k1, p3, k2, p1, k2, p6, k2, turn.
Row 23 P2, k6, p2, sl 1, p2, C3L, [k1, p1] 4 times, k1, C3R, p2, sl 1, p2, k6, p3, k1, turn.

Row 24 P2, k2, p6, k2, p1, k3, p3, [k1, p1] 3 times, k1, p3, k3, p1, k2, p6, k2, p2 — 45 sts.
Row 25 K1, p1, M1, pm, p2, k6, p2, sl 1, p3, C3L, [k1, p1] 3 times, k1, C3R, p3, sl 1, p2, k6, p2, pm, M1, p1, k1. Cuff shaping is complete. Place marker each side of row. Measure lengths above this marker. Cont in pats as established, inc 1 st each side (working inc sts into seed st before first marker and after 2nd marker) every 4th row 10 (13, 16) times, every 6th row 12 (10, 8) times— 91 (93, 95) sts. Work even until piece measures 14"/35.5cm above markers, end with a WS row.

Cap shaping

Bind off 4 (6, 7) sts at beg of next 2 rows, 3 sts at beg of next 0 (18, 14) rows, 4 (4, 2) sts at beg of next 18 (4, 14) rows. Bind off rem 11 sts.

FINISHING

Block pieces to measurements. K 33 (33, 37) sts of each front shoulder tog with 33 (33, 37) sts of back shoulder for shoulder seams. Set in sleeves. Sew side and sleeve seams.

Neckband

With WS facing and with smaller needle, pick up and k 53 sts along left front neck, k 41 sts from back neck holder, pick up and k 53 sts along right front neck —147 sts.
Next row (RS) K1, *p1, k1; rep from * to end.

Beg short rows

Next row Rib to last 4 sts, turn.
Next row Sl 1, rib to last 4 sts, turn.
Next row Sl 1, rib to last 8 sts, turn.
Next row Sl 1, rib to last 8 sts, turn. Cont in this way to work 4 sts less at end of next 20 rows. Then work 5 sts less at end of next 2 rows. There are 41 sts worked on last short row.
Next row Sl 1, rib 47, turn.
Next row 1 Sl 1, rib 53, turn. Cont in this way to work 6 more sts at end of next 14 rows, then 5 sts more at end of

next 2 rows. Rib 1 row on all 147 sts. Bind off in rib.

FROGS (make 2)
With dpn, cast on 3 sts. Make I-cords as foll: two 8"/20.5cm for button side and two 10"/25.5cm for loop side. Sew

front edge closed or sew several hook and eyes along front edge to close. Use the illustration as a guide to position the cord. Begin with the cast-on edge and follow the arrows, pinning the cord in place as you work. Tack frogs at points where cords cross. Sew frogs to fronts

(see photo for placement).

BUTTONS (make 2)
Make two 2"/5cm I-cords and knot twice to make buttons. Sew inside the shorter cord loop.

Chart 1
10 sts

Chart 3
10 sts

Chart 2
21 sts

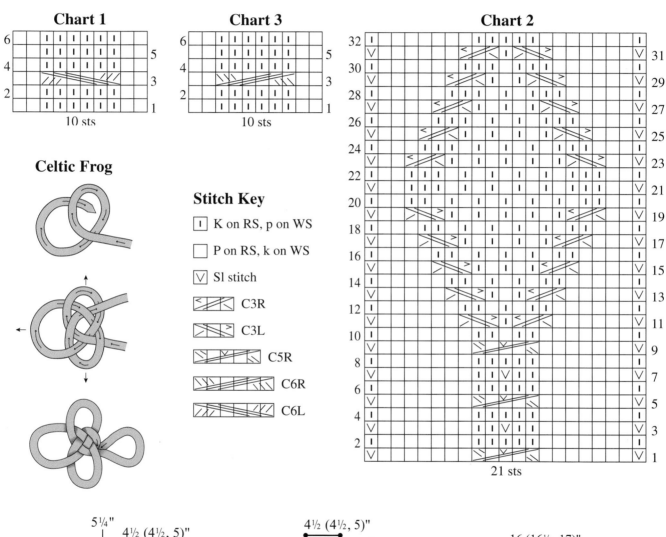

Celtic Frog

Stitch Key

I	K on RS, p on WS
	P on RS, k on WS
V	Sl stitch
	C3R
	C3L
	C5R
	C6R
	C6L

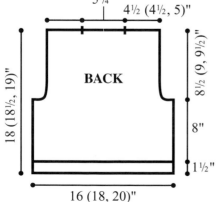

BACK

5¼"
4½ (4½, 5)"
18 (18½, 19)"
8½ (9, 9½)"
8"
1½"
16 (18, 20)"

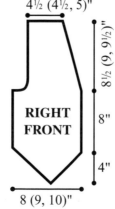

RIGHT FRONT

4½ (4½, 5)"
8½ (9, 9½)"
8"
4"
8 (9, 10)"

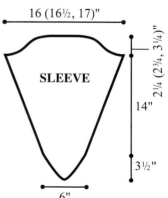

SLEEVE

16 (16½, 17)"
2¼ (2¾, 3¼)"
14"
3½"
6"

A Victorian paper doll and her wardrobe embellished with lace, buttons, and beads give this child's sweater cut-out charm. Designed for sizes four through ten, the pullover has drop shoulders and delicate lace ribbing along the collar, cuffs, and lower edge. Shown in size 6. The Paper-Doll Sweater first appeared in the Winter '92/93 issue of *Vogue Knitting.*

Paper-Doll Sweater

FOR EXPERIENCED KNITTERS

SIZES
To fit 23 (25, 27, 29)"/58 (63, 68, 74)cm chest OR child's size 4 (6, 8, 10). Directions are for smallest size with larger sizes in parentheses. If there is only one figure, it applies to all sizes.

KNITTED MEASUREMENTS
● Chest at underarm 32 (34, 37, 40)"/81.5 (86.5, 94, 101.5)cm.
● Length 18 (20, 22, 23)"/45.5 (51, 56, 58.5)cm.
● Sleeve width at upper arm 12 (14, 16, 18)"/30.5 (35.5, 40.5, 45.5)cm.

MATERIALS
Original Yarn
● 6 (7, 8, 9) 1¾oz/50g balls (each approx 109yd/100m) of Plymouth Yarns *Cleo* (cotton 4) in #411 seafoam (MC)
● 1 ball each in #385 black (A), #439 violet (B), #500 ecru (C), #435 yellow (D), #419 pink (E), #409 rose (F), #019 blue (G), #378 brown (H) and #403 peach (J)
Substitute Yarn
● 5 (6, 7, 8) 1¾oz/50g balls (each approx 136yd/123m) of Plymouth Yarns *Wildflower* (cotton/acrylic 3) in #42 seafoam (MC)
● 1 ball each in #47 black (A), #50 vio-let (B), #40 ecru (C), #48 yellow (D), #53 pink (E), #32 rose (F), #71 blue (G), #68 brown (H) and #52 peach (J)
● One pair each sizes 4 and 5 (3.5 and 3.75mm) needles OR SIZE TO OBTAIN GAUGE
● Bobbins and stitch markers
● Assorted buttons, beads and ribbons
Note
The original yarn used for this sweater is no longer available. A comparable substitution has been made, which is available at the time of printing. Check gauge of substitute yarns very carefully before beginning.

GAUGE
21 sts and 28 rows to 4"/10cm over St st using size 5 (3.75mm) needles. FOR PERFECT FIT, TAKE TIME TO CHECK GAUGE.

STITCH GLOSSARY
Lace Rib (multiple of 7 sts + 2 extra)
Row 1 (RS) P2, *k5, p2; rep from *.
Row 2 and 4 (WS) K2, *p5, k2; rep from *.
Row 3 P2 *k2tog, yo, k1, yo, ssk, p2; rep from *. Rep rows 1-4 for lace rib.

Note
When changing colors, twist yarns on WS to prevent holes. To avoid long loose strands, weave or twist yarns not in use around working yarn every 3 or 4 sts. Use separate bobbins for large blocks of color.

BACK
With smaller needles and MC, cast on 79 (86, 93, 100) sts. Work 4-row rep of lace rib 3 (5, 5, 5) times, inc 5 (4, 5, 4) sts evenly across last WS row—84 (90, 98, 104) sts. Change to larger needles and St st. Work even until piece measures 18 (20, 22, 23)"/45.5 (51, 56, 58.5)cm from beg, end with a WS row. Bind off.

FRONT
Work lace rib as for back. Change to larger needles and St st. Work 0 (4, 10, 14) rows.
Beg front chart: Row 1 (RS) K5 (8, 12, 15) MC, place marker (pm), work 71 sts of chart, pm, k8 (11, 15, 18) MC. Cont to work chart through row 100 (104, 108, 108) and sts outside chart with MC—piece measures approx 16 (18, 19½, 20)"/40.5 (45.5, 49.5, 51)cm from beg, end with a WS row.

Neck shaping
Next row (RS) Cont in chart pat, work 31 (32, 36, 39) sts, join 2nd ball of yarn and bind off 22 (26, 26, 26) sts, work to end. Working both sides at once, dec 1 st at each neck edge every other row 5 times—26 (27, 31, 34) sts, AT SAME TIME, when row 108 of chart is complete, work in MC only until same length as back to shoulder. Bind off.

SLEEVES
With smaller needles and MC, cast on 37 (37, 44, 44) sts. Work 4-row rep of lace rib 3 (3, 4, 4) times, inc 7 (9, 8, 8) sts evenly across last row—44 (46, 52, 52) sts. Change to larger needles and St st, inc 1 st each side every 4th row 0 (7, 1, 11) times, every 6th row 6 (7, 15, 10) times, then every 8th row 4 (0, 0, 0) times—64 (74, 84, 94) sts, AT SAME TIME, when piece measures 2 (2½, 3, 4½)"/5 (6.5, 7.5, 11.5)cm from beg, end with a WS row—44 (48, 54, 58) sts.
Beg chart: Row 1 (RS) K2 (3, 6, 8) MC, work chart through st 42 (45, 48, 48), k0 (0, 0, 2) MC. Cont to work chart until 66

Sleeve Chart

Front Chart

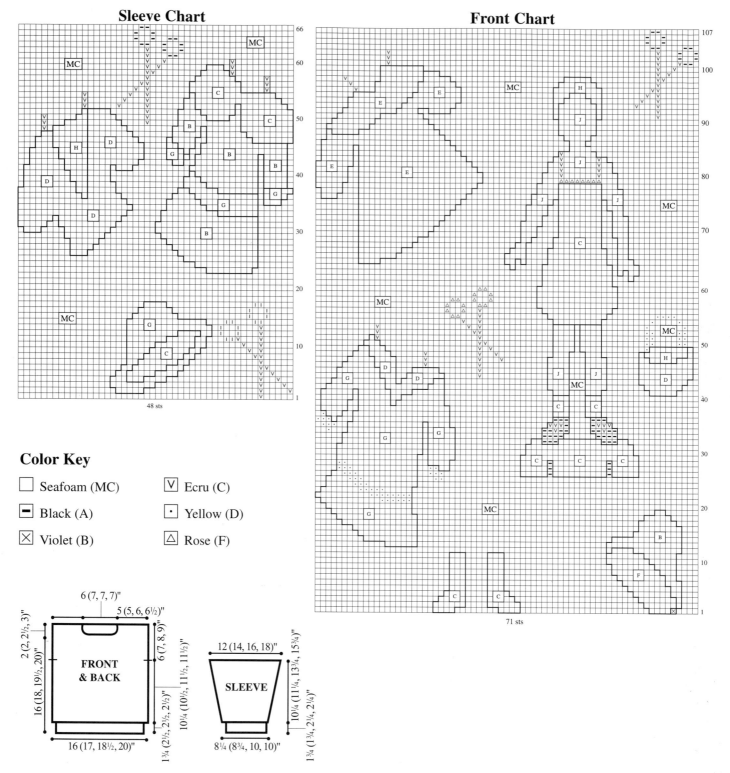

48 sts

71 sts

Color Key

☐ Seafoam (MC)	Ⓥ Ecru (C)
⊟ Black (A)	· Yellow (D)
⊠ Violet (B)	△ Rose (F)

Schematic measurements

FRONT & BACK
6 (7, 7, 7)"
5 (5, 6, 6½)"
2 (2, 2½, 3)"
6 (7, 8, 9)"
16 (18, 19½, 20)"
1¾ (2½, 2½, 2½)"
10¼ (10½, 11½, 11½)"
16 (17, 18½, 20)"

SLEEVE
12 (14, 16, 18)"
10¼ (11¼, 13¾, 15¾)"
10¼ (11¼, 2¼, 2¼)"
1¾ (1¾, 2¼, 2¼)"
8¼ (8¾, 10, 10)"

rows are complete, cont incs as established, then work in MC only until piece measures 12 (13, 16, 18)"/30.5 (33, 40.5, 45.5)cm from beg. Bind off.

FINISHING

Block pieces. Sew right shoulder seam. With H, make 4 braids, each 2"/5cm long. Tack 2 to each side of doll's head.

Embroider straight st eyes and mouth on face. With F, straight st lines on slip top. Cut ribbons and trims to outline yokes, socks, for baskets and hats. Use small beads as buttons. Add cameo and heart buttons as faux jewelry.

Neckband

With RS facing, smaller needles and

MC, pick up and k86 (93, 93, 100) sts evenly around neck edge. Work 4-row rep of lace rib 3 times. Bind off loosely. Sew left shoulder including lace rib band. Place markers 6 (7, 8, 9)"/15 (17.5, 20.5, 23)cm down from shoulders on front and back for armholes. Sew top of sleeves between markers. Sew side and sleeve seams.

This check-pattern chenille pullover with appliquéd leaves is perfect in the stylish cropped version shown here, or add another tier of motifs for a long look. It's standard-fitting with a rollneck and bobble edging. Shown in size Medium. The Chenille Leaf Pullover first appeared in the Fall '97 issue of *Vogue Knitting*.

Chenille Leaf Pullover

SIZES
To fit X-Small (Small, Medium, Large). Directions are for smallest size with larger sizes in parentheses. If there is only one figure, it applies to all sizes.

KNITTED MEASUREMENTS
● Bust 36 (39, 43, 46)"/91.5 (99, 109, 117)cm.
● Length 18½ (18½, 18½, 20)"/47 (47, 47, 51)cm.
● Sleeve width at upper arm 18 (18, 18, 20)"/46 (46, 46, 51)cm.

MATERIALS
● 10 (11, 12, 13) 1¾oz/50g balls (each approx 140yd/130m) of GGH/Meunch Yarns *Cotton Velour* (cotton 4) in #28 rust
● One pair each sizes 3 and 4 (3.25 and 3.5mm) needles OR SIZE TO OBTAIN GAUGE
● Size 3 (3.25mm) circular needle, 16"/40cm long

Chenille Leaf Pullover

GAUGES
● 19 sts and 32 rows to 4"/10cm over St st, using size 4 (3.5mm) needles.
● 19 sts and 30 rows to 4"/10cm over garter check chart, using size 4 (3.5mm) needles. FOR PERFECT FIT, TAKE TIME TO CHECK GAUGES.

STITCH GLOSSARY
Make Bobble (MB)
Make 5 sts in one st (k into front, back, front, back, front of same st); [turn, k5; turn, p5] twice, turn, k2tog, k1, k2tog; turn, p3tog.

BACK
With larger needles, cast on 83 (89, 101, 107) sts. K 1 row on WS.
Next (bobble) row (RS) K2, *MB, k5; rep from * to last 3 sts, MB, k2. Change to smaller needles. K 7 rows, inc 2 (4, 1, 3) sts evenly on last row—85 (93, 102, 110) sts. Change to larger needles. K 1 row, p 1 row. Beg and end as indicated, work garter check chart until piece measures 18½ (18½, 18½, 20)"/46 (46, 46, 51)cm from beg. Bind off all sts.

FRONT
Work as for back until piece measures 16½ (16½, 16½, 18)"/42 (42, 42, 46)cm from beg, end with a WS row.

Neck shaping
Next row (RS) Work across 37 (40, 43, 47) sts, join 2nd ball of yarn and bind off center 11 (13, 16, 16) sts, work to end. Working both sides at once, bind off from each neck edge 4 sts once, 3 sts once, 2 sts once. Dec 1 st at each neck edge every other row 1 (1, 2, 2) times. Work even until piece measures same length as back to shoulders.

Bind off rem 27 (30, 32, 36) sts each side for shoulders.

SLEEVES
With larger needles, cast on 47 sts. K 1 row on WS.
Next (bobble) row (RS) K2, *MB, k5; rep from * to last 3 sts, MB, k2. Change to smaller needles. K 7 rows. Change to larger needles. K 1 row, p 1 row, inc 1 st—48 sts. Beg and end as indicated for sleeve, work garter check chart, AT SAME TIME, inc 1 st each side (working incs into pat) every 4th row 0 (0, 0, 14) times, every 6th row 19 (19, 19, 10) times—86 (86, 86, 96) sts. Work even until piece measures 17½"/44.5cm from beg. Bind off all sts.

LEAF
With larger needles, cast on 5 sts. Work 24 rows of leaf chart. Fasten off last st.

FINISHING
Block pieces. Sew shoulder seams.

Neckband
With RS facing and circular needle, beg at left shoulder, pick up and k66 (66, 78, 78) sts evenly around neck edge. Join, place marker and work in garter st (p 1 rnd, k 1 rnd) for 2"/5cm, end with a p rnd. Turn and work 1 row on WS as foll: K3, *MB, k5; rep from * to last 3 sts, MB, k2. K 1 row on RS. Bind off. Place markers 9 (9, 9, 10)"/23 (23, 23, 25.5)cm down from shoulders on front and back for armholes. Sew top of sleeves between markers. Sew side and sleeve seams. Make a leaf for each complete (or nearly complete) block of St st on garter check pat. Sew one leaf on each block.

Leaf Chart

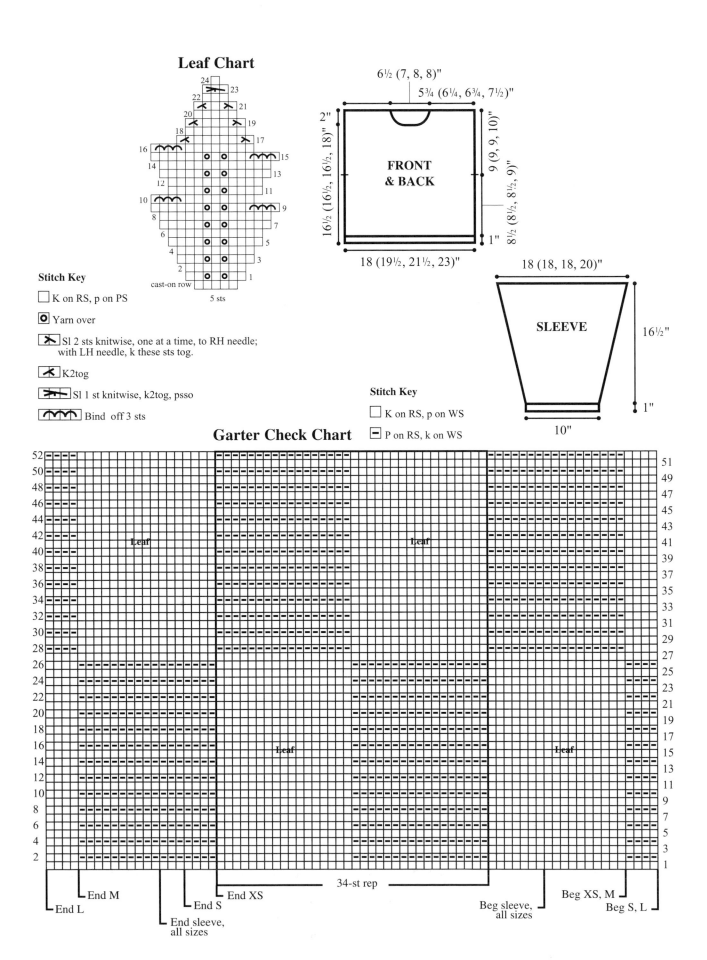

24
23
22
21
20
19
18
17
16
15
14
13
12
11
10
9
8
7
6
5
4
3
2
1

cast-on row

5 sts

Stitch Key

☐ K on RS, p on PS

⊙ Yarn over

⤨ Sl 2 sts knitwise, one at a time, to RH needle; with LH needle, k these sts tog.

⤡ K2tog

⤟ Sl 1 st knitwise, k2tog, psso

〰〰 Bind off 3 sts

FRONT & BACK

6½ (7, 8, 8)"

5¾ (6¼, 6¾, 7½)"

2"

9 (9, 9, 10)"

16½ (16½, 16½, 18)"

8½ (8½, 8½, 9)"

1"

18 (19½, 21½, 23)"

SLEEVE

18 (18, 18, 20)"

16½"

1"

10"

Stitch Key

☐ K on RS, p on WS

— P on RS, k on WS

Garter Check Chart

52 50 48 46 44 42 40 38 36 34 32 30 28 26 24 22 20 18 16 14 12 10 8 6 4 2

51 49 47 45 43 41 39 37 35 33 31 29 27 25 23 21 19 17 15 13 11 9 7 5 3 1

Leaf Leaf Leaf Leaf

End M
End L
End S
End XS
End sleeve, all sizes
34-st rep
Beg sleeve, all sizes
Beg XS, M
Beg S, L

Norah Gaughan

Norah Gaughan learned to knit as a teenager but never imagined it becoming a career. A science and math whiz in school, Norah attended Brown University in Providence, Rhode Island, with dreams of becoming a scientist. It wasn't until after college, when Norah was working in a sweater store, that the seeds of her future career as a handknit designer would start to take root.

"I had a design published in high school and maybe one or two things published when I was in college, but it still hadn't occurred to me that I could do this for a living," she says. Fortunately, there were two professional handknit designers also living in Providence at the time—Deborah Newton and Margery Winter. "I answered Margery's ad for a knitter," she remembers, "and she said that I shouldn't be knitting, that I should be designing, so she sent me away! A year later I contacted her again and said 'no, I really need this.'"

So Norah began working with Margery Winter. "It was the best thing I did, making those contacts," she says. "It was incredible. The next thing I knew Margery became editor of *McCall's Needlework and Craft*, and that was like graduate school for me—instead of

knitting, I was designing for her. Then, I began designing for other knitting publications that Deborah recommended me to."

Like many other designers, Norah came from an artistic home. Her mother is an illustrator who specializes in home decorating and crafts and her father is well-known science fiction illustrator. Yet neither parent taught Norah how to knit—in fact, her mother didn't learn to knit until years after Norah did. "It was my grandmother who taught me how to knit and crochet," she says. "Mom didn't learn until years afterwards when she was illustrating a knitting book. She's a perfectionist and she wanted the drawings to be right, so she learned how to knit."

It's no wonder that Norah took to designing at such a young age. As a child, she sewed regularly as a member of the 4-H. She turned to knitting as a teenager, looking for a way to fill time with a friend on a rainy summer afternoon. But it wasn't until Norah discovered Elizabeth Zimmermann's books that she became truly enamored with knitting.

"The first sweater I ever published was for *Ladies Home Journal Needle and Craft*. It was the last issue published," she says. "That came about because my mother was working as an illustrator for them, and she brought in a sweater that I had designed and they decided to publish it."

Since then, Norah has become a prolific designer, who has been known to produce well over sixty sweater designs a year. "It *is* a huge volume," she admits. "But I don't worry about running out of ideas. What I do worry about is repeating myself. Sometimes you can be inspired by two completely different things and still come up with something very similar—occasionally two pathways collide. There's an evolutionary term for it: convergent evolution," the scientist in her coming out.

For years, Norah sustained a thriving freelance career, designing for knitting magazines and yarn companies. "I remember season after season, sending thirteen to fifteen sketches and swatches to *Vogue Knitting*," she recalls. "They used to send this wonderful design inspiration package and they would have these meetings where everyone would be invited to come and look at slides and color boards. It was really nice."

For a period of time, Norah developed swatches for the garment industry. "That was the most incredible, creative part of my life," she recalls. "With swatches, I could work through a series of

"I am more interested in the evolution of the pattern stitch than the garment. A nice garment is the outcome."

thoughts and often would come up with several more ideas in the process."

Nowadays, Norah is design director at JCA, which distributes Reynolds, Unger, and Adrienne Vittadini yarns. Instead of computers, Norah uses graph paper and the photocopy machine to chart out her patterns, and she makes swatches. "Swatching is the most important part for me," she says. "Working on the fabric comes first; the overall look of the sweater is almost always secondary. I am more interested in the evolution of the pattern stitch than the garment. A nice garment is the outcome, but that is not how I think of it."

An illustration of stitch-driven design resulting in a beautiful garment is the Dragonfly Pullover on page 72. At the time, Norah was experimenting with manipulating cables and filling in cables with other stitches. Meanwhile, *Vogue Knitting* was looking for insect motifs for a summer issue. "I was experimenting with cables and stitches and they needed an insect. It all came together," she says.

As for the future, Norah doesn't believe in looking too far ahead. "I have short-term goals that move me forward," she says. "But as far as anything long-term, I prefer watching things unfold!"

Knit in a smoky, classic grey wool, this richly textured sweater vest is a wardrobe-builder you'll reach for year after year. The vest is loose-fitting with bold cables and a flattering shawl collar. Shown in size 34. The Cabled Vest first appeared in the Fall '92 issue of *Vogue Knitting*.

Cabled Vest

FOR INTERMEDIATE KNITTERS

SIZES
To fit 32 (34, 36, 38-40)"/81 (86, 91, 96-106)cm. Directions are for smallest size with larger sizes in parentheses. If there is only one figure, it applies to all sizes.

KNITTED MEASUREMENTS
● Bust at underarm (buttoned) 36 (39¼, 43¼, 47)"/91.5 (99.5, 110, 119.5)cm.
● Length 18½ (20, 21½, 22½)"/47 (51, 54.5, 57)cm.

MATERIALS
● 5 (5, 6, 6) 3½oz/100g balls (each approx 170yd/153m) of Reynolds/ JCA *Candide* (wool 4) in #74 charcoal
● One pair each sizes 7 and 9 (4.5 and 5.5mm) needles OR SIZE TO OBTAIN GAUGE
● Stitch markers and cable needle (cn)
● Four ⅞"/22mm buttons

GAUGE
22 sts and 26 rows to 4"/10cm over chart #1 and #2 using size 9 (5.5mm) needles. (Note: To work gauge swatch, work pats as foll: P1, work 4-st rep of chart #1 twice, 8 sts of chart #2, 5 sts of chart #1.) FOR PERFECT FIT, TAKE TIME TO CHECK GAUGE.

STITCH GLOSSARY
6-St Front Cable Sl 3 sts to cn and hold to *back* of work, k3, k3 from cn.

BACK
With smaller needles, cast on 80 (90, 98, 106) sts. Work in k1, p1 rib for 2"/5cm, end with a RS row. P 1 row, inc 3 (1, 1, 1) sts evenly across—83 (91,

99, 107) sts. Change to larger needles.
Beg chart pats: Row 1 (RS) Work 4-st rep of chart #1 for 1 (2, 3, 4) times, work last st of chart #1, [work 8-st rep of chart #2, work 5 sts of chart #1] 5 times, work 8-st rep of chart #2, then 4-st rep of chart #1 for 1 (2, 3, 4) times, then work last st of chart #1. Cont to work in pat as established, inc 1 st each side every 6th row 6 (7, 8, 9) times (working inc sts into chart #1)—95 (105, 115, 125) sts. Work even until piece measures 8½ (9, 10½, 11)"/21.5 (23, 26.5, 28)cm from beg, end with a WS row.

Armhole shaping
Bind off 4 sts at beg of next 2 (2, 4, 4) rows, 3 sts at beg of next 4 (6, 6, 6) rows, 2 sts at beg of next 4 (4, 2, 4) rows. Dec 1 st each side every other row 2 (1, 2, 1) times, every 4th row once, every 6th row once, then every 8th row once—57 (63, 67, 75) sts. Work even in pat until armhole measures 10 (11, 11, 11½)"/25.5 (28, 28, 29)cm. Bind off all sts.

LEFT FRONT
With smaller needles, cast on 42 (46, 50, 54) sts. Work in k1, p1 rib for 2"/5cm, end with a RS row. P 1 row. Change to larger needles.
Beg chart pats: Row 1 (RS) Work 4-st rep of chart #1 for 1 (2, 3, 4) times, work last st of chart, [work 8-st rep of chart #2, work 5 sts of chart #1] twice, work 8-st rep of chart #2, work sts 1-3 of chart #1. Cont in pat as established, inc 1 st at beg of RS rows (side edge) every 6th row 6 (7, 8, 9) times—48 (53, 58, 63) sts. Cont to work until same length as back to armhole, end with a WS row.

Armhole and neck shaping
Shape armhole at side edge only (beg of RS rows) as for back, AT SAME TIME, when piece measures 9 (10, 11½, 11½)"/23 (25.5, 29, 29)cm, work neck shaping as foll: Cont to work armhole shaping, dec 1 st at end of every other RS row (neck edge) twice, then every 4th row 13 (14, 14, 16) times. When piece measures same length as back to shoulder, bind off rem 14 (16, 18, 20) sts.

RIGHT FRONT
Work rib as for left front.
Beg chart pats: Row 1 (RS) Work sts 3-5 of chart #1, [work 8-st rep of chart #2, work 5 sts of chart #1] twice, work 8-st rep of chart #2, work 4-st rep of chart #1 for 1 (2, 3, 4) times, work last st of chart #1. Cont as for left front, reversing all shaping.

FINISHING
Block pieces. Sew shoulder seams.

Armhole bands (make two)
With smaller needles, cast on 7 sts.
Row 1 K2, p1, k1, p1, k2.
Row 2 K1, [p1, k1] 3 times. Rep rows 1 and 2 until rib measures 21 (23, 23, 24)"/53 (58.5, 58.5, 61)cm from beg. Bind off. Sew armhole band around armhole, easing to fit. Sew side seams, including bands.

Front bands and collar
(Note: When working band and collar, RS of collar becomes WS when sewn in place.) With smaller needles, cast on 8 sts (for lower left front edge).
Row 1 [P1, k1] 3 times, k2.

Row 2 K2, [p1, k1] 3 times. Rep last 2 rows until piece measures 9 (10, 11½, 11½)"/23 (25.5, 29, 29)cm from beg, end with row 2. Change to larger needles.

Next row Cast on 2 sts (neck edge), work to end.

Next row Cont in rib on 8 sts, place marker, beg with row 9 and st 2 of chart #2, work sts 2-3. Cont to work in pats, casting on 2 sts at neck edge every other row 7 times more, then inc 1 st at neck edge every other row 15 times (working inc sts in pat as foll: 7 sts of chart #2, 5 sts of chart #1, 8 sts of chart #2, [4-st rep of chart #1] twice, then sts 1-3 of chart #1). Cont in pats on 39 sts for 7 (7, 7½, 8½)"/18 (18, 19, 21.5)cm more.

Dart shaping

Cont in pat, AT SAME TIME, bind off 2 sts at neck edge 13 times—13 sts.

Next row Pick up 2 sts in 2 bound-off sts, work to end. Cont to pick up 2 sts in bound-off sts 12 times more (working picked up sts in pat rows to mirror bound-off sts)—39 sts. Work even until 7 (7, 7½, 8½)"/18 (18, 19, 21.5)cm from dart shaping.

Right collar

Cont to work in pat, dec 1 st at neck edge every other row 15 times, then bind off 2 sts at neck edge 8 times—8 sts. Place markers on left front band for 4 buttons with first 1"/2.5cm from lower edge, the last 1"/2.5cm below beg of collar shaping and 2 evenly spaced between. Change to smaller needles. Cont in rib pat, working buttonholes opposite markers as foll:

Row 2 K2, p1, k1, bind off 2 sts, work to end. On next row, cast on 2 sts over bound-off sts. Work even until same length as left front band. Bind off. Sew collar and bands around front and neck edges, easing to fit around neck. Sew on buttons.

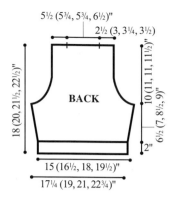

BACK

5½ (5¾, 5¾, 6½)"
2½ (3, 3¼, 3½)
18 (20, 21½, 22½)"
10 (11, 11, 11½)"
6½ (7, 8½, 9)"
2"
15 (16½, 18, 19½)"
17¼ (19, 21, 22¾)"

LEFT FRONT

2½ (3, 3¼, 3½)"
9½ (10, 10, 11)"
2"
9 (10, 11½, 11½)"
10 (11, 11, 11½)"
6½ (7, 8½, 9)"
2"
7½ (8¼, 9, 9¾)"
8¾ (9½, 10½, 11½)"

CHART 1

2
1
4-st rep

CHART 2

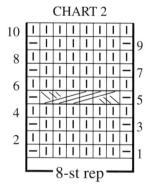

10
9
8
7
6
5
4
3
2
1
8-st rep

Stitch Key

☐ K on RS, p on WS

☐ P on RS, k on WS

◺◹◸◿ 6-st Front Cable

A-Line Tunic

Knit in one piece from the neck down, this roomy, trapeze-shaped pullover has a distinctive pyramid-shaped clock pattern on the front. Oversized, the pullover has darted raglan sleeve shaping, a ribbed funnelneck, and cuffs with rolled edging. Shown in size 36-38. The A-Line Tunic first appeared in the Fall '89 issue of *Vogue Knitting*.

A-Line Tunic

SIZES
To fit 32-34 (36-38, 40)"/81-86 (91-96, 101)cm bust. Directions are for smallest size with larger sizes in parentheses. If there is only one figure, it applies to all sizes.

KNITTED MEASUREMENTS
● Finished bust measurement at underarm 40 (43, 46)"/100 (108, 115)cm.
● Length 25 (26, 27)"/63 (66, 68.5)cm.
● Sleeve width at upper arm 15½ (16, 16½)"/39 (40, 41.5)cm.

MATERIALS
Original Yarn
● 12 (13, 14) 1¾oz/50g balls (each approx 92yd/84m) of Bernat *Rusticale* (wool/mohair 5) in #14042 off white
Substitute Yarn
● 14 (15, 16) 1¾oz/50g balls (each approx 83yd/75m) of JCA/Reynolds *Contessa* (wool/angora/polyamid 5) in #10 ecru
● Sizes 7 and 9 (4.5 and 5.5mm) circular needles, 29"/80cm long OR SIZE TO OBTAIN GAUGE
● Sizes 7 and 9 (4.5 and 5.5mm) circular needles, 16"/40cm long
● Stitch markers and stitch holders
● Cable needle (cn)

Note
The original yarn used for this sweater is no longer available. A comparable substitution has been made, which is available at the time of printing. Check gauge of substitute yarns very carefully before beginning.

GAUGE
16 sts and 24 rows to 4"/10cm over St st using size 9 (5.5mm) needles. FOR PERFECT FIT, TAKE TIME TO CHECK GAUGE.

Note
Sweater is knit in one piece from the neck down.

STITCH GLOSSARY
M1 Knitwise Insert LH needle into horizontal strand between last st worked and next st on needle, k this strand tbl.
M1 Purlwise Insert LH needle into horizontal strand between last st worked and next st on needle, p this strand tbl.
2-st Right Cross Sl 1 st to cn and hold to *back*, k1 tbl, k1 from cn.
2-st Left Cross Sl 1 st to cn and hold to *front*, k1, k1 tbl from cn.
2-st Twisted Right Cross Sl 1 st to cn and hold to *back*, k1 tbl, k1 tbl from cn.
2-st Twisted Left Cross Sl 1 st to cn and hold to *front*, k1 tbl, k1 tbl from cn.
2-st Right Purl Cross Sl 1 st to cn and hold to *back*, k1 tbl, p1 from cn.
2-st Left Purl Cross Sl 1 st to cn and hold to *front*, p1, k1 tbl from cn.
3-st Right Cross Sl 1 st to cn and hold to *back*, k2 tbl, k1 from cn.
3-st Left Cross Sl 2 sts to cn and hold to *front*, k1, k2 tbl from cn.
3-st Twisted Right Cross Sl 1 st to cn and hold to *back*, k2 tbl, k1 tbl from cn.
3-st Twisted Left Cross Sl 2 sts to cn and hold to *front*, k1 tbl, k2 tbl from cn.
3-st Right Purl Cross Sl 1 st to cn and hold to *back*, k2 tbl, p1 from cn.
3-st Left Purl Cross Sl 2 sts to cn and hold to *front*, p1, k2 tbl from cn.
4-st Right Cable Sl 2 sts to cn and hold to *back*, k2 tbl, k2 tbl from cn.

Notes on working charts
Chart #1
Work chart #1 on center front only through row 29. Mark center 4 sts on front. On row 30, work 4-st cable in center of chart #2 on these sts and 13 sts each side in chart #1. Rep rows 31-50 of chart #1 and cont working chart #2 in center (except for p st on each side of chart).
Chart #2
Work row 1 of chart #2 over center 6 sts on back. After row 26 of chart #2, cont to inc 1 st inside of twisted side sts every 4th row, alternating inc between left side and right side.

Notes
1 For ease in working, use different color markers to denote raglan and dart incs and for chart sts.
2 Beg with 16"/40cm circular needle and change to 29"/80cm when enough sts have been inc.

BODY
With smaller 16"/40cm needle, beg at top of highneck, cast on 76 (80, 84) sts. Join, taking care not to twist sts on needle. Place marker for end of rnd, and sl marker every rnd. K 4 rnds.
Twisted rib: Rnd 1 (RS) *K1 tbl, p1; rep from * around. Rep rnd 1 for twisted rib for 3"/7.5cm. Change to larger 16"/40cm needle. K next rnd, dec 8 sts evenly around—68 (72, 76) sts.
Next rnd K22 (24, 24) for front, place

raglan marker; k6 (6, 7), place sleeve dart marker, k6 (6, 7) for right sleeve, place raglan marker; k22 (24, 24) for back, place raglan marker; k6 (6, 7), place sleeve dart marker, k6 (6, 7) for left sleeve, change end of rnd marker to raglan marker. (Note: Work inc each side of markers as foll: On right side of marker, work to 1 st before marker, m1, k1; on left side of marker, k1, m1.) Work inc and chart pats as foll: On body sides of raglan markers, inc 1 st on next rnd, then every other rnd 24 (26, 29) times more, every 4th rnd 1 (1, 0) time; on sleeve sides of raglan markers, inc 1 st every 4th rnd 12 (10, 9) times, every 6th rnd 1 (3, 4) times; on each side of sleeve dart markers, inc 1 st every other rnd 9 times, AT SAME TIME, work St st on all sts for 4 rnds, then mark center 2 sts on front to correspond to center 2 sts on chart #1, and work chart #1 on center front only, through rnd 29. Beg chart #2 as foll: Mark center 6 sts on back and center 4 sts on front and work chart #2 on

back and center front (between chart #1) and rem sts in St st. After all incs have been worked, work until piece measures 9½ (10, 10½)"/24 (25.5, 26.5)cm above rib—there are 83 (90, 95) sts on front, 79 (86, 91) sts on back and 56 (58, 58) sts on each sleeve.

Divide for back, front and sleeves
Cast on 3 (3, 4) sts, work to right sleeve marker, remove marker, place sts of sleeve on holder, cast on 3 (3, 4) sts, place marker for side seam, cast on 3 (3, 4) sts, work to left sleeve marker, remove marker, place sts of sleeve on holder, cast on 3 (3, 4) sts, sl marker (2nd side seam). Cont in pats, inc 1 st each side of each side seam marker every 8th row 9 times. Work even until piece measures 13½ (14, 14½)"/34 (35.5, 37)cm from dividing point. Change to smaller needles.

Lower edge rib
Next rnd Inc 1 st in every 4th st to

front chart, then dec 1 st, k12 sts instead of chart #1, work chart #2 as established, k12 sts instead of chart #1, dec 1 st, inc 1 st in every 4th st to back chart, work chart #2, inc 1 st in every 4th st to end of rnd. Work in twisted rib for 2"/5cm. Bind off in rib.

SLEEVES
With larger 16"/40cm circular needle, work across sts of sleeve as foll: With larger needle, cast on 3 (3, 4) sts, k sts from holder, cast on 3 (3, 4) sts, place marker for sleeve seam—62 (64, 66) sts. Join and work in St st, dec 1 st each side of marker every 6th rnd 12 (11, 10) times, every 8th rnd 0 (1, 2) times—38 (40, 42) sts. Work even until sleeve measures 12½ (13, 13½)"/31.5 (33, 34)cm. Change to smaller needles. Work in twisted rib for 3"/7.5cm. Work 4 rows in St st. Bind off.

FINISHING
Sew underarm and sleeve seams.

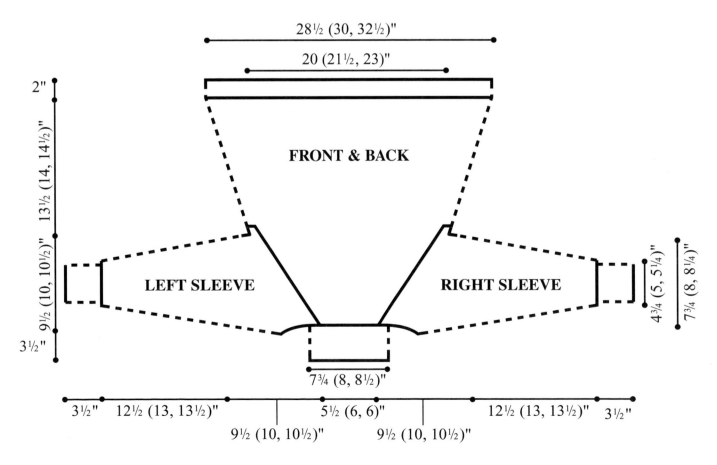

Chart 2

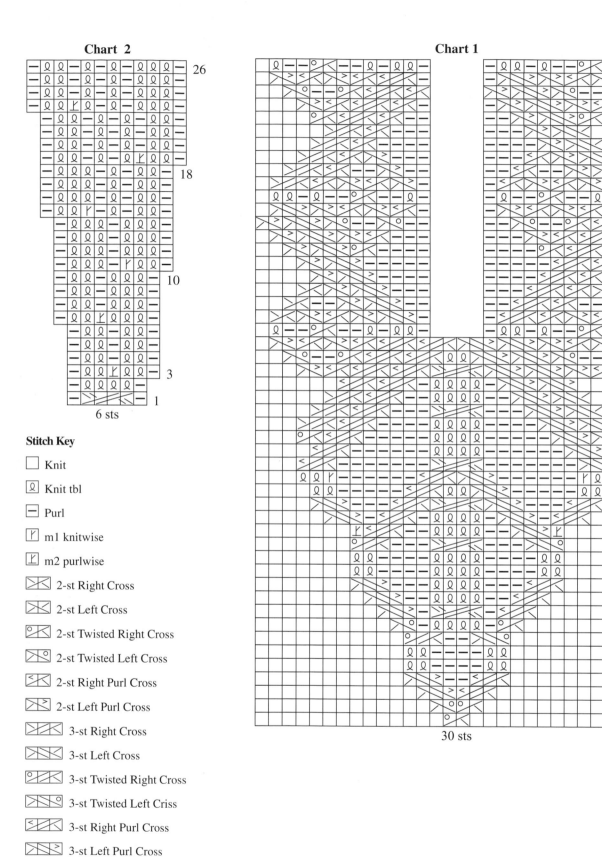

6 sts

Chart 1

30 sts

Stitch Key

☐ Knit

Ω Knit tbl

⊟ Purl

Ⴑ m1 knitwise

Ⴑ m2 purlwise

⊠ 2-st Right Cross

⊠ 2-st Left Cross

⊠ 2-st Twisted Right Cross

⊠ 2-st Twisted Left Cross

⊠ 2-st Right Purl Cross

⊠ 2-st Left Purl Cross

⊠ 3-st Right Cross

⊠ 3-st Left Cross

⊠ 3-st Twisted Right Cross

⊠ 3-st Twisted Left Criss

⊠ 3-st Right Purl Cross

⊠ 3-st Left Purl Cross

⊠ 4-st Right Cable

Ribbed Cardigan

The cardigan redefined! Handsomely elegant, this boxy, cartridge-ribbed jacket is oversized with drop shoulders, shawl collar and hemmed edges. Shown in size Medium. The Ribbed Cardigan first appeared in the Fall '90 issue of *Vogue Knitting*.

Ribbed Cardigan

FOR EXPERIENCED KNITTERS

SIZES
To fit Small (Medium, Large). Directions are for smallest size with larger sizes in parentheses. If there is only one figure, it applies to all sizes.

KNITTED MEASUREMENTS
● Bust at underarm (buttoned) 41½ (46, 50½)"/102.5 (114.5, 126.5)cm.
● Length 20½ (21, 22)"/52 (53, 55.5)cm.
● Sleeve width at upper arm 19 (20, 21)"/48 (50, 53)cm.

MATERIALS
Original Yarn
● 14 (15, 16) 1¾oz/50g balls (each approx 92yd/84m) of Bernat® *Rusticale* (wool/mohair 5) in #14058 oatmeal
Substitute Yarn
● 16 (17, 18) 1¾oz/50g balls (each approx 83yd/75m) of Reynolds/JCA *Contessa* (wool/angora/polyamid 5) in #84 camel
● One pair each sizes 7 and 9 (4.5 and 5.5mm) needles OR SIZE TO OBTAIN GAUGE
● Stitch markers
● Four 2"/5cm long horn buttons

Note
The original yarn used for this sweater is no longer available. A comparable substitution has been made, which is available at the time of printing. Check gauge of substitute yarns very carefully before beginning.

GAUGE
17 sts and 24 rows to 4"/10cm over pat st using size 9 (5.5mm) needles. FOR PERFECT FIT, TAKE TIME TO CHECK GAUGE.

STITCH GLOSSARY
Pat St (multiple of 5 sts + 2 extra)
Row 1 (RS) K3, *p1, k4; rep from *, end last rep k3.
Row 2 *P2, k3; rep from *, end p2. Rep rows 1 and 2 for pat st.

BACK
With smaller needles, cast on 86 (94, 106) sts. Work in k2, p2 rib for 3"/7.5cm, inc 1 (3, 1) sts on last row—87 (97, 107) sts. Change to larger needles. Work in pat st until piece measures 22 (22½, 23½)"/56 (57, 59.5)cm from beg. Bind off.

LEFT FRONT
With smaller needles, cast on 42 (46, 50) sts. Work in k2, p2 rib for 3"/7.5cm, inc 0 (1, 2) sts on last row—42 (47, 52) sts. Change to larger needles. Work in pat st until piece measures 13 (13½, 14½)"/33 (34, 36.5)cm from beg, end with a WS row.

Neck shaping
Dec 1 st at end of next (RS) row and rep dec every 4th row 9 (12, 12) times, every 6th row 2 (0, 0) times—30 (34, 39) sts. Work even until same length as back. Bind off.

RIGHT FRONT
Work to correspond to left front, reversing neck shaping.

SLEEVES
With smaller needles, cast on 46 (46, 50) sts. Work in k2, p2 rib for 3"/7.5cm, inc 1 (1, 2) sts on last row—47 (47, 52) sts. Change to larger needles. Work in pat st, inc 1 st each side (working inc sts into pat st) every 4th row 6 (10, 10) times, every 6th row 11 (9, 9) times—81 (85, 90) sts. Work even until piece measures 19 (19½, 19½)"/47.5 (49, 49)cm from beg. Bind off.

FINISHING
Block pieces. Sew shoulder seams. Place markers 9½ (10, 10½)"/24 (25, 26.5)cm down from shoulders on front and back for armholes. Sew side seams to markers. Fold lower edge rib in half to WS and sew in place.

Front bands and collar

(Note: When working band and collar, RS of collar becomes WS when sewn in place.) With smaller needles, cast on 5 sts (for lower left front edge).
Row 1 (RS) [P1, k1tbl] twice, k1.
Row 2 K1, [p1, k1tbl] twice. Rep last 2 rows until piece measures 9½ (10, 11)"/24 (25, 27.5)cm from beg, end with a WS row. Change to larger needles.
Next row (RS) Cast on 2 sts (mark as neck edge), p1, k1, place marker, rib to end.
Next row Rib 5, sl marker, k2.
Next row Cast on 2 sts, k1, p2, k1, rib 5.
Next row Rib 5, k4.
Next row Cast on 2 sts, k3, p2, k1, rib 5.
Next row (row 1 of pat) Rib 5, k4, p1, k1.
Next row (row 2 of pat) Cast on 2 sts, p2, k3, p2, k1, rib 5. Cont to inc at neck edge, (working inc sts into pat st as established, beg with a row 1 of pat and keeping 5 sts at front edge in established rib) by casting on 2 sts 7 times more, then inc 1 st at same edge every other row 6 times, every 4th row twice—35 sts. Work even in pats until straight edge measures 20½ (21, 22)"/52 (53, 55.5)cm from beg, end at straight edge. Work short rows as foll:
*Next row (WS) Work 5 sts, wrap next st, turn, work to end.
Next row (WS) Work 10 sts, wrap next st, turn, work to end. Cont in this way to work 5 more sts at end of every WS row 3 times more, end with a RS row. Work 6 rows even on all sts.* Rep between *'s 7 times more. Work even on 35 sts for 4"/10cm. Dec 1 st at end of RS rows on next row, then every 4th row twice, every other row 5 times. Bind off at same edge 2 sts 11 times. Work in rib on rem 5 sts for 9½ (10, 11)"/24 (25, 27.5)cm. Bind off. With WS of collar facing RS of body, baste bands and collar in place. Place markers on left front band for 4 buttons, first marker ½"/1.5cm from lower edge, last marker at first collar cast-on, and 2 others evenly between. Sew bands and collar in place, leaving unsewn openings on right front band opposite markers for buttonholes. Sew sleeve seams. Set in sleeves. Fold rib at lower edge of cuffs in half to WS and sew in place. Sew on buttons.

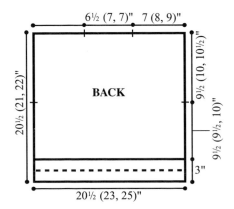

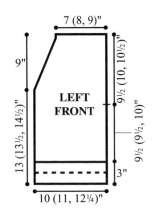

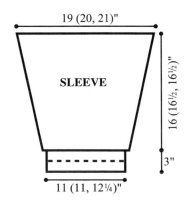

A lacy cable and open-work dragonfly is the focal point on this summer charmer. The circular-knit tunic is oversized with drop shoulders and crew neck. Shown in size Large. The Dragonfly Pullover first appeared in the Spring/Summer '97 issue of *Vogue Knitting*.

Dragonfly Pullover

FOR EXPERT KNITTERS

SIZES
To fit Small (Medium, Large, X-Large). Directions are for smallest size with larger sizes in parentheses. If there is only one figure, it applies to all sizes.

KNITTED MEASUREMENTS
● Bust 41 (43, 45, 47)"/104 (109, 114, 119)cm.
● Length 28"/71cm.
● Sleeve width at upper arm 15"/38cm.

MATERIALS
Original Yarn
● 12 (13, 13, 14) 1¾oz/50g balls (each approx 120yd/110m) of Missoni/Stacy Charles *Caprera* (cotton 3) in #146 green
Substitute Yarn
● 11 (12, 12, 13) 1¾oz/50g balls (each approx 136yd/125m) of Filatura di Crosa/Tahki•Stacy Charles, Inc. *Millefili Fine* (cotton 3) in #149 green
● One pair each sizes 1 and 3 (2 and 3mm) needles, OR SIZE TO OBTAIN GAUGE
● Sizes 1 and 3 (2 and 3mm) circular needles, 29"/74cm long
● Cable needle (cn)
● Stitch markers
Note
The original yarn used for this sweater is no longer available. A comparable substitution has been made, which is available at the time of printing. Check gauge of substitute yarns very carefully before beginning.

GAUGE
24 sts and 33 rows to 4"/10cm over St st using size 3 (3mm) needles. FOR A PERFECT FIT, TAKE TIME TO CHECK GAUGE.

STITCH GLOSSARY
1/1 Left Twist (1/1 LT)
With RH needle behind work, k 2nd st on LH needle through back lp (tbl), leave st on needle; then k first and 2nd sts tog tbl.
2/1 Right Cross (2/1 RC)
Sl 1 st to cn and hold to *back*, k2, then k1 from cn.
2/1 Left Cross (2/1 LC)
Sl 2 sts to cn and hold to *front*, k1, then k2 from cn.
2/1 Right Purl Cross (2/1 RPC)
Sl 1 st to cn and hold to *back*, k2, then p1 from cn.
2/1 Right Yarnover Inc Cross (2/1 RYIC)
Sl 1 st to cn and hold to *back*, k2, then yo, k1 from cn (1 st inc'd).
2/1 Left Yarnover Inc Cross (2/1 LYIC)
Sl 2 sts to cn and hold to *front*, k1, yo, then k2 from cn (1 st inc'd).
2/2 Right Cable (2/2 RC)
Sl 2 sts to cn and hold to *back*, k2, then k2 from cn.
2/2 Left Cable (2/2 LC)
Sl 2 sts to cn and hold to *front*, k2, then k2 from cn.
2/2 Left Purl Cable (2/2 LPC)
Sl 2 sts to cn and hold to*front*, p2, then k2 from cn.
2/2 Right Yarnover Cable (2/2 RYC)
Sl 2 sts to cn and hold to *back*, k2, then yo, p2tog, from cn.
2/2 Left Yarnover Cable (2/2 LYC)
Sl 2 sts to cn and hold to *front*, yo, p2tog, then k2 from cn.
2/2 Right Dec Cable (2/2 RDC)
Sl 2 sts to cn and hold to *back*, k2, then p2tog from cn (1 st dec'd).
2/2 Right Yarnover Inc Cable (2/2 RYIC)
Sl 2 sts to cn and hold to *back*, k2, then from cn: yo, k1, k yo of previous row tbl (1

st inc'd). (Note: On next row, k yo tbl.)
2/2 Left Yarnover Inc Cable (2/2 LYIC)
Sl 2 sts to cn and hold to *front*, yo, k1, k yo of previous row tbl, then k2 from cn (1 st inc'd). (Note: On next row, k yo tbl.)
2/3 Right Cable (2/3 RC)
Sl 3 sts to cn and hold to *back*, k2, then k3 from cn.
2/3 Left Cable (2/3 LC)
Sl 2 sts to cn and hold to *front*, k3, then k2 from cn.
2/3 Left Purl Cable (2/3 LPC)
Sl 2 sts to cn and hold to *front*, p3, then k2 from cn.
2/3 Right Dec Cable (2/3 RDC)
Sl 3 sts to cn and hold to *back*, k2tog, then k3tog from cn (3 sts dec'd).
2/3 Left Dec Cable (2/3 LDC)
Sl 2 sts to cn and hold to *front*, k3tog, then ssk from cn (3 sts dec'd).
2/3 Right Yarnover Dec Cable (2/3 RYDC)
Sl 3 sts to cn and hold to *back*, k2, then yo, p3tog from cn (1 st dec'd).
2/3 Left Yarnover Dec Cable (2/3 LYDC) Sl 2 sts to cn and hold to *front*, yo, p3tog, then k2 from cn (1 st dec'd).
3/3 Left Cable (3/3 LC)
Sl 3 sts to cn and hold to *front*, k3, then k3 from cn.
3/3 Left Purl Cable (3/3 LPC)
Sl 3 sts to cn and hold to *front*, p3, then k3 from cn.
Note
Body of sweater is worked circularly to underarms, then divided for front and back and worked at the same time with separate balls.

BODY
With smaller circular needle, cast on 300 (312, 324, 336) sts. Join, place marker

and work in rnds of k2, p2 rib for
1½"/4cm. Change to larger circular needle and work in St st, dec 43 sts evenly
around on first rnd—257 (269, 281, 293)
sts. K 3 rnds.
Next rnd K to 14 sts before end of rnd,
place marker (pm), work rnd 1 of
Dragonfly chart over 154 sts, pm, k to
end. Cont to work in St st and Dragonfly
chart through chart row 140—247 (259,
271, 283) sts rem. K1 rnd, dec 1 st—246
(258, 270, 282) sts. Work even in St st
until piece measures 18½"/47cm from
beg, end 4 sts before rnd marker.

Armhole shaping
Bind off next 8 sts (underarm), k until
there are 115 (121, 127, 133) sts for
front, join 2nd ball and bind off next 8 sts
(underarm), k until there are 115 (121,
127, 133) sts for back. Working front and
back at same time with separate balls
(now working back and forth), bind off
from each armhole edge 3 sts once, 2
sts once. Dec 1 st every RS row 3 times
(dec by k2, k2tog, k to last 4 sts, ssk,
k2)—99 (105, 111, 117) sts. Work even
until armhole measures 4½"/11.5cm, end
with a WS row.

Front neck shaping
Cont to work straight on back sts, shape
front neck as foll:
Next row (RS) K41 (44, 47, 50) sts, join
2nd ball and bind off center 17 sts, work
to end. Working both sides at same time,
bind off from each neck edge 4 sts
once, 3 sts once, 2 sts twice, dec 1 st 4
times. Work even until armhole measures
8½"/21.5cm, end with a WS row.

Shoulder and back neck shaping
Bind off at each shoulder edge of front
and back 6 (7, 8, 8) sts 2 (3, 4, 1) times,
7 (8, 0, 9) sts 2 (1, 0, 3) times, AT SAME
TIME, bind off center 23 sts of back for
neck and, working both sides at same
time, bind off from each neck edge 4 sts
3 times.

SLEEVES
With smaller straight needles, cast on 90
sts. Work in k2, p2 rib for 3½"/9cm, end
with a WS row. Change to larger straight

needles. Work in St st until piece measures 16"/40.5cm from beg, end with a WS row.

Cap shaping
Bind off 4 sts at beg of next 2 rows, 2 sts at beg of next 4 rows.
Next row (RS) K2, k2tog, k to last 4 sts, ssk, k2. Rep last row every other row 3 times more, every 4th row twice, then every other row 4 times. Work 1 row even. Bind off 2 sts at beg of next 4 rows, 3 sts at beg of next 2 rows, 4 sts at beg of next 2 rows. Bind off rem 32 sts.

FINISHING
Block pieces (stretching dragonfly motif flat). Sew shoulder and side seams. Sew sleeve seams. Set in sleeves.

Neckband
With smaller straight needles, cast on 12 sts.
Row 1 (RS) K3, p2, k2, p2, k3.
Row 2 P3, k2, p2, k2, sl 3 with yarn in front. Rep rows 1 and 2 until short side measures 21"/53.5cm from beg. Bind off. Sew ends tog. Sew neckband around neck edge, placing seam at center back neck.

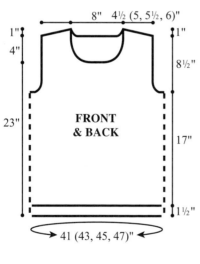

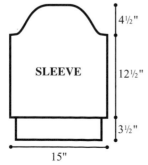

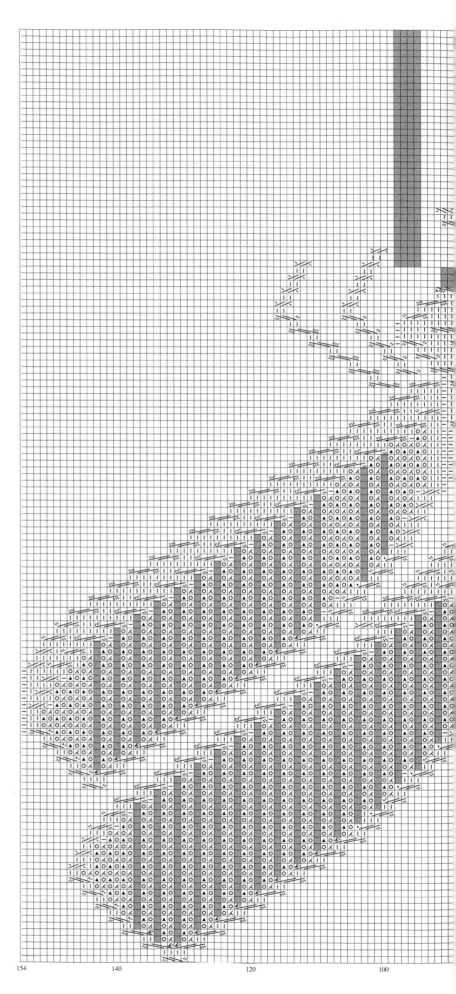

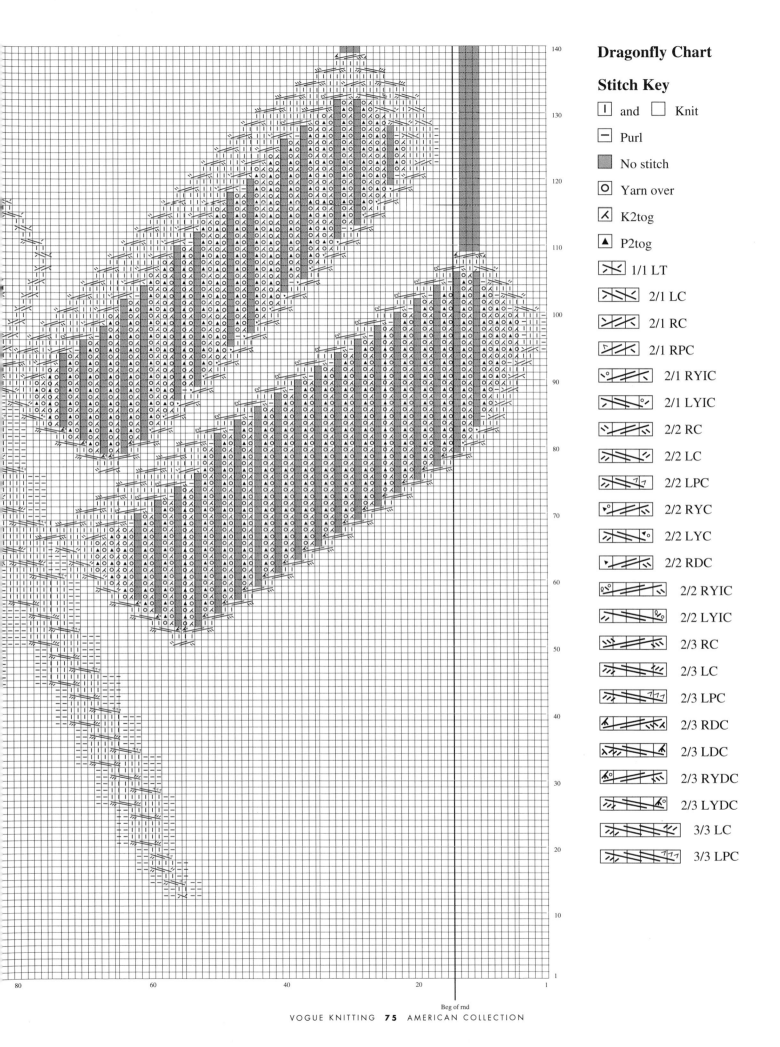

Dragonfly Chart

Stitch Key

| | and | | Knit

| − | Purl

No stitch

| O | Yarn over

| ⊠ | K2tog

| ▲ | P2tog

1/1 LT

2/1 LC

2/1 RC

2/1 RPC

2/1 RYIC

2/1 LYIC

2/2 RC

2/2 LC

2/2 LPC

2/2 RYC

2/2 LYC

2/2 RDC

2/2 RYIC

2/2 LYIC

2/3 RC

2/3 LC

2/3 LPC

2/3 RDC

2/3 LDC

2/3 RYDC

2/3 LYDC

3/3 LC

3/3 LPC

Beg of rnd

Kristin Nicholas

As the creative director of Classic Elite Yarns, Kristin Nicholas's introduction to *Vogue Knitting* was different from those of most other designers. She was already an established figure in the industry when the magazine came knocking on her door, rather than the other way around. "Because we're a yarn company," she explains, "I'll call them and say, 'Can you use this this year?' We want to get an editorial because they sell yarn. Then I will volunteer to make the sweater for them, so they don't have to worry about anything; they know the instructions and everything will be all right."

Kristin's relationship with *Vogue Knitting* goes back many years. She can name all the editors, past and present, and knows off the top of her head which sweaters were the biggest sellers. "It's a great magazine," she adds. "They are always right on top of the fashion cycle. I think that's really nice—it makes knitting hip and fashionable. Handknits never have a frumpy look when they come from *Vogue Knitting*. That's their place in the publishing and knitting world.

"We love to have our yarns in *Vogue Knitting*," she continues. "They want to use your newest and most luxurious fiber. Coming from the yarn company perspective, working with the magazine is a group effort. They're about keeping the excitement in the whole knitting population, and so are we."

Like many accomplished designers, Kristin came from a creative household. Her mother was an enthusiastic sewer and gardener, and her grandmother had a gift for needlework. "There was always handmade stuff around," she says. "My sisters and I were always making things."

Kristin began sewing as a child, making clothes in school and as a member of the 4-H club. She went on to major in textile and clothing design in college, taking classes in subjects such as fashion illustration and fiber arts, eventually earning a master's degree. It was during her college years, after completing a course in handspinning, that Kristin decided she wanted to learn how to knit. "I had all this yarn, and I didn't know what to do with it. So I got Elizabeth Zimmermann's book, *Knitting Without Tears*, and basically read that and figured out how to design my own sweaters from her really great instructions," she says. "Her attitude of just plunging right in fit with what I wanted to do. So that's when I started designing sweaters and started really knitting a lot."

After graduation, Kristin moved to the New York area to pursue a career in textile manufacturing. For years, Kristin would spend weekends in Massachusetts with her long-time boyfriend, Mark Duprey. Together they were raising sheep, with Kristin using the sheeps' wool to

"We have nice, beautiful yarns and the fact that I can pick them out and bring them to the knitting public is really great."

make sweaters. This eventually led to a small mail-order business through which Kristin sold her yarns, patterns, and some simple notions. As her reputation in the yarn industry grew, Kristin was offered several high-ranking positions back in the city. She decided to take a job at a fledgling yarn company in nearby Lowell, and she and Mark got married.

That young company grew to become Classic Elite Yarns, today one of this country's leading yarn manufacturers. As Creative Director for the last sixteen years, Kristin has become one of the best-known designers in the field. "Taking that job was a chance to make it a national brand," she relates. "As their creative person, I do all the colors, I decide on the yarns, then put the direction to the whole handknitting pattern collection. I also do a lot of graphic design. It's a real varied job."

As a yarn company executive, Kristin has a unique approach to designing. "I look at the yarn and I kind of let it say to me what it does," she explains. "I usually start out with a stockinette-stitch swatch just to feel the yarn and to see if it works nicely in stockinette—if it's soft, has a nice drape to it, if it's stiff. Then I decide what I am then going to move that yarn into, whether it is a cable or an allover texture stitch. It definitely starts with the yarn."

When designing a garment, Kristin puts comfort above all else. "I think most of the people who knit, knit to wear it on weekends, when you put your favorite sweater on to kick around in," she says. "The stuff I tend to do has that feeling to it."

She doesn't envision herself leaving the yarn industry or her job with Classic Elite anytime soon. "We have nice, beautiful yarns," she says, "and the fact that I can pick them out and bring them to the knitting public is really great. I like the texture and all the colors—it's still fresh and fun." She feels that knitting in recent decades has taken on a life of its own, with more and more people becoming interested in it and pushing the boundaries. "The group of people knitting now are really smart and intelligent. If I ever see someone knitting in an airport or someplace, I will always sit down next to them and talk to them. They usually have very interesting jobs and want to know all they can about knitting."

Nowadays, as parents of a young daughter, Kristin and Mark still farm and raise sheep, but out of sheer love rather than as a means of income. The family lives on a farm just a few miles from Mark's childhood home. "We moved out here so my daughter can grow up in the countryside," she remarks. In her free time, Kristin likes to explore creative interests outside of knitting. She likes to paint, make pottery, and garden when she can. "It's a good life," she declares.

● **Kristin Nicholas**

Cropped and cabled woman's sweater with ribbed sleeves and deep turtleneck. Shown in size Medium. Man's oversized pullover with cabled front and back and classic crew neck. Shown in size Medium. The His-and-Hers Pullovers first appeared in the Fall '96 issue of *Vogue Knitting*.

His–and–Hers Pullovers

FOR INTERMEDIATE KNITTERS

SIZES
Woman's Pullover Extra-Small (Small, Medium, Large). Directions are for smallest size with larger sizes in parentheses. If there is only one figure, it applies to all sizes.

KNITTED MEASUREMENTS
● Bust 36 (38, 40, 42)"/91.5 (96.5, 101.5, 106.5)cm.
● Length 17 (17½, 18, 19)"/43 (44.5, 46, 48)cm.
● Upper arm 16 (16½, 17, 17)"/40.5 (42, 43, 43)cm.

MATERIALS
Original Yarn
● 6 (6, 7, 7) 3½oz/100g balls (each approx 176yd/160m) each Classic Elite Yarns *Mackensie* (wool/silk 4) in #4275 oatmeal
Substitute Yarn
Note: This lighter yarn will give a looser, more relaxed look to the fabric.
● 9 (9, 11, 11) 1¾oz/50g balls (each approx 123yd/113m) of Classic Elite Yarns *Devon* (wool/silk 3) in #2875 oatmeal
● One pair each sizes 6 and 8 (4 and 5mm) needles OR SIZE TO OBTAIN GAUGE.
● Size 6 (4mm) circular needle, 16"/40cm long
● Stitch holders

Note
The original yarn used for this sweater is no longer available. A comparable substitution has been made, which is available at the time of printing. Check gauge of substitute yarns very carefully before beginning.

WOMAN'S PULLOVER

GAUGE
18 sts and 24 rows to 4"/10cm using with size 8 (5mm) needles over P3, K2 rib. FOR PERFECT FIT, TAKE TIME TO CHECK GAUGE.

STITCH GLOSSARY
Small Cable (over 8 sts)
Row 1 (RS) P2, k4, p2.
Row 2 (WS) K the knit sts, p the purl sts.
Row 3 P2, sl 2 to cn, hold to *back*, k2, k2 from cn, p2.
Row 4 Rep Row 2. Rep rows 1-4 for small cable.

Open Rope Cable (over 10 sts)
Row 1 (RS) K3, p4, k3.
Row 2 (WS) K the knit sts, p the purl sts.
Rows 3 and 4 Rep rows 1 and 2.
Row 5 Sl 3 to cn hold to *front*, p2, k3 from cn, sl 2 to cn, hold to *back*, k3,

p2 from cn.
Row 6 Rep row 2.
Row 7 P2, sl 3 to cn, hold to *back*, k3, k3 from cn.
Rows 8-10 Rep row 2.
Row 11 P2, sl 3 to cn, hold to *back*, k3, k3 from cn, p2.
Row 12 Rep row 2.
Row 13 Sl 2 to cn, hold to *back*, k3, p2 from cn, sl 3 to cn, hold to *front*, p2, k3 from cn.
Rows 14-16 Rep row 2. Rep rows 1-16 for open rope cable.

Diamond Rib Cable (over 34 sts)
Row 1 (RS) P2, k3, p9, k2, sl 2 to cn, hold to *back*, k2, k2 from cn, p9, k3, p2.
Row 2 and all WS rows K the knit sts, p the purl sts.
Row 3 P2, sl 3 to cn, and hold to *front*, k2, k3 from cn, p7, sl 2 to cn, hold to *front*, k2, k2 from cn, k2, p7, sl 2 to cn, hold to *back*, k3, k2 from cn, p2.
Row 5 P2, k2, sl 3 to cn, hold to *front*, p2, k3 from cn, p5, k2, sl 2 to cn, hold

to *back*, k2, k2 from cn, p5, sl 2 to cn, hold to *back*, k3, p2 from cn, k2, p2.
Row 7 P2, k2, p2, sl 3 to cn, hold to *front*, k2, k3 from cn, p3, sl 2 to cn, hold to *front*, k2, k2 from cn, k2, p3, sl 2 hold to *back*, k3, k2 from cn, p2, k2, p2.
Row 9 [P2, k2,] twice, sl 3 to cn, hold to *front*, p2, k3 from cn, p1, k2, sl 2 to cn hold to *back*, k2, k2 from cn, p1, sl 2 to cn, hold to *back*, k3, p2 from cn, [k2, p2] twice.
Row 11 [P2, k2] twice, p2, k3, p1, sl 2 to cn, hold to *front*, k2, k2 from cn, k2, p1, k3, [p2, k2] twice, p2.
Row 13 [P2, k2] twice, sl 2 to cn, hold to *back*, k3, p2 from cn, p1, k2, sl 2 to cn hold to *back*, k2, k2 from cn, p1, sl 3 to cn, hold to *front*, p2, k3 from cn, [k2, p2] twice.
Row 15 P2, k2, p2, sl 2 to cn, hold to *back*, k3, p2 from cn, p3, sl 2 to cn, hold to *front*, k2, k2 from cn, k2, p3, sl 3 to cn, hold to *front*, p2, k3 from cn, p2, k2, p2.
Row 17 P2, k2, sl 2 to cn, hold to *back*, k3, p2 from cn, p5, k2, sl 2 to cn, hold

to *back*, k2, k2 from cn, p5, sl 3 to cn, hold to *front*, p2, k3 from cn, k2, p2.
Row 19 P2, sl 2 to cn, hold to *back*, k3, p2 from cn, k2 p7, sl 2 to cn, hold to *front* k2, k2 from cn, p7, sl 3 to cn, hold to *front*, p2, k3 from cn, p2.
Row 20 Rep row 2. Rep rows 1-20 for diamond rib cable.

Complex Rope Cable (over 20 sts)
Rows 1 and 5 P2, k3, p2, k6, p2, k3, p2.
Row 2 and all WS rows K the knit sts and p the purl sts.
Row 3 P2, k3, p2, sl 3 to cn, hold to *back*, k3, k3 from cn, p2, k3, p2.
Row 7 P2, sl 3 to cn, hold to *front*, p2, k3 from cn, sl 3 to cn, hold to *back*, k3, k3 from cn, sl 2 to cn, hold to *back*, k3, p2 from cn, p2.
Row 9 P4, sl 3 to cn, hold to *back*, k3, p3 from cn, sl 3 to cn, hold to *front*, p3, k3 from cn, p4.
Row 11 P2, sl 2 to cn, hold to *back*, k3, p2 from cn, p6, sl 3 to cn, hold to *front*, p2, k3 from cn, p2.
Row 13 Sl 2 to cn, hold to *back*, k3, p2 from cn, p10, sl 3 to cn, hold to *front*, p2, k3 from cn.
Row 15 K3, p14, k3.
Row 17 Sl 3 to cn, hold to *front*, p2, k3 from cn, p10, sl 2 to cn, hold to *back*, k3, p2 from cn.
Row 19 P2, sl 3 to cn, hold to *front*, p2, k3 from cn, p6, sl 2 to cn, hold to *back*, k3, p2 from cn, p2.
Row 21 P4, sl 3 to cn, hold to *front*, k3, k3 from cn, sl 3 to cn, hold to *back*, k3, k3 from cn, p4.
Row 23 P2, sl 2 to cn, hold to *back* , k3, p2 from cn, sl 3 to cn, hold to *back*, k3, k3 from cn, sl 3 to cn, hold to *front*, p2, k3 from cn, p2.
Row 24 Rep Row 2. Rep rows 1-24 for complex rope cable.

BACK
With smaller needles, cast on 90 (94, 98, 102) sts.
Beg pats: Next row (WS) Work in k1, p1 rib over 10 (12, 14, 16) sts, work 8 sts in simple cable, work 10 sts in open rope cable, work 34 sts in diamond cable, work 10 sts in open rope cable,

work 8 sts in simple cable, work p1, k1 rib over 10 (12, 14, 16) sts. Cont in pats as established, for 1½"/4cm, end with a WS row.
Next row (RS) Change to larger needles. P10 (12, 14, 16) sts, work all cables as established, ending with p10 (12, 14, 16) sts. Maintain first and last 10 (12, 14, 16) sts as reverse St st, cont cables as established. Work until piece measures 7½ (8, 8, 8½)"/19 (20, 20, 21.5) cm from beg, end with a WS row.

Armhole shaping
Bind off 4 sts at beg of next 2 rows, 2 sts at beg of next 2 rows, dec 1 st at beg of next 4 (4, 6, 6) rows—74 (78, 80, 84) sts. Work until armhole measures 8½, (8½, 9, 9½)"/21.5 (21.5, 23, 24)cm end with a WS row.

Shoulder and neck shaping
Bind off 6 (7, 7, 7) sts at beg of next 4 rows, then 6 (6, 6, 7) sts, at beg of next 2 rows, AT SAME TIME, sl center 34 (34, 36, 38) sts to holder, working both sides at once dec 1 st at neck edge *every* row twice.

FRONT
Work same as back until piece measures 14 (14½, 15, 16)"/35.5 (37, 38, 40.5)cm from beg, end with a WS row.

Neck shaping
Work 23 (25, 25, 27) sts, sl center 28 (28, 30, 30) sts to holder, join 2nd ball of yarn, work to end. Working both sides at once, bind off 2 sts at each neck edge once, then 1 st 3 (3, 3, 4) times—18 (20, 20, 21) sts each shoulder. When same length as back to shoulder, shape shoulder as for back.

SLEEVES
With smaller needles, cast on 37 sts.
Row 1 K2, *p3, k2, rep from * to last 2 sts, end k2. Work for 1½"/4cm in p3, k2 rib. Change to larger needles and cont in rib pat. AT THE SAME TIME, inc 1 st each side (working incs into rib pat) every 5th row 19 (20, 21, 23) times—75 (77, 79, 83) sts. Work until piece mea-

sures 19½ (20, 20, 21)"/48 (50.5, 50.5, 53.5)cm from beg, end with a WS row.

Cap shaping
Bind off 6 sts at beg of next 2 rows, 6 (5, 5, 6) sts at beg of next 2 rows, 7 (5, 5, 5) sts at beg of next 4 rows, 0 (4, 5, 5) sts at beg of next 2 rows. Bind off rem 23 (27, 27, 29) sts.

FINISHING
Sew shoulder seams. With circular needle, pick up and k 85 (85, 90, 90) sts evenly around neckline. Join and work in p3, k2 rib for 8"/20cm. Bind off all sts loosely. Sew in sleeves. Sew side seams and sleeve seams.

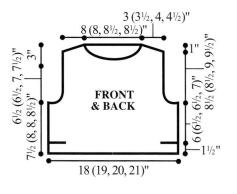

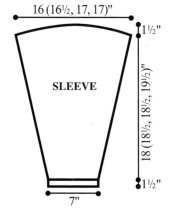

MAN'S PULLOVER

SIZES
To fit Small (Medium, Large, X-Large). Directions are for smallest size with larger sizes in parentheses. If there is only one figure, it applies to all sizes.

KNITTED MEASUREMENTS
• Chest 46 (50, 54, 58)"/117 (127, 137, 147.5)cm.
• Length 26 (27, 27½, 28)"/66 (68.5, 69, 71)cm.
• Upper arm 18 (18½, 19½, 20)"/46 (47, 50, 51)cm.

MATERIALS
Original Yarn
• 8 (8, 9, 9, 10) 3½oz./100g skeins (each approx 185yd/169m) of Classic Elite Yarns *Kelso* (wool 4) in #9286 brown tweed
Substitute Yarn
Note: This lighter yarn will give a looser, more relaxed look to the fabric.
• 6 (6, 7, 7) 1¾oz/50g balls (each approx 123yd/113m) of Classic Elite Yarns *Devon* (wool/silk 3) in #2878 brown tweed
• One pair each sizes 6 and 8 (4 and 5mm) needles OR SIZE TO OBTAIN GAUGE
• Cable needle (cn)
• Size 6 (4mm) circular needle, 16"/40cm long
• Stitch holders
Note
The original yarn used for this sweater is no longer available. A comparable substitute has been made, which is available at the time of printing. Check gauge of substitute yarns very carefully before beginning.

GAUGE
18 sts and 24 rows to 4"/10cm over p3, k2 rib using size 8 (5mm) needles. FOR PERFECT FIT, TAKE TIME TO CHECK GAUGE.

STITCH GLOSSARY

See woman's pullover, above, for pattern stitches.

BACK

With smaller needles, cast on 126 (136, 146, 156) sts.

Beg pat

Work 8 (13, 18, 23) sts in p3, k2 rib, work complex rope cable over 20 sts, work simple cable over 8 sts, work open rope cable over 10 sts, work diamond rib cable over 34 sts, work open rope cable over 10 sts, work simple cable over 8 sts, work complex rope cable over 20 sts, work 8 (13, 18, 23) in p3, k2 rib. Work in pat as established until piece measures 2"/5cm from beg. Change to larger needles. Work until piece measures 26 (27, 27½, 28½)"/66 (68.5, 69, 71)cm from beg. Bind off all sts.

FRONT

Work same as back until piece measures 23½ (24½, 25, 25½)"/58.5 (62.5, 63.5, 65)cm from beg.

Neck shaping

Work 47 (51, 55, 60) sts, sl center 32 (34, 36, 36) sts to holder, join 2nd ball of yarn and work to end. Working both sides at once, dec 1 st at each neck edge every other row 4 (3, 3, 4) times—43 (48, 52, 56) sts. When same length as back, bind off all sts.

SLEEVES

With smaller needles, cast on 50 sts.

Beg pat

Work simple cable over 8 sts, work diamond rib cable over 34 sts, work simple cable over 8 sts. Cont in pat as established until piece measures 2"/5cm from beg. Change to larger needles and beg inc (working incs as p3, k2 rib). Inc 1 st each side every 5th row 10 (4, 0, 0) times, then every 4th row 9 (16, 21, 22) times—88 (90, 92,

94) sts. Work until piece measures 18"/45.5cm from beg. Bind off.

FINISHING

Sew shoulder seams. With circular needle, pick up and k 100 (105, 105, 110) sts evenly around neck. Join and work p3, k2 rib for 1½"/4cm. Bind off all sts loosely. Place markers for armholes 9 (9¼, 9¾, 10)"/23 (23.5, 25, 25.5)cm down from shoulder seams. Sew sleeves between markers. Sew side and sleeve seams.

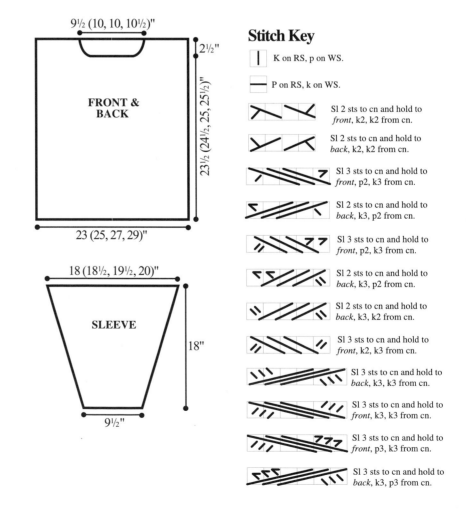

Stitch Key

	K on RS, p on WS.
—	P on RS, k on WS.

Sl 2 sts to cn and hold to *front*, k2, k2 from cn.

Sl 2 sts to cn and hold to *back*, k2, k2 from cn.

Sl 3 sts to cn and hold to *front*, p2, k3 from cn.

Sl 2 sts to cn and hold to *back*, k3, p2 from cn.

Sl 3 sts to cn and hold to *front*, p2, k3 from cn.

Sl 2 sts to cn and hold to *back*, k3, p2 from cn.

Sl 2 sts to cn and hold to *back*, k3, k2 from cn.

Sl 3 sts to cn and hold to *front*, k2, k3 from cn.

Sl 3 sts to cn and hold to *back*, k3, k3 from cn.

Sl 3 sts to cn and hold to *front*, k3, k3 from cn.

Sl 3 sts to cn and hold to *front*, p3, k3 from cn.

Sl 3 sts to cn and hold to *back*, k3, p3 from cn.

FRONT & BACK

9½ (10, 10, 10½)"

2½"

23½ (24½, 25, 25½)"

23 (25, 27, 29)"

SLEEVE

18 (18½, 19½, 20)"

18"

9½"

Diamond Rib Cable Chart

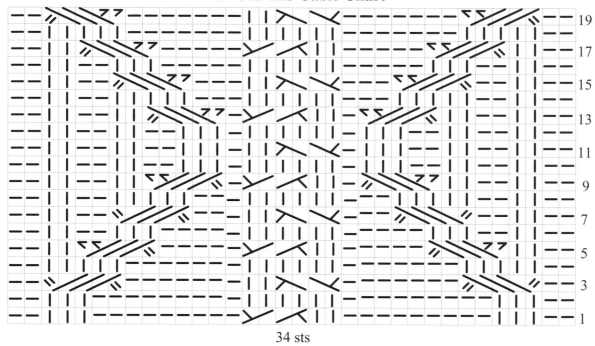

34 sts

Complex Rope Cable Chart

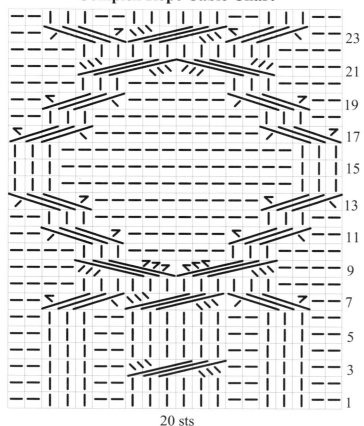

20 sts

Open Rope Cable Chart

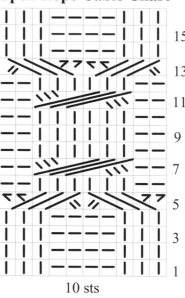

10 sts

Simple Cable Chart

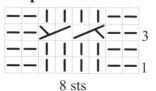

8 sts

Criss-crossing vines, accented with berries, trail their way up from diamond-shaped leaves on this beautifully textured pullover. An organic interpretation of classic cable work, the sweater features drop shoulders and a turtleneck. Shown in size Small. The Leaf Pullover first appeared in the Winter '99/00 issue of *Vogue Knitting*.

Leaf Pullover

FOR EXPERIENCED KNITTERS

SIZES
To fit Small (Medium,Large). Directions are for smallest size with larger sizes in parentheses. If there is only one figure, it applies to all sizes.

KNITTED MEASUREMENTS
● Bust 42(47,50)"/106.5(119,127) cm.
● Length 26 (26½, 27)"/66 (67, 68.5)cm.
● Upper arm 17(18,19)"/43 (45.5,48)cm.

MATERIALS
● 10 (10, 11) 3½oz/100g hanks (each approx 128yd/118m) of Classic Elite Yarns *Montera* (wool/llama 4) in #3816 white
● One pair each sizes 7 and 9 (4.5 and 5.5mm) needles OR SIZE TO OBTAIN GAUGE
● Size 7 (4.5mm) circular needle, 16"/40cm long
● Cable needle (cn)

GAUGES
● 20 sts and 23 rows to 4"/10cm over cable pat foll charts using size 9 (5.5mm) needles.
● 22 sts and 23 rows to 4"/10cm over St st using size 9 (5.5mm) needles.
FOR PERFECT FIT, TAKE TIME TO CHECK GAUGES.

STITCH GLOSSARY
Make Bobble (MB)
Make bobble by k1 into front, back and front of st (3 sts), turn, k3, p3, SK2P.

5-st RPC Sl 1 st to cn and hold to *back*, k4, p1 from cn.
5-st LPC Sl 4 sts to cn and hold to *front*, p1, k4 from cn.
6-st RPC Sl 2 sts to cn and hold to *back*, k4, p2 from cn.
6-st LPC Sl 4 sts to cn and hold to *front*, p2, k4 from cn.
7-st RPC Sl 3 sts to cn and hold to *back*, k4, p3 from cn.
7-st LPC Sl 4 sts to cn and hold to *front*, p3, k4 from cn.
8-st LC Sl 4 sts to cn and hold to *front*, k4, k4 from cn.

BACK
With larger needles, cast on 106 (118, 126) sts.
Next row (WS) K2 (selvage sts), k3 (6, 8), *work 32-st rep of chart 2 from left to right, k0 (3, 5); rep from * once, work 32-st rep of chart, k3 (6, 8), k2 (selvage sts). Cont to foll chart through row 5.
Row 6 Work foll chart, inc as indicated—112 (124, 132) sts. Cont to foll chart through row 46. On row 47, dec as indicated—100 (112, 120) sts. Then foll rows 48-63 only (16 rows), cont pat until piece measures 18"/45.5cm from beg, end with a WS row.

Armhole shaping
Dec 1 st each side of next row, then every other row 3 (4, 5) times more—92 (102, 108) sts. Work even until armhole measures 8 (8½, 9)"/20.5 (21.5, 23)cm. Bind off. With smaller needles pick up and k 1 st in every st on lower edge. K 1 row, p 1 row. Bind off.

FRONT
Work as for back until armhole measures 5½ (6, 6½)"/14 (15, 16)cm.

Neck shaping
Next row (RS) Work 33 (36, 39) sts, join 2nd ball of yarn and bind off center 26 (30, 30) sts, work to end. Working both sides at once, dec 1 st at each neck edge every other row 4 times. When same length as back, bind off rem 29 (32, 35) sts each side for shoulders. Work two rows at lower edge as for back.

SLEEVES
With smaller needles, cast on 54 sts. Work chart 1 as foll:
Row 1 (WS) Beg with st 19 (and working selvage st each side), work to st 1 then work 21-st rep twice ending 2nd rep with st 8. Foll chart through row 11. Change to larger needles and cont foll chart, AT SAME TIME, inc 1 st each side (inside selvage sts) every other row 27 (29, 32) times—108 (112, 118) sts. Work even until piece measures 17½"/44.5cm from beg.

Cap shaping
Dec 1 st each side of next row, then every other row 3 (4, 5) times more—100 (102, 106) sts. Bind off.

FINISHING
Block pieces to measurements. Using 2 strands of yarn, embroider straight st across large St st diamond then back st down center. Work ch-st all around diamonds (see chart and photo). Sew shoulder seams.

Turtleneck

With circular needle, pick up and k 96 (104, 104) sts evenly around neck edge. Join and work in k4, p4 rib for 6"/15cm. Bind off in rib. Sew in sleeves. Sew side and sleeve seams.

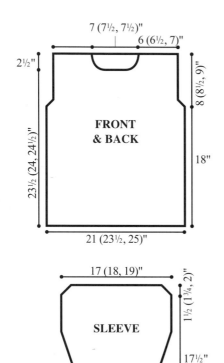

FRONT & BACK

SLEEVE

Chart 2

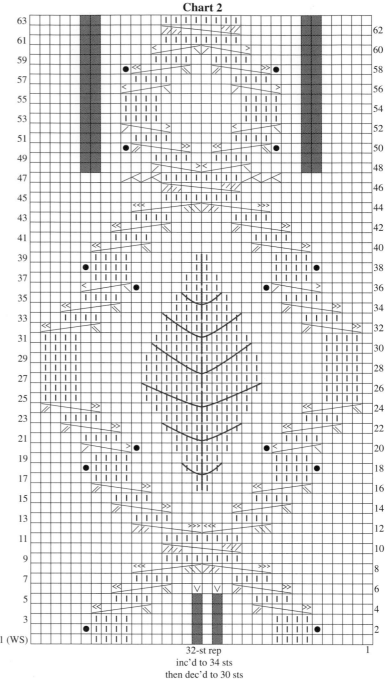

32-st rep
inc'd to 34 sts
then dec'd to 30 sts

Chart 1

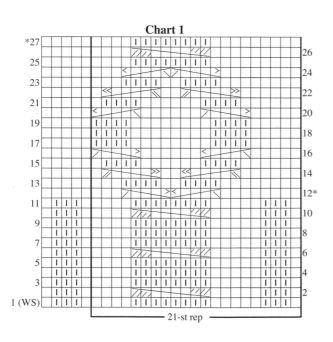

21-st rep

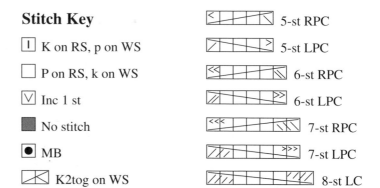

Stitch Key

- $\boxed{\text{I}}$ K on RS, p on WS
- $\square$ P on RS, k on WS
- $\boxed{\text{V}}$ Inc 1 st
- ■   No stitch
- ●   MB
- ⧄   K2tog on WS

- 5-st RPC
- 5-st LPC
- 6-st RPC
- 6-st LPC
- 7-st RPC
- 7-st LPC
- 8-st LC

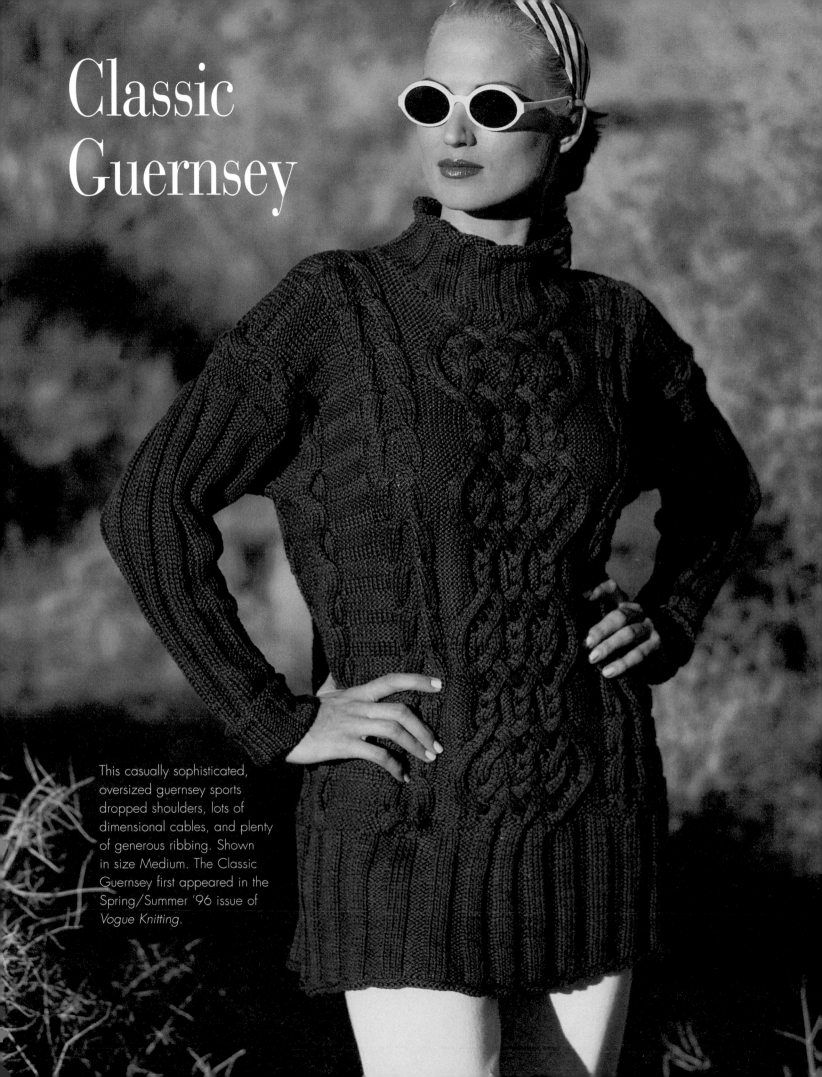

Classic
Guernsey

This casually sophisticated, oversized guernsey sports dropped shoulders, lots of dimensional cables, and plenty of generous ribbing. Shown in size Medium. The Classic Guernsey first appeared in the Spring/Summer '96 issue of *Vogue Knitting*.

Classic Guernsey

FOR EXPERIENCED KNITTERS

SIZES
To fit Small (Medium, Large). Directions are for smallest size with larger sizes in parentheses. If there is only one figure, it applies to all sizes.

KNITTED MEASUREMENTS
- Bust 39 (42, 44)"/99 (107, 112)cm.
- Length (above St st rolled edge) 27 (28, 28)"/68.5 (71, 71)cm.
- Sleeve width at upper arm 18 (18, 20)"/45.5 (45.5, 51)cm.

MATERIALS
Original Yarn
- 10 (10, 11) 4½oz/125g hanks (each approx 192yd/173m) of Classic Elite Yarns *Camden Cotton* (cotton 4) in #7110 marine blue

Substitute Yarn
- 28 (28, 31) 1¾oz/50g skeins (each approx 70yd/64m) of Classic Elite Yarns *Newport Cotton* (cotton 4) in #2092 periwinkel
- One pair each sizes 4 and 6 (3.5 and 4mm) needles OR SIZE TO OBTAIN GAUGE
- Size 4 (3.5mm) circular needle, 16"/40cm long
- Cable needle (cn)
- Stitch markers

Note
The original yarn used for this sweater is no longer available. A comparable substitution has been made, which is available at the time of printing. Check gauge of substitution yarns very carefully before beginning.

GAUGES
- 19 sts and 23 rows to 4"/10cm over K4, P4 Rib pat (slightly stretched), using size 6 (4mm) needles.
- 64 sts of Center Cable to 7½"/19cm wide, using size 6 (4mm) needles.

FOR PERFECT FIT, TAKE TIME TO CHECK GAUGES.

STITCH GLOSSARY
5-st Back Purl Cross (BPC) Sl 1 st to cn and hold to *back*, k4, then p1 from cn.
5-st Front Purl Cross (FPC) Sl 4 sts to cn and hold to *front*, p1, then k4 from cn.
6-st Back Purl Cross (BPC) Sl 2 sts to cn and hold to *back*, k4, then p2 from cn.
6-st Front Purl Cross (FPC) Sl 4 sts to cn and hold to *front*, p2, then k4 from cn.
7-st Back Purl Cross #1 (BPC) Sl 3 sts to cn and hold to *back*, k4, then p3 from cn.
7-st Front Purl Cross #1 (FPC) Sl 4 sts to cn and hold to *front*, p3, then k4 from cn.
7-st Back Purl Cross #2 (BPC) Sl 3 sts to cn and hold to *back*, p3, k1, then k3 from cn.
7-st Front Purl Cross #2 (FPC) Sl 4 sts to cn and hold to *front*, k3, then k1, p3 from cn.
8-st Back Cross (8-st BC) Sl 4 sts to cn and hold to *back*, k4, then k4 from cn.
8-st Front Cross (8-st FC) Sl 4 sts to cn and hold to *front*, k4, then k4 from cn.
8-st Back Purl Cross (BPC) Sl 4 sts to cn and hold to *back*, k4, then p4 from cn.
8-st Front Purl Cross (FPC) Sl 4 sts to cn and hold to *front*, p4, then k4 from cn.

K4, P4 Rib Pat (multiple of 8 sts)
Row 1 (RS) *P2, k4, p2; rep from * to end.
Row 2 K the knit sts and p the purl sts. Rep last row for K4, P4 rib pat.

BACK
With larger needles, cast on 104 (112, 120) sts. Work 4 rows in St st (beg with a k row). Work in K4, P4 rib pat until piece measures 5 (6, 6)"/12.5 (15, 15)cm above St st rolled edge, end with a RS row. P 2 rows, k 1 row. K next row on RS, inc 26 (24, 22) sts evenly across—130 (136, 142) sts.

Beg chart pats
Next row (WS) Work 1 (4, 7) sts in rev St st, snake cable over 8 sts, ladder pat over 12 sts, lobster cable over 14 sts, center cable over 60 sts, lobster cable over 14 sts, ladder pat over 12 sts, snake cable over 8 sts, 1 (4, 7) sts in rev St st. Cont in pat as established until piece measures 18 (19, 18)"/45.5 (48, 45.5)cm above St st rolled edge. Place markers each side of row for armhole. Work until piece measures 27 (28, 28)"/68.5 (71, 71)cm above St st rolled edge. Bind off all sts.

FRONT
Work as for back until piece measures 6½ (6½, 7½)"/16.5 (16.5,19)cm above armhole markers, end with a WS row.

Neck shaping
Next row (RS) Work 48 (49, 52) sts, join 2nd ball of yarn and bind off center 34 (38, 38) sts, work in pat to end. Working both sides at once, dec 1 st at each neck edge every other row 6 times. Work even until same length as back. Bind off rem 42 (43, 46) sts each side for shoulders.

SLEEVES
With smaller needles, cast on 40 (40, 48) sts. Work 4 rows in St st (beg with a k row). Work in K4, P4 rib pat until piece measures 2"/5cm above St st rolled edge. Change to larger needles and cont in K4, P4 rib pat, inc 1 st each side (working inc sts into pat) every 4th row 20 (20, 23) times, every 6th row 3 (3, 1) times—86 (86, 96) sts. Work even until piece measures 19"/48cm above St st rolled edge. Bind off all sts.

FINISHING
Block pieces lightly. Sew shoulder seams.

Collar

With circular needle, beg at left shoulder, pick up and k 80 (88, 88) sts evenly around neck edge. Join, place marker and work in rnds of K4, P4 rib until collar measures 3"/7.5cm. Work 4 rnds of St st (k every rnd). Bind off all sts knitwise on next rnd. Sew sleeves between markers. Sew side and sleeve seams.

Lobster Chart

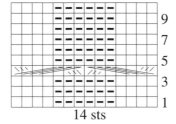

14 sts

Ladder Pattern

12 sts

Stitch Key

☐ K on RS, p on WS
⊟ P on RS, k on WS
M1
K2tog on WS
Skp on WS
5-st BPC
5-st FPC
6-st BPC
6-st FPC
7-st BPC #1
7-st FPC #1
7-st BPC #2
7-st FPC #2
8-st FC
8-st FC
8-st BPC
8-st FPC

Snake Cables

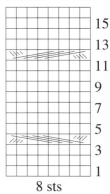

8 sts

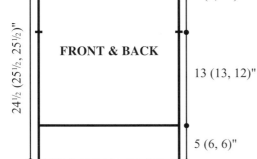

2½"

7 (7½, 7½)" 6¼ (6¾, 7¼)"

9 (9, 10)"

24½ (25½, 25½)"

FRONT & BACK

13 (13, 12)"

5 (6, 6)"

19½ (21, 22)"

18 (18, 20)"

SLEEVE

17"

2"

8½ (8½, 10)"

Center Cable

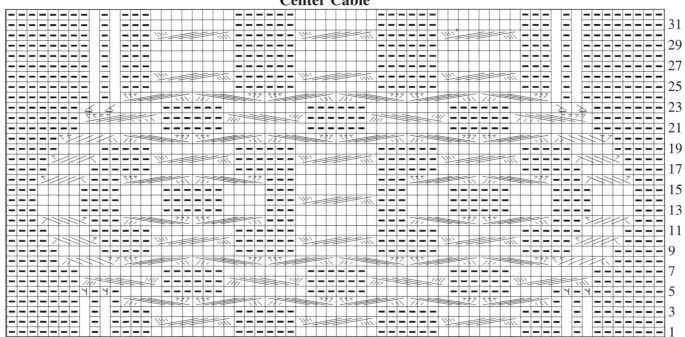

6 sts increased to 64 sts

Vibrant colorwork and offbeat design elements conspire to create this eyecatching pillow. The pillow features a knitted front with a vase of flowers motif set against a patterned background, a garter striped border and fabric back. The Embroidered Pillow first appeared in the Fall '97 issue of *Vogue Knitting*.

Embroidered Pillow

FOR INTERMEDIATE KNITTERS

KNITTED MEASURMENTS
- 13" x 14½"/33cm x 37cm

MATERIALS
- 3 1¾oz/50g hanks (each approx 95yd/86m) of Classic Elite Yarns *Tapestry* (wool/mohair 4) in #2285 couscous gold (A)
- 2 hanks in #2295 Punjab purple (C)
- 1 hank each in #2226 Persian purple (B) and #2204 tile turquoise (D)
- Small amounts of #2260 Kani teal (E), #2246 loomed teal (F), #2232 museum magenta (G), #2279 Istanbul marketplace (H), #2298 spice cabinet (I), #2205 interwined pink (J), #2294 Medici green (K), #2272 gobelin green (L), #2217 Caspian Sea (M), #2276 Dardarnelles brown (N) and #2251 Tibetan gold (O)
- One pair size 7 (4.5mm) needles OR SIZE TO OBTAIN GAUGE
- Three size 7 (4.5mm) circular needles, 60"/150cm long
- Stitch markers
- Tapestry needle (for embroidery)
- 12" x 12"/30.5cm x 30.5cm pillow form
- Fabric for backing

GAUGE

20 sts and 22 rows to 4"/10cm over St st, using size 7 (4.5mm) needles. TAKE TIME TO CHECK GAUGE.

STITCH GLOSSARY

Border Stripe Pat

Pick up with N and p 1 rnd. With I, k 1 rnd, p 2 rnds. With D, k 1 rnd, p 1 rnd. With A, k 1 rnd, p 1 rnd. Bind off purlwise in A.

PILLOW

With straight needles, cast on 63 sts. Work foll chart, working major shapes in colors as indicated with A stranded behind throughout (use duplicate stitch for small motifs when pillow top is complete). When row 72 of chart is complete, bind off all sts.

EMBROIDERY

Work French knot embroidery in N randomly on background of entire pillow. At base of vase, chain and back stitch stripes of L and D. Work French knots directly above the stripes in I. Chain stitch swirls on base of vase in O. Work elongated Lazy Daisy leaves on left flower stem in F. Decorate center of middle flower with back stitch and French knots in assorted colors. Use photo for inspiration.

FINISHING

With circular needle and N, *pick up and k 61 sts at bottom edge of pillow, pick up corner st, pick up every 2nd, 3rd, and 4th row at side of pillow, mark corner stitch;* using 2nd circular needle rep bet *'s once. With the 3rd circular needle, work in border stripe pat, AT SAME TIME, miter the corners: work to st before marked st, inc 1, work marked st as knit st, inc 1. Repeat at each corner. Cut piece of fabric to same size as pillow inside border adding ½"/1.5cm seam allowance. Press ¼"/.5cm to WS twice and hem. Sew to back of pillow inside border leaving one seam open. Stuff with pillow form and stitch closed.

Pillow Chart

Color Key

- ☐ Couscous gold (A)
- + Persian purple (B)
- V Punjab purple (C)
- × Tile turquoise (D)
- / Kani teal (E)
- O Loomed teal (F)
- = Museum magenta (G)
- F Istanbul marketplace (H)
- ˥ Spice cabinet (I)
- Λ Interwined pink (J)
- I Medici green (K)
- – Gobelin green (L)
- • Caspian sea (M)

Following photo, embellish with:

Tibetan gold (vase)

Dardanelles brown (background)

Deborah Newton

Deborah Newton entered the field of knitwear design just when the iron was hot. Young, without major responsibilities, she started freelancing full time after selling only a few sweaters. "I was very lucky, the timing was right," she says. "There were a lot of knitting magazines being published, and they were buying lots of designs. People liked my work and one thing led to another."

When Deborah sent her first design to *Vogue Knitting*, editor Nancy Thomas returned the sweater, saying that it wasn't right for the current issue but that it was very nice. She encouraged her to send it elsewhere, which Deborah did with success. Thus began Deborah's relationship with the magazine, which has extended over almost two decades of publications. Even though knitting seemed natural to Deborah, she barely knit at all before college, when she was inspired by Elizabeth Zimmermann's books on the subject. "I found her books very intriguing," she explains. "They were sort of an invitation to take knitting into my own arena, as a form of self-expression." From there, Deborah started reading Barbara Walker's knitting dictionaries, experimenting with the different pattern stitches and learning the various techniques.

Deborah started designing her own sweaters almost immediately, and it was not long after that she began contemplating a career in knitwear design. "I was working for a costume designer at the time," she says. "I had done a couple of sweaters and somebody said to me, gee, those are as nice as anything I've seen published. That gave me the idea. I sold a couple of sweaters and I thought, this is interesting, I wonder if I could do this for a living? So I took the plunge."

As her career took off, Deborah quickly recognized that she would have to change some of her work habits. "I didn't realize when I first began that editors were working very specifically," she recalls. "I thought you had to knit a sweater up and sell it that way. But an editor wants a certain color, look, whatever—everything has to be made from scratch. That's when I realized that I was going to have to develop some kind of sketching and swatching presentation to be able to sell my stuff. I couldn't make up every sweater ahead of time, then have it reknit to spec [specifications]."

Deborah also soon felt the need to hire other knitters to help her keep up with the high demand. "When you're freelancing as a designer, you're doing a million different things at once," she explains. "There were times when I had anywhere from two to ten sweaters going a month, and that's pretty hairy. You're submitting work for future jobs, you're getting instructions ready for sweaters that are in the works, you're planning out gauges and sizing, sometimes doing instructions in various sizes, as well as knitting and doing finishing. For a long time it was a real juggling act to do all those things at once. But I had a lot of really wonderful knitters working with me and that made things a little bit easier. You really need to be able to count on people to finish things when there are short deadlines."

With her background in costume-making, Deborah approaches knit design from a different angle than most. "Most of the things I was interested in making were more dressmaker-inspired," she says. "I came from a background of wanting to make sweaters look more like sewn clothes. At the same time, I was very interest-

> "It's the designer's role to interpret the culture, what is happening fashionwise, and to make it into something a knitter wants to make."

ed in everything knitting had to offer—all of the traditional patterns and techniques—but I also have a great deal of interest in any kind of garment. I love all kinds of fabrics and fibers."

Likewise, she attributes her strong emphasis on process to her sewing background. She methodically works through each design, taking an idea from sketch to swatch to construction. "You can start a design in many different ways," she says. "You can start it because you're interested in creating a certain garment shape, so therefore you have to find a fabric that suits it. Or you can start with the fabric and ask what this fabric would be best suited for."

Reluctant to call herself an artist, Deborah sees herself as a craftsperson, making functional garments that look good and are fun to make. She identifies her three basic concerns: "First, you satisfy yourself from a creative point of view. Second, you are designing for a knitter, so it has to be interesting for them, and third, your work is being portrayed in a magazine or book form, so it has to look good in the photo. All of those things are equally important to me. I want to satisfy an editor, a knitter, and myself."

Over the years, Deborah's designs have evolved from complicated constructions to simpler and more streamlined ones. She attributes the change partly to her own evolving interests and partly to fashion trends. "It's the designer's role

to interpret the culture, what is happening fashionwise, and to make it into something a knitter wants to make," she explains. "Everyone has a little bit of fashion intuition, and I'm always looking in newspapers and magazines. You have to when you're doing it professionally, because you can't fall back on the same old thing over and over again. You have to be conscious of what the silhouette of the season is, and what things everyone is tuned into, whether consciously or unconsciously."

After years of designing professionally, Deborah now enjoys spending more time pursuing her own creative interests. "Now that I'm not designing professionally as much, the knitting that I do is a little more freeform. I don't have to meet the market needs, I'm meeting my own needs," she says. "Nowadays, I like to do one sweater at a time and I like to knit it myself. I get a real charge being able to knit the sweater myself, because for years I couldn't."

Still, Deborah admits to being a perfectionist who would never settle for something being just okay. "You can't always know how many stitches are going to work out for a collar or a buttonband, and when you want it to be really precise you have to be willing to tear it out a time or two until you get it just right."

It's that degree of technical excellence that has earned Deborah her ranking as one of this country's master knitters.

Brimming with elegance, this shapely, close-fit pullover has vintage flair and alluring details—a graceful peplum with two pleats in front and one in back; tiny slits at the cuffs; flirty tacked-on bows and a deep, scooped back neck. Shown in size 34. The Pleated Pullover with Bows first appeared in the Holiday '86 issue of *Vogue Knitting*.

Pleated Pullover with Bows

FOR EXPERIENCED KNITTERS

SIZES
To fit 32 (34, 36, 38)"/81 (86, 91, 96)cm bust. Directions are for smallest size with larger sizes in parentheses. If there is only one set of figures, it applies to all sizes.

KNITTED MEASUREMENTS
● Finished bust measurement at underarm 34 (36, 38, 40)"/84 (90, 94, 100)cm.
● Length 23 (24, 25, 26)"/58 (60, 63, 65)cm.
● Sleeve width at upper arm 13½ (14, 14½, 15)"/34 (35, 36, 37)cm.

MATERIALS
Original Yarn
● 12 (12, 13, 14) 2oz/60g balls (each approx 100yd/90m) of Melrose *Cablenella* (wool/rayon 3) in copper
Substitute Yarn
● 13 (13, 14, 15) 1¾oz/50g balls (each approx 96yd/89m) of Berroco, Inc. *SensuWool* (wool/rayon 4) in #6554 burgundy
● One pair each 4 and 6 (3.5 and 4mm) needles OR SIZE TO OBTAIN GAUGE
● Stitch markers
● ¼yd/.25m black velvet fabric for bows (optional)
● Sewing needle and black thread.

Note
The original yarn used for this sweater is no longer available. A comparable substitution has been made, which is available at the time of printing. Check gauge of substitute yarns very carefully before beginning.

GAUGE
20 sts and 28 rows to 4"/10cm over St st using size 6 (4mm) needles. FOR PERFECT FIT, TAKE TIME TO CHECK GAUGE.

Note
Always knit first and last st of every row for selvage sts to aid in seaming. Do not count these sts at seam edges when measuring pieces. Work incs and decs at edges inside of these sts.

PLEAT
(panel of 32 sts dec to 2 sts)
Row 1 (RS) Sl 1 wyib, k7, p1, k14, p1, k7, sl 1 wyib.
Row 2 and all WS rows P, slipping p sts of previous row wyib.
Rows 3 and 5 Rep row 1.
Row 7 Sl 1 wyib, k4, k2tog, place marker (pm), k1, p1, k1, ssk, k8, k2tog, k1, p1, k1, pm, ssk, k4, sl 1 wyib.
Rows 9 and 11 Sl 1 wyib, k6, p1, k12,

p1, k6, sl 1 wyib.
Row 13 Sl 1 wyib, k to 2 sts before marker, k2tog, sl marker, k1, p1, k1, ssk, k to 2 stitches before next marker, k2tog, sl marker, k1, p1, k1, ssk, k to last st, sl 1 wyib. Cont in this way to dec 1 st each side of markers, every 6th row, until there are 12 sts.
Next row (WS) Sl 1, k2tog, p1, ssk, k2tog, p1, ssk, sl 1—8 sts. Work 4 rows even.
Next row K1, bind off center 6 sts—2 sts rem.

BACK
With larger needles, cast on 118 (122, 128, 132) sts. P 1 row.
Beg pat: Row 1 (RS) K1 (selvage st), k42 (44, 47, 49), pm, work pleat over next 32 sts, pm, k42 (44, 47, 49), k1 (selvage st). Cont working St st outside markers and pleat inside markers for 12 rows. Cont working pleat, dec 1 st each side of next row, then every 12 (12, 10,

10) rows 2 (2, 3, 3) times more. After all pleat rows have been worked, p next row over all 82 (86, 90, 94) sts. (**Note:** Hole formed by 6 bound-off sts at top of pleat can be sewn closed after piece is complete.)

Waist rib
Next row (RS) K1, [k1, p1] 16 (17, 18, 19) times, pm, k16, pm, [p1, k1] 16 (17, 18, 19) times, k1.
Next row K the knit sts end p the purl sts. Rep last 2 rows twice more.
Next (inc) row (RS) Rib to first marker, sl marker, k2, m1, k12, m1, k2, sl marker, work to end. Cont in this way to inc 2 sts between markers (working inc sts into St st) every 4th row 0 (1, 1, 2) times more, every 6th row once—86 (92, 96, 102) sts. Work 1 row even.
Next row (RS) Work to last p st in first rib section, k1, k to first p st of next rib section, k1, rib to end. Cont in this way to work 1 less st in rib in each rib sec-

tion every other row (working rib st in St st), until all sts are worked in St st. Cont in St st until piece measures 8 (8½, 9, 9½)"/20.5 (21.5, 23, 24)cm from beg of waist rib.

Armhole shaping
Bind off 5 sts at beg of next 2 rows. Dec 1 st each side every other row 5 times—66 (72, 76, 82) sts. Work even until armhole measures 4½ (5, 5½, 6)"/11.5 (12.5, 14, 15)cm.

Neck shaping
Inc 1 st each side of next row, then every 4th row 4 times more, and AT SAME TIME, bind off center 14 (16, 16, 20) sts for neck and working both sides at once, bind off from each neck edge 4 sts twice, 3 sts twice, 2 sts once, 1 st 3 times—12 (14, 16, 17) sts each side. Work even until armhole measures 8 (8½, 9, 9½)"/20.5 (21.5, 23, 24)cm.

Shoulder shaping
Bind off at beg of next row 4 sts 3 (1, 0, 0) times, 5 sts 0 (2, 2, 1) times, 6 sts 0 (0, 1, 2) times.

FRONT
With larger needles, cast on 148 (152, 158, 162) sts. P 1 row.
Beg pat: Row 1 (RS) K1 (selvage st), k19 (20, 22, 23), pm, work pleat over next 32 sts, pm, k44 (46, 48, 50), pm, work pleat over next 32 sts, pm, k19 (20, 22, 23), k1 (selvage st). Cont in this way working St st and pleats and work dec at side edges as for back until all pleat rows have been worked. P next rows over all 82 (86, 90, 94) sts. Work waist rib (including inc sts) and armhole dec and inc as for back until armhole measures 7 (7½, 8, 8½)"/17.5 (18.5, 20, 21)cm.

Neck shaping
Bind off center 26 (28, 28, 32) sts for neck and working both sides at once, bind off from each neck edge 4 sts once, 3 sts once, 2 sts 3 times, AT SAME TIME, when same length as back to shoulder, shape shoulder as for back.

SLEEVES

With larger needles, cast on 19 (20, 20, 21) sts, with 2nd ball of yarn, cast on 19 (20, 20, 21) sts. Work both pieces at once for slit cuff as foll: Work in St st for 4 rows.

Next row (RS) K1 (selvage st), k2, m1, k to end of first section, k to last 3 sts of 2nd section, m1, k2, k1 (selvage st). P 1 row.

Join sections: Next row (RS) K to end of first section, with same strand, cast on 2 sts, k to end of 2nd section dropping 2nd ball—42 (44, 44, 46) sts. Cont in St st on all sts, inc 1 st each side every 6th row 4 (2, 4, 2) times, every 8th row 10 (12, 11, 13) times—70 (72, 74, 76) sts. Work even until piece measures 16½ (17, 17½, 18)"/41.5 (42.5, 43.5, 45)cm from beg.

Cap shaping

Bind off 5 sts at beg of next 2 rows. Dec 1 st each side every other row 15 (17, 18, 20) times. Bind off 2 sts at beg of next 4 rows, 3 sts at beg of next 2 rows. Bind off 16 (14, 14, 12) sts.

FINISHING

Block pieces. Sew left shoulder seam.

Sleeve trim

With RS facing and larger needles, pick up and k18 (19, 20, 21) sts along lower edge of first section, pick up 1 st in corner and mark, pick up 6 sts along side of slit. K 2 rows, inc 1 st each end of marked st on RS row. Bind off. Work trim along other section in same way. Overlap trim at top of slit and tack.

Lower edge trim

With RS facing and larger needles, pick up and k1 st in each cast-on st along lower edge of front (except sl sts in pleats). K 2 rows. Bind off. Work lower edge of back in same way.

Neckband

With RS facing and smaller needles, beg at right shoulder, pick up and k68 (70, 70, 72) sts along back neck, 54 (56, 56, 58) sts along front neck—122

(126, 126, 130) sts. K 2 rows. Bind off. Sew right shoulder seam, including neckband. Sew in sleeves. Sew side and sleeve seams.

BOWS

Note: Instructions are given for fabric or knit bows which can be done in matching or contrasting fabric or yarn.

Fabric bows (make 5)
Cut velvet fabric 4 x 5½"/10 x 14cm. With WS facing, fold in half lengthwise. Leaving ½"/1.5cm seam allowance, stitch edge leaving center ¾"/2cm unsewn. Centering seam, fold back seam allowance, press lightly. Sew upper and lower edges with a ⅜"/1cm seam allowance. Trim seam allowances and turn to RS through opening. Steam lightly. With seam at back of bow, take running st through center and sew in place with 1 bow above each pleat and 1 at each sleeve cuff above slit.

Knitted bows (make 5)
With larger needles, cast on 13 sts. K 3 rows.
Next row (WS) P6, sl 1 wyib, p6.
Next row K 3, sl 1 wyib, k2, p1, k2, sl 1 wyib, k3. Rep last 2 rows for 2¾"/7cm, end with a WS row.
Next row K6, p1, k6. K 2 rows. Bind off. Tack center of pleated piece to form bow. Sew on for fabric bow.

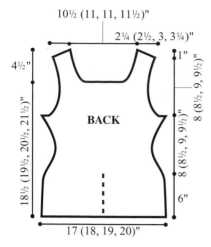

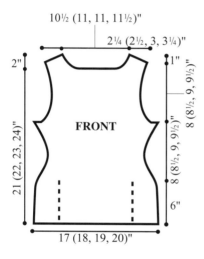

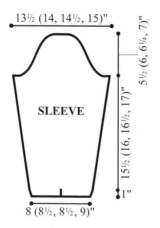

Cashmere Pullover

A stunning interlocking cable panel is the centerpiece of this lush cashmere pullover. Eyelets punctuate the cables, and are echoed in lace bands and at the edges. Shown in size Medium. The Cashmere Pullover first appeared in the Fall '99 issue of *Vogue Knitting*.

Deborah Newton

Cashmere Pullover

FOR PERFECT FIT, TAKE TIME TO CHECK GAUGES.

Note
When working cable panel chart, rep rows 1-16 for first and last 8 sts, rep rows 1-24 for center 20 sts.

SIZES
To fit Small (Medium, Large). Directions are for smallest size with larger sizes in parentheses. If there is only one figure, it applies to all sizes.

KNITTED MEASUREMENTS
● Bust 42 (46, 50)"/106.5 (116.5, 127)cm.
● Length 23½ (24, 24½)"/59.5 (61, 62)cm.
● Upper arm 15½ (16½, 17½)"/39.5 (42, 44.5)cm.

MATERIALS
● 15 (16, 18) 1¾oz/50g balls (each approx 66yd/60m) of Filatura Di Crosa/Takhi•Stacy Charles Collection *Melville* (cashmere 6) in #16 natural
● One pair each size 9 and 10 (5.5 and 6mm) needles OR SIZE TO OBTAIN GAUGE
● Sizes 9 and 10 (5.5 and 6mm) circular needles, 16"/40cm long
● Cable needle (cn)
● Stitchmaker

GAUGES
● 13 sts and 20 rows to 4"/10cm over St st using size 10 (6mm) needles.
● 36 sts to 8"/20.5cm over cable panel using size 10 (6mm) needles.

STITCH GLOSSARY
4-st RC
Sl 2 sts to cn and hold to *back*, k2, k2 from cn.
4-st LC
Sl 2 sts to cn and hold to *front*, k2, k2 from cn.
8-st RC
Sl 4 sts to cn and hold to *back*, k4, k4 from cn.
8-st LC
Sl 4 sts to cn and hold to *front*, k4, k4 from cn.

BACK
With smaller needles, cast on 70 (74, 82) sts.
Next row (WS) P2, *k2, p2; rep from * to end. Cont in k2, p2 rib as established for 2 rows more.
Eyelet row (RS) K2, *yo, p2tog, k2; rep from * to end. P next row, inc 4 (6, 4) sts evenly spaced across 74 (80, 86) sts. Change to larger needles.

Establish pats
Next row (RS) Work 10 (12, 14) sts in St st, work 4 sts eyelet panel chart, 5 (6, 7) sts in St st, 36 sts cable panel chart, 5 (6, 7) sts in St st, 4 sts eyelet panel chart, 10 (12, 14) sts in St st. Cont in pats as established for 9 rows more.
Next (dec) row (RS) K3, ssk, work to last 5 sts, k2tog, k3. Rep dec row every 6th row 3 times more 66 (72, 78) sts. Work even until piece measures

9½"/24cm from beg, end with a WS row.
Next (inc) row (RS) K3, M1, work to last 3 sts, M1, k3. Rep inc row every 6th row 3 times more 74 (80, 86) sts. Work even until piece measures 15"/38cm from beg, end with a WS row.

Armhole shaping
Bind off 3 (4, 5) sts at beg of next 2 rows.
Next row (RS) K2, ssk, work to last 4 sts, k2tog, k2. Work 1 row even. Rep last 2 rows 3 (4, 5) times more 60 (62, 64) sts. Work even until armhole—measures 7½ (8, 8½)"/19 (20.5, 21.5)cm.

Shoulder and neck shaping
Bind off 4 sts at beg of next 4 rows, 4 (4, 5) sts at beg of next 2 rows, AT SAME TIME, bind off center 20 (22, 22) sts for neck and working both sides at once, bind off from each neck edge 4 sts twice.

FRONT
Work as for back until armhole measures 6 (6½, 7)"/15 (16.5, 17.5)cm.

Neck and shoulder shaping
Next row (RS) Work 21 (21, 22) sts, join 2nd ball of yarn and bind off center 18 (20, 20) sts, work to end. Working both sides at once, bind off from each neck edge 2 sts 4 times, 1 st once, AT SAME TIME, when same length as back to shoulder, shape shoulder as for back.

SLEEVES
With smaller needles, cast on 30 (30, 34) sts. Work in k2, p2 rib as for 3 rows as for back. P next row on WS, inc 4 (6, 4) sts evenly spaced across—34 (36, 38) sts. Change to larger needles.

Establish pats

Next row (RS) Work 6 sts in St st, [4 sts in eyelet panel chart, 5 (6, 7) sts in St st] twice, 4 sts in eyelet panel chart, 6 sts in St st. Cont in pats as established for 7 rows more.

Inc row (RS) K2, M1, work to last 2 sts, M1, k2. Cont to work inc row (working inc sts into St st) every 8th row 1 (1, 6) times more, every 10th row 6 (6, 2) times—50 (52, 56) sts. Work even until piece measures 17½"/44.5cm from beg, end with a WS row.

Cap shaping

Bind off 4 sts at beg of next 2 rows. Work dec row as for back armhole shaping on next row, then every other row 8 (9, 10) times more.

Next row (RS) Work dec row.

Next row P2, p2tog, work to last 4 sts, p2tog tbl, p2. Rep last 2 rows twice more. Bind off rem 12 (12, 14) sts.

FINISHING

Block pieces to measurements. Sew shoulder seams.

Turtleneck

With RS facing and larger circular needle, pick up and k 50 (52, 52) sts along back neck and 62 (64, 64) sts along front neck 112 (116, 116) sts. Join, mark beg of rnd. Work in k2, p2 rib for 1 rnd.

Eyelet rnd *K2, p2tog, yo; rep from * around. Cont in k2, p2 rib until turtleneck measures 3"/7.5cm. Change to smaller circular needle and rib for ½"/1.5cm. Bind off, work p2tog in every other p2 rib across back neck, then p2tog in every p2 rib across front neck while binding off. Sew in sleeves. Sew side and sleeve seams.

Cable Panel

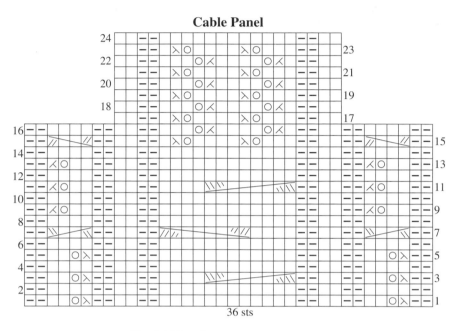

36 sts

Eyelet Panel

4 sts

Stitch Key

☐ K on RS, p on WS

– P on RS, k on RS

O Yo

K2tog on RS, p2tog on WS

Ssk

4-st RC

4-st LC

8-st RC

8-st LC

FRONT & BACK

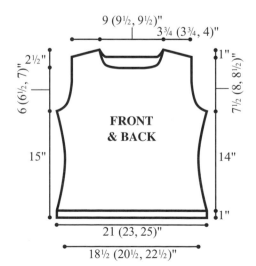

9 (9½, 9½)"
3¾ (3¾, 4)"
2½"
6 (6½, 7)"
1"
7½ (8, 8½)"
15"
14"
1"
21 (23, 25)"
18½ (20½, 22½)"

SLEEVE

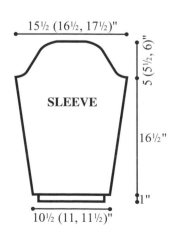

15½ (16½, 17½)"
5 (5½, 6)"
16½"
1"
10½ (11, 11½)"

Three different pattern panels—thick cables broken with blocks of ribbing, tiny twists and textured ribs—make up this roomy, shawl-collared cardigan. A classic look to wear year-round, the sweater is trimmed with leather buttons and I-cord streamers. Shown in size Medium. The Shawl-Collared Cardigan first appeared in the Winter '99/00 issue of *Vogue Knitting*.

Shawl-Collared Cardigan

FOR INTERMEDIATE KNITTERS

SIZES
To fit Small (Medium, Large). Directions are for smallest size with larger sizes in parentheses. If there is only one figure, it applies to all sizes.

KNITTED MEASUREMENTS
- Bust (closed) 45 (47, 49)"/114 (119, 124.5)cm.
- Length 27 (28, 28)"/68.5 (71, 71)cm.
- Upper arm 17¼ (19¼, 19¼)"/44 (49, 49)cm.

MATERIALS
- 17 (20, 21) 1¾oz/50g balls (each approx 137yd/126m) of Classic Elite Yarns *Waterspun* (wool 4) in #5016 natural
- One pair each sizes 6 and 8 (4 and 5mm) needles OR SIZE TO OBTAIN GAUGE
- One set (2) size 8 (5mm) double-pointed needles (dpn)
- Cable needle
- Two ¾"/20mm leather buttons
- One large (white) covered hook and eye

GAUGES
- 26 sts and 26 rows to 4"/10cm over pats following charts using size 8 (5mm) needles.
- 22 sts and 26 rows to 4"/10cm over rev St st using size 8 (5mm) needles.
FOR PERFECT FIT, TAKE TIME TO CHECK GAUGES.

STITCH GLOSSARY
Seed Stitch
Row 1 (RS) *K1, p1; rep from * to end.
Row 2 K the purl sts and p the knit sts.

Rep row 2 for seed st.

LC Sl 1 st to cn and hold to *front*, k1, k1 from cn.
RC Sl 1 st to cn and hold to *back*, k1, k1 from cn.
8-st RC Sl 4 sts to cn and hold to *back*, k4, k4 from cn.

BACK
With larger needles, cast on 153 (159, 165) sts.
Row 1 K3, *p3, k3; rep from * to end. Cont in k3, p3 rib as established for 2"/5cm. P next WS row, dec 8 sts evenly across—145 (151, 157) sts.

Beg pats
Row 1 (RS) K2 (2 selvage sts in St st), p6 (9, 12), *work 3-st small cable panel, 11-st textured rib panel, 3-st small cable panel, 11-st large cable panel; rep from * 3 times more, work 3-st small cable panel, 11-st textured rib panel, 3-st small cable panel, p6 (9, 12), k2 (2 selvage sts in St st). Cont in pat as established until piece measures 17"/43cm from beg.

Armhole shaping
Bind off 3 (2, 3) sts at beg of next 2 rows, 2 sts at beg of next 6 (10, 12) rows—127 sts. Keeping first and last 2 sts as St st selvage sts, work even until armhole measures 9 (10, 10)"/23 (25.5, 25.5)cm.

Shoulder and neck shaping
Bind off 13 sts at beg of next 6 rows, AT SAME TIME, bind off center 29 sts and working both sides at once, bind off 5 sts from each neck edge twice.

LEFT FRONT
With larger needles, cast on 69 (75, 75) sts. Work in k3, p3 rib as for back for 2"/5cm. P next WS row, dec 3 (6, 3) sts evenly spaced—66 (69, 72) sts.

Beg pats
Row 1 (RS) K2 (2 selvage sts in St st), p6 (9, 12), *work 3-st small cable panel, 11-st textured rib panel, 3-st small cable panel, 11-st large cable panel; rep from * once, k2 (2 selvage sts in St st). Cont in pats until piece measures 17"/43cm from beg.

Armhole and neck shaping
Next row (RS) Bind off 3 (2, 3) sts, work to last 3 sts, k2tog, k1. Cont to shape armhole binding off 2 sts every other row 3 (5, 6) times and dec 1 st at neck edge every 4th row 14 (17, 17) times more, then every other row 3 (0, 0) times—39 sts. When same length as back, shape shoulder as for back.

RIGHT FRONT
Work to correspond to left front, reversing pat placement and shaping.

SLEEVES
With larger needles, cast on 63 sts. Work in k3, p3 rib for 2"/5cm. P next WS row, dec 4 sts evenly spaced—59 sts.

Beg textured rib pat
Row 1 (RS) K2 (2 selvage sts in St st), work sts 1 to 5 of textured rib pat chart, rep sts 4 and 5 24 times, work sts 6 and 7, k2 (2 selvage sts in St st). Cont to work pat in this way, inc 1 st each side (by M1 inside of selvage sts and working sts into pat) every 4th row until

there are 73 sts, end with row 5 of 3rd 12-row rep. Mark center 11 sts.
Next row (WS) [P4, M1] 7 times, p3, work center 11 sts in pat, p3, [M1, p4] 7 times—87 sts.

Beg pats
Row 1 (RS) K2, p5, *[work 3-st small cable panel, 11-st large cable panel] twice, 3-st small cable panel*, 11-st textured rib panel; rep between *'s once, p5, k2. Cont in pats as established, cont to inc every 4th row 10 (15, 15) times more—107 (117, 117) sts. Work even until piece measures 17"/43cm from beg.

Cap shaping
Bind off 2 sts at beg of next 20 rows, 3 sts at beg of next 4 rows. Bind off rem 55 (65, 65) sts.

FINISHING
Block pieces to measurements. Sew shoulder seams. Sew in sleeves. Sew side and sleeve seams.

Right front band
With RS facing and smaller needles, pick up and k 82 sts along left front to beg of neck shaping.
Row 1 (WS) K2, work seed st over 78 sts, k2. Rep this row 3 times more. P 1 row, k 1 row, p 1 row. Bind off. Work left front band to correspond.

Collar
With larger needles, cast on 201 (213, 213) sts.
Row 1 (RS) K3, *p3, k3; rep from * to end. Cont in k3, p3 rib for 6"/15cm. Bind off 8 sts at beg of 8 (20, 20) rows, 7 sts at beg of next 12 (0, 0) rows. Bind off rem 53 sts. Sew bound-off (shaped) edge of collar around neck edge. Sew first ½"/1.5cm of collar to top of front bands.

I-cord
With 2 dpn, cast on 4 sts. K4, do not turn. *Bring yarn from back, sl sts to beg of needle and k4. Rep from * until I-cord measures 16"/40.5cm. Bind off.

Fold cord in half at center and pick up and k 4 sts at fold. Work another I-cord for 8"/20cm. Bind off. Sew to top of right front. Sew on button at center. Rep I-cords for left front. Sew on hook and eye closure underneath buttons on WS.

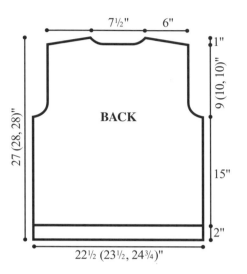

BACK

7½"   6"

1"

9 (10, 10)"

15"

2"

27 (28, 28)"

22½ (23½, 24¾)"

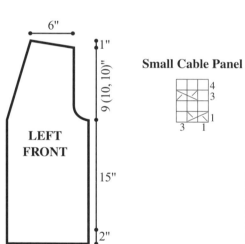

LEFT FRONT

6"

1"

9 (10, 10)"

15"

2"

10½ (11, 11½)"

Small Cable Panel

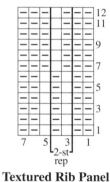

SLEEVE

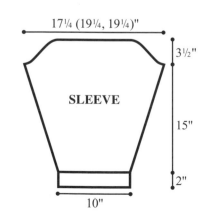

17¼ (19¼, 19¼)"

3½"

15"

2"

10"

Large Cable Panel

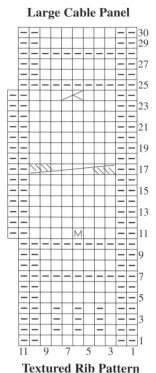

Textured Rib Pattern

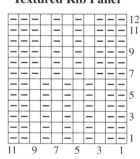

Textured Rib Panel

Stitch Key
- ☐ K on RS, p on WS
- ⊟ P on RS, k on WS
- Ⓜ M1 st
- ⧄ K2tog
- RT
- LT
- 8-st RC

Pink Pullover

Pretty in pink! Lacy stitchwork
and a drawstring tie put a
romantic spin on the traditional
tee. Shown in size Medium.
The Pink Pullover first appeared
in the Spring/Summer '00
issue of *Vogue Knitting*.

Pink Pullover

FOR INTERMEDIATE KNITTERS

SIZES
To fit Small (Medium, Large).
Directions are for smallest size
with larger sizes in parentheses.
If there is only one figure, it applies
to all sizes.

KNITTED MEASUREMENTS
● Bust 34 (39, 44)"/86.5 (99, 112)cm.
● Waist 31 (36, 41½)"/79 (91.5,
105.5)cm.
● Length 23½ (24½, 25½)"/60 (62,
65)cm.
● Upper arm 15 (16, 17)"/38 (40.5,
43)cm.

MATERIALS
● 4 (4, 5) 1¾oz/50g balls (each
approx 115yds/106m) of Classic Elite
Yarns *Avignon* (cotton/silk 3) in #3189
peach
● One pair each sizes 6 and 7 (4 and
4.5mm) needles OR SIZE TO OBTAIN
GAUGE
● Size 6 (4mm) circular needle,
24"/60cm long
● Stitchmarker
● Size F/5 (4mm) crochet hook

GAUGE
22 sts and 29 rows to 4"/10cm over
main pat (slightly stretched) using size
7 (4.5mm) needles. FOR PERFECT FIT,
TAKE TIME TO CHECK GAUGE.

STITCH GLOSSARY
Eyelet Panel (over 4 sts)
Row 1 (RS) P1, yo, SKP, p1.
Rows 2 and 4 K1, p2, k1.
Row 3 P1, k2tog, yo, p1. Rep rows 1-4
for eyelet panel.

Eyelet/Rib Pattern (over 10 sts)
Rows 1, 3, 5, 7 and 9 (RS) K2, [p2,
k2] twice.
Rows 2, 4, 6, 8 and 10 P2, [k2,
p2] twice.
Row 11 K2, [k2tog, yo, k2] twice.
Rows 12, 14, 16, 18, 20 and 22 Purl.
Row 13 K1, [k2tog, yo, k2] twice, k1.
Row 15 [K2tog, yo, k2] twice, k2.
Row 17 K1, [yo, SKP, k2] twice, k1.
Row 19 K2, [yo, SKP, k2] twice.
Row 21 K1, [k2, yo, SKP] twice, k1.
Rep rows 1-22 for eyelet/rib pat.

BACK
With smaller needles, cast on 88 (101,
114) sts.
**For sizes Small and Large only: Next
row (WS)** *P1, k1; rep from * to end.
For size Medium only: Next row (WS)
K1, *p1, k1; rep from * to end.
For all sizes: Next row (RS) K the knit
sts and p the purl sts.
Next (inc) row (WS) Rib 11, inc 1 into
next st, [rib 12, inc 1 into next st] 5 (6,
7) times, rib 11—94 (108, 122) sts.
Change to larger needles.

Beg main pat
Next row (RS) Work eyelet/rib pat
over 10 sts, [work eyelet panel over 4
sts, work eyelet/rib pat over 10 sts] 6
(7, 8) times. Cont as established for 21
rows more.

Shape sides
Next (dec) row (RS) K2, ssk, work in pat
to last 4 sts, k2tog, k2—92 (106, 120)
sts. Cont in pat as established, work
dec row every 8th row 3 times more—
86 (100, 114) sts. Work even for 2 (2½,
3)"/5 (6.5, 7.5)cm, end with WS row.
Next (inc) row (RS) K2, inc 1, work to
last 3 sts, inc 1, k2—88 (102, 116) sts.
Work inc row every 10th row 3 times
more—94 (108, 122) sts. Work even
until piece measures 16½ (17, 17½)"/42
(43, 44.5)cm from beg.

Armhole shaping
Bind off 5 (6, 7) sts at beg of next 2
rows, 2 sts at beg of next 2 rows. Dec 1
st each side on next row, then every
other row twice more—74 (86, 98) sts.
Work even until armhole measures 5½
(6, 6½)"/14 (15, 16.5)cm, end with a
WS row.

Neck and shoulder shaping
Next row (RS) Work 28 (31, 37) sts, join
2nd ball of yarn and bind off center 18
(24, 24) sts, work to end. Working both
sides at once, bind off 4 sts from each
neck edge 4 times, AT SAME TIME,
after 4 rows of shaping have been
worked, bind off 4 (5, 7) sts from each
shoulder edge 3 times.

FRONT

Work as for back until armhole measures 5¼ (5¾, 6¼)"/13.5 (14.5, 16)cm, end with a WS row.

Neck and shoulder shaping

Next row (RS) Work 22 (25, 31) sts, join 2nd ball of yarn and bind off center 30 (36, 36) sts, work to end. Working both sides at once, bind off 2 sts from each neck edge 5 times, AT SAME TIME, when same length as back to shoulder, shape shoulder as for back.

SLEEVES

With smaller needles, cast on 62 (75, 75) sts.

For size Small only: Next row (WS) *P1, k1; rep from * to end.

For sizes Medium and Large only: Next row (WS) K1, *p1, k1; rep from * to end.

For all sizes: Next row (RS) K the knit sts and p the purl sts.

Next (inc) row (WS) Rib 11, inc 1 into next st, [rib 12, inc 1 into next st] 3 (4, 4) times, rib 11—66 (80, 80) sts. Change to larger needles.

Beg main pat

Next row (RS) Work eyelet/rib pat over 10 sts, [work eyelet panel over 4 sts, work eyelet/rib pat over 10 sts] 4 (5, 5) times. Cont in pat as established until piece measures 1½"/4cm from beg. Cont in pats as established, inc 1 st each side (working inc sts into pat) every 2nd (4th, 2nd) row 6 (2, 3) times, every 4th (6th, 4th) row 2 (2, 4) times—82 (88, 94) sts. Work even until piece

measures 5 (5, 5½)"/12.5 (12.5, 14)cm from beg, end with a WS row.

Cap shaping

Bind off 5 (6, 7) sts at beg of next 2 rows, 2 sts at beg of next 2 rows.

Next row (RS) Work 1 st, ssk, work to last 3 sts, k2tog, work 1 st. Work 1 row even. Rep last 2 rows 5 (7, 9) times more—56 sts.

**Next row (RS) Work 1 st, ssk, work to last 3 sts, k2tog, work 1 st.

Next row (WS) Work 1 st, p2tog, pat to last 3 sts, p2tog tbl, work 1 st. Work 1 more dec row. Work 1 row even.** Rep from ** to ** 4 times more. Bind off rem 26 sts.

FINISHING

Block pieces to measurements. Sew shoulder seams. Set in sleeves. Sew side and sleeve seams.

Neckband

With RS facing and circular needle, pick up and k 158 (164, 164) sts evenly around neck edge. Join, mark beg of rnd. Work in k1, p1 rib for 2 rnds. Bind off in rib.

Drawstring

With crochet hook, make a ch 46 (50, 54)"/117 (127, 137)cm long or desired length. Turn, sl st into each ch. Fasten off. Thread drawstring through eyelets 11½ (12, 12½)"/29 (30.5, 32)cm from beg or as desired.

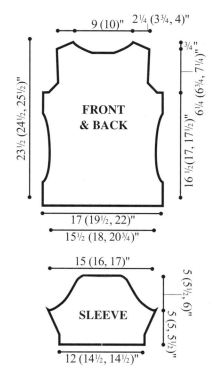

Aran accessories to take the chill out and put the chic into winter dressing: The stylish and warm gauntlet gloves with corded pompom ties are paired with a toque hat with ruched side and corded pompom tassels. The Gauntlet Gloves & Hat first appeared in the Fall/Winter '86 issue of *Vogue Knitting*.

Gauntlet Gloves & Hat

FOR EXPERT KNITTERS

SIZES
One size fits all.

KNITTED MEASUREMENTS
● Finished circumference of gloves at cuff edge 14"/35.5cm.
● Finished hat circumference at lower edge 20-22"/51-56cm.
● Finished hat height 7½"/19cm.

MATERIALS
GLOVES:
Original Yarn
● 4 1¾ oz/50g balls (each approx 135yd/125m) of Berger du Nord *Douceur No.4* (wool/mohair 3) in #8524 ecru

Substitute Yarn
● 4 1¾ oz/50g balls (each approx 155yd/141m) of Dale of Norway *Daletta* (wool 3) in #0020 ecru
● One set (4) each sizes 4 and 5 (3.5 and 3.75mm) double-pointed needles (dpn) OR SIZE TO OBTAIN GAUGE
● Cable needle (cn)
● Stitch marker and holder

HAT:
Original Yarn
● 6 1¾ oz/50g balls (each approx 70yd/65m) of Berger du Nord *Douceur No.5* (wool/mohair 4) in #8524 ecru

Substitute Yarn
● 4 1¾ oz/50g balls (each approx 110yd/100m) of Dale of Norway *Heilo* (wool/mohair 4) in #0020 ecru
● Size 7 (4.5mm) circular needle, 16"/40cm long
● One pair and one set of 5 double-pointed size 7 (4.5mm) needles (dpn) OR SIZE TO OBTAIN GAUGE.
● Stitch markers and cable needle (cn)

Note
The original yarns used for the gloves and hat are no longer available. Comparable substitutions have been made, which are available at the time of printing. Check gauge of substitute yarns very carefully before beginning.

GAUGE
Gloves:
● 24 sts and 32 rows to 4"/10cm over St st using size 5 (3.75mm) needles.
Hat:
● 20 sts and 24 rows to 4"/10cm over St st using size 7 (4.5mm) needles.
FOR PERFECT FIT, TAKE TIME TO CHECK GAUGES.
Note
As chart pats have varying row reps, keep careful count of rows.

STITCH GLOSSARY
Mock Cable (over 2 sts)
On straight needles:
Rows 1 and 3 (WS) P2.
Row 2 (RS) K2tog but leave sts on needle, insert RH needle between the 2 sts and k the first st again, sl both sts from needle.
Row 4 K2. Rep rows 1-4 for mock cable.
On circular needle:

Rnds 1, 3 end 4 (RS) K2.
Rnd 2 Work as for straight needles.
Rep rnds 1-4 for mock cable.

GLOVES

LEFT GLOVE
With smaller dpn, cast on 120 sts and divide evenly over 3 needles. Join, taking care not to twist sts on needles. Place marker for beg of rnd.
Beg cuff edge: Rnd 1 (RS) *K2, p2; rep from * over first 40 sts, place marker (pm), [k4, p4] twice, k4, p2 (center 2 sts), k4, [p4, k4] twice, pm, *p2, k2; rep from * over last 38 sts. (Note: Slip markers (sm) every rnd. Work rnds 1-4 only when working chart #1.)
Rnd 2 [Work rnd 2 of mock cable over next 2 sts, p2] 10 times to marker, working rnd 2 of chart #1 over each k4 section and p sts in between, work to next marker, [p2, work rnd 2 of mock

cable over next 2 sts] 9 times, p2.
Rnds 3-10 Work in pats. Change to larger dpn.

Gauntlet/Cuff
Rnd 11 Work 11 sts in pat, m1, work 20 sts in pat, m1, work to next marker, work rnd 3 of chart #1 over next 4 sts, m1, working 4 k sts instead of cable twist, work to 1 st before center 2 sts, [k2tog] twice, work to 4 sts before next marker, m1, work rnd 3 of chart #1 over next 4 sts, work 9 sts, m1, work 20 sts, m1, work to end—124 sts. (Note: When working chart #1, cont chart through rnd 6, then rep rnds 1-6 of chart.)
Rnd 12 [Work mock cable over 2 sts, pm, p3, pm, work rnd 2 of chart #3 over 13 sts, pm, p3] twice, sm, work rnd 4 of chart #1 over 4 sts, pm, p3, pm, work rnd 2 of chart #4 over center 28 sts, pm, p3, pm, work rnd 4 of chart #1 over 4 sts, sm, p3, pm, work rnd 2

of chart #3 over 13 sts, pm, p3, pm, work mock cable over 2 sts, pm, p3, pm, work rnd 2 of chart #3 over 13 sts, pm, p3. Cont in pats, working sts between chart pats in rev St st, and AT SAME TIME, dec 1 st in each section every 16 rnds twice, then every 8 rnds once—94 sts. Work even through rnd 2 of 3rd rep of chart #4. (Note: Markers are to aid in dec and can be removed if not needed.)

Wrist shaping
Next rnd [Work mock cable, p3tog, k3tog, p1, k3tog tbl, p3tog tbl] twice, work rnd 5 of chart #1, work, keeping in pat to next 4-st cable, work rnd 5 of chart #1, *p3tog, k3tog, p1, k3tog tbl, p3tog tbl*, work mock cable; rep between *'s once—62 sts.

Wrist ribbing
Change to smaller dpn.
Next rnd [Work mock cable, p1, k1, p1, k1, p1] twice, work 4-st cable, work rnd 4 of chart #4, work 4-st cable, [p1, k1] twice, p1, work mock cable, [p1, k1] twice, p1. (Note: Rnds will be given according to rnd of chart #4. Be sure to work all other pats with correct rnd rep.)
Rnds 5-14 Work in pats.
Rnd 15 Work mock cable, *p1, k3, p1, work mock cable, p1, k3, p1,* work 4-st cable, work rnd 15 of chart #4, work 4-st cable, rep between *'s once.

Hand
Change to larger dpn.
Rnds 16-21 Work in pats.

Thumb gusset
Rnd 22 Work through 2nd mock cable, p1, k1, pm, m1, k1, m1, pm (thumb sts), work to end of rnd—64 sts.
Rnds 23 and 24 Work even, k the inc sts.
Rnd 1 Work to marker, sm, m1, k3, m1, sm, work to end of rnd—66 sts.
Rnds 2 and 3 Work even, k the inc sts. Cont in this way to inc 2 sts inside of markers every 3 rnds until there are 15 sts between markers, end with rnd 16 of chart #4.
Rnd 17 Work even.

Thumb
(Note: When measuring thumb and fingers, measure from cast-on sts. Measure your

own fingers or try on gloves while knitting for best fit.)

Next rnd Work to thumb sts, k15 sts and divide them onto 2 dpn, place all but thumb sts on a holder. With 3rd dpn and same strand, cast on 5 sts. Join and place marker for beg of rnd.

Next 2 rnds Knit.

Next rnd K to 3rd needle, k2tog, k to end. Rep last 3 rnds 3 times more—16 sts. Work 4 rnds even.

Shape top

Change to smaller dpn. K 1 rnd.

Next rnd K2tog around. K 1 rnd.

Next rnd K2tog around. Fasten off by drawing yarn through rem sts, pull tog tightly and secure. Cont with hand as foll:

Rnd 18 With palm facing, sl sts from beg of rnd to thumb onto larger dpn, with new strand, pick up and k8 sts in 5 cast-on sts of thumb, work pat to end of rnd—69 sts.

Rnd 19 [Work mock cable, p1, k3, p1] 3 times, work pats to end of rnd. Work even in pats until this rep of chart #4 has been worked, then work through rnd 10 of chart #4.

Rnd 11 [K2, k2tog, k1, ssk] twice, k2, k2tog, k2, p1, k2tog, k2, beg chart #4 and work dec simultaneously, p2tog, k2tog, k2 p2tog, p2, k4 (now at center of chart #4), k4, p1 (stop working chart #4), p2, k2tog, k2, p2tog, p1, ssk, k1, [ssk, k2] twice, k2tog, k1, ssk—53 sts. Discontinue working all charts and cables. (Note: When working fingers, k the knit sts and p the purl sts.) Cont as foll:

Rnd 12 Work 26 sts, work 8-st front cable over next 8 sts (center of back hand), work 11 sts, sl last 8 sts of rnd plus first 15 sts of rnd to dpn for palm sts, sl rem 30 sts to dpn for back of hand.

Fingers

Index finger Work to last 6 sts of palm, work these sts and place them on a separate dpn, work first 8 sts of back of hand on a 2nd dpn, sl rem sts to holder. Cast on 3 sts on 3rd dpn. Join and place marker—17 sts. Work 3 rnds even.

Rnd 4 Work to p st, k2tog, work to end of rnd—16 sts. K around on all sts until finger measures 1¼"/3cm from cast-on sts. Dec 1 st at inner finger—15 sts. K until finger measures 2½"/6.5cm, or desired length. Shape top as for thumb.

Little finger Sl 5 sts of palm to separate dpn, sl 8 sts of back of hand to 2nd dpn, cast on 2 sts on 3rd dpn. Join and place marker—15 sts. Work 1 rnd even.

Next rnd K2, ssk, work to end of rnd—14 sts. Work 2 rnds even.

Next rnd Work to p st, k2tog, work to end of rnd—13 sts. K around on all sts until finger measures 1¼"/3cm. Dec 1 st at inner finger—12 sts. K until finger measures 1¾"/4.5cm, or desired length. Shape top as for thumb.

Ring finger Sl 6 sts of palm to separate dpn, sl 7 sts of back of hand to 2nd dpn. Beg at palm, work 6 sts, cast on 3 sts, join and work across 7 sts of back hand, pick up 2 sts in cast-on sts of little finger. Join and place marker—18 sts. Work 1 rnd even.

Next rnd K to last st of 3 cast-on sts, p next st, k3, ssk, work to end of rnd. Work to next p st, SFC, work to end. Work 5 rnds even.

Next rnd Work to last k st of SFC, ssk, work to end—16 sts. Work 2 rnds even.

Next rnd Work to 2nd p st, k2tog, work to end. Work 2 rnds even.

Next rnd Work to k st before p st, ssk, work to end. K around on all sts until finger measures 2½"/6.5cm, or desired length. Shape top as for thumb.

Middle finger Sl 6 sts of palm to separate dpn, sl 7 sts of back of hand to 2nd dpn. Beg at palm, work 6 sts, pick up 3 sts in cast-on sts of index finger, work across 7 sts of back hand, pick up 2 sts in cast-on sts of ring finger. Join and place marker—18 sts.

Next rnd Work to first st of 2 cast-on sts, p next st, work to end of rnd. Work to p st before 4 k sts, k2tog, work to end. Work to p st before 4 k sts, SBC, work to end. Work 5 rnds even.

Next rnd Work to first p st of SBC, k2tog, work to end—16 sts. Work 2 rnds even.

Next rnd Work to 2nd p st, k2tog, work

to end. Work 2 rnds even.

Next rnd Work to p st, k2tog, work to end. K around on all sts until finger measures 3"/7.5cm, or desired length. Shape top as for thumb.

RIGHT GLOVE

Work to correspond to left glove, reversing placement of pats, thumb and fingers. Make 4 twisted cords and 4 pompoms. Attach pompom to one end of each cord and sew other end to side of wrist. Tie cords at back of hand through center cable twist of chart #4.

HAT

VERTICAL CABLE PANELS (make 3)

With straight needles, beg at top of panel, cast on 46 sts.

Row 1 (RS) [P1, k1] selvage stitch, place marker (pm), work row 1 of chart #1 over 4 sts, pm, k3, pm, work row 1 of chart #4 over 28 sts, pm, k3, pm, work row 1 of chart #2 over 4 sts, pm, [k1, p1] (selvage stitch). Cont in pats until 10 rows have been worked.

Next row (RS) Work to first 3-st section, k1, ssk, work to last 2 sts of 2nd 3-st section, k2tog, work to end. Cont in this way to dec 1 st in each section as before every 12 rows twice more—40 sts. Work even until row 2 of 3rd rep of chart #4 has been worked. Bind off in pat, dec 10 sts evenly across at same time.

HORIZONTAL CABLE SECTION

With straight needles, cast on 46 sts.

Row 1 (WS) K1, *work row 1 of chart #1 over 4 sts, k4, work row 1 of chart #2 over 4 sts, k4; rep from *, end working row 1 of chart #2 over 4 sts, k1. Cont in pats until piece measures 2½"/6.5cm from beg. Dec 1 st in each p-4 section on next row. Work even for 2"/5cm more. Inc 1 st in each p-4 section—46 sts. Work even until piece measures 6½"/16.5cm from beg. Bind off.

TOP OF HAT

With dpn, cast on 8 sts and divide evenly over 4 needles (2 sts each). Join and place marker for beg of rnd. (Note: Work with a 5th dpn. Keep the same number of sts on each needle. Instructions are written for one needle only. Work rnds on each of 4 dpn.)

Rnd 1 K2 tbl.

Rnd 2 K into front and back of each st—4 sts each needle.

Rnds 3-5 K1, p2, k1.

Rnd 6 M1 purlwise, k1, m1 knitwise, p2, m1 knitwise, k1, m1 purlwise—8 sts each needle.

Rnds 7-11 P1, k2, p2, k2, p1.

Rnd 12 M1 purlwise, p1, m1 knitwise, k2, m1 knitwise, bring yarn to front of work over RH needle (not between needles) then to back again between needles (backward loop-BL), p2, BL, m1 knitwise, k2, m1 knitwise, p1, BL—16 sts, each needle.

Rnds 13-19 P2, work chart #1 over 4 sts, p4, work chart #2 over 4 sts, p2.

Rnd 20 [P1 , m1 purlwise] twice, work 4 sts, [m1 purlwise, p1] 4 times, work 4 sts, [m1 purlwise, p1] twice—24 sts.

Rnds 21-24 P4, work 4 sts, p8, work 4 sts, p4.

Rnd 25 [P2, m1 purlwise] twice, work 4 sts, [m1 purlwise, p2] twice, [p2, m1 purlwise] twice, work 4 sts, [m1 purlwise, p2] twice—32 sts each needle. Change to circular needle and work on all 128 sts as foll:

Rnds 26-28 [P6, work 4 sts, p12, work 4 sts, p6] 4 times.

Trim edging: Last rnd Wyib cast on 3 sts to LH needle, *k2, k2tog, sl 3 sts from RH to LH needle; rep from * until 3 sts rem on RH needle, sl 3 sts back to LH needle and bind off.

FINISHING

Sew 1 vertical panel to each side of horizontal panel, then sew last vertical panel between other 2. Pin wider (cast-on) edge of panels evenly to edge of top of hat. From RS, sew lower sections of hat to under edge of top so that trim extends only slightly. Pick up 1 st at center top of hat and make a bobble. Weave end to inside.

Lower edging

With RS facing and circular needle, pick up and k24 sts along each vertical panel and 32 sts along horizontal panel—104 sts. Wyib, cast on 3 sts to LH needle. *K2, k2tog tbl, sl 3 sts from RH to LH needle; rep from * until 3 sts rem on RH needle, sl 3 back to LH needle and bind off. Join to beg of edging. Make 3 twisted cords and 3 pompoms and attach under bobble at top of hat.

Stitch Key

St st (k on RS, p on WS)

Rev St st (p on RS, k on WS)

4-st Back Cable: Sl 2 sts to cn and hold to back, k2, k2 from cn.

4-st Front Cable: Sl 2 sts to cn and hold to front, k2, k2 from cn.

Back Cross: Sl p st to cn and hold to back, k3, p st from cn.

Front Cross: Sl 3 sts to cn and hold to front, p1, k3 from cn.

7-st Back Cable: Sl 4 sts to cn and hold to back, k3, p1, k3 from cn.

8-st Back Cable: Sl 4 sts to cn and hold to back, k4, k4 from cn.

8-st Front Cable: Sl 4 sts to cn and hold to front, k4, k4 from cn.

Single Back Cross (SBC): Sl 1 st to cn and hold to back, k4, p1 from cn.

Single Front Cross (SFC): Sl 4 sts to cn and hold to front, p1, k4 from cn.

Make bobble: k1, [yo, k1] twice (5 sts made in one st); turn and p5; turn and ssk, k1, k2tog; turn and p3; turn and sl 2 tog knitwise, k1, pass 2 sl sts over.

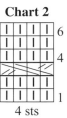

Chart 1

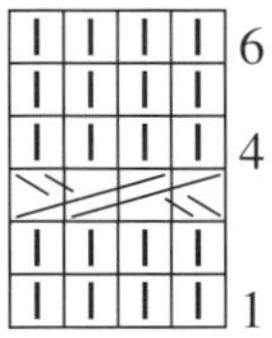

4 sts

Chart 2

4 sts

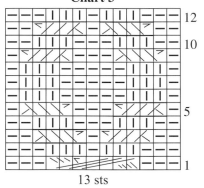

Chart 3

13 sts

Chart 4

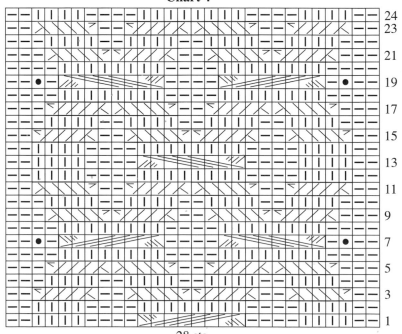

28 sts

Mari Lynn Patrick

In 1981, Mari Lynn Patrick was living abroad in Ankara, Turkey. Although she worked as a French translator while living there, she hadn't abandoned her dreams of continuing as a handknit designer. During a trip back to the United States, she heard that *Vogue Knitting* magazine was starting up again. "I brought the sweaters in and they bought every one," she recalls. "One of those sweaters was actually one of the best sellers of all time."

Nowadays, Mari Lynn's presence can be felt from cover to cover in every issue of *Vogue Knitting*. She not only designs knitwear, but also writes numerous articles on the subject and is one of the best instruction writers in the country.

It was Mari Lynn's grandmother who taught her to knit. She remembers being struck, even as a child, by the degree of pleasure her grandmother derived from handcrafts. "She was prolific," she says. "She made these intensely exquisite things. Not just knitting—she also did quite a bit of deep lace crochet and white cutwork embroidery. She was from Russia. She would visit in the summers, and each summer she came I would learn a couple more things. She taught me the basics, then I learned more from books and after that from just doing it myself—knitting, knitting, knitting. Tearing things out and making them again."

Mari Lynn recalls reading the old *Vogue Knitting* magazines of the sixties back when she was a preteen. "My friend's mother got *Vogue Knitting*, and I remember reading them at her house. I loved looking at all the dresses and the couture-looking

designs," she says. "The sweaters weren't as interesting to me. I liked the idea of high-fashion clothing. That's where I got my interest not just in knitting, but the whole clothing concept—fashion."

Mari Lynn decided then and there that she wanted to work in the knitting and yarn industry. Not only that, she wanted to do it in a big way. While still a teenager, she started applying for design jobs, first with a local yarn company, then writing to the editors at *Vogue Knitting*. "I was knitting-crazy," she remembers. "In the graduation yearbook in 1969, it said 'Mari Lynn looks forward to a career in handknitting design.' I knew back then."

During college, Mari Lynn started writing to knitting schools to inquire about their programs. "That's how I ended up going to school at Leicester Polytechnic in England," she says. "The school was for knitwear design and textile technology, so it wasn't so much for handknitting. It was really designing for the machine-knitting industry in England, which is quite large in the Midlands. A lot of it was about the cut-and-sew of knitted fabric, charting and stitches, chemical testing and dyeing of yarns. It was intense 'only-knitting' and that's what I really liked."

When designing garments, Mari Lynn draws her inspiration mainly from studying what's around her. She examines how garments are structured and thinks of ways to apply what she sees to the handknitting area. "I'm influenced by what is happening in the high-fashion design industry versus the hand-

"As much as designing, I like to write up the instructions. I like to write them so they are clear and comprehensible to the handknitter."

knitting design industry—for example, the French and American designers," she says. "I am always looking at their direction and then trying to give some of those concepts to handknitters."

But Mari Lynn's contribution doesn't end with the design. "As much as designing, I like to write up the instructions," she says. "I like to size and to have them fit exactly. I like to write them so that they are clear and comprehensible to the handknitter." With Mari Lynn's instructions, patterns are always clearly and logically spelled out, and absolutely accurate. She has an elaborate system of checks, often working closely with her sister, *Vogue Knitting*'s executive editor, Carla Patrick Scott. "We have the same mind," she explains. "Our father is an engineer. We think in the same technical way, and we have the same quality of patience—we like the math, we like the words."

Mari Lynn is actually one of the people responsible for standardizing the language and symbols used in many knitting instructions today. During the early seventies she served on a committee along with several other experienced writers and together they addressed those concerns. "It has had a really big influence," she says. "We standardized measurements and the language, so there wasn't a misinterpretation of symbols and brackets and other editorial fine points. At that time, instructions weren't so straightforward."

She started writing instructions for *Vogue Knitting* at the same time she started designing for the magazine. "After I moved to Baltimore from Turkey," she remembers, "I used to commute up to New York for three days a week to work in the office. At that time, I emphasized the importance of schematics and finished measurements and saw to it that the instructions included all of the various kinds of information knitters need in order to visualize what the finished garment would look like."

"There are so many things you have take into consideration with hand knitwear," she explains. "It's so stretchable. You have to be careful what you add or subtract if you want to keep within the concept of the original design for each of the sizes you include. It's tricky."

"I learned much less in school than I have through experience over the years," she adds. "Seeing how well things work. Since I write other people's patterns, I'm schooled not only by my mistakes, but by other peoples' mistakes and successes as well."

As for the future, Mari Lynn hopes to keep contributing to the handknitting yarn industry. "I'd love to see some new directions, some new avenues for doing this, but I can't see leaving the instruction-driven design area that I am in," she says. "I like what I contribute to the industry, and I hope to be able to do this for the rest of my life."

Mari Lynn Patrick

Interior shaping—formed by slants and decorative eyelet details—gives this warm-weather tunic a flattering, body-skimming silhouette. Perfect for long walks on the beach, the ribbed tunic is knit in a stunning shade of ocean blue. Shown in size Medium. The Summer Tunic first appeared in the Spring/Summer '98 issue of *Vogue Knitting*.

Summer Tunic

FOR EXPERIENCED KNITTERS

SIZES
To fit Small (Medium, Large/X-Large). Directions are for smallest size with larger sizes in parentheses. If there is only one figure, it applies to all sizes.

KNITTED MEASUREMENTS
● Bust 34 (37, 42)"/86 (94,106.5)cm.
● Lower edge 47 (50, 55)"/119 (127, 139.5)cm.
● Length 25¾ (26¾, 28¼)"/65.5 (68, 72)cm.
● Upper arm 13 (14, 14½)"/33 (35.5, 37)cm.

MATERIALS
● 17 (18, 21) 1¾oz/50g balls (each approx 85yd/78m) of Skacel *Hillary* (rayon 4)) in #9 turquoise
● One pair each sizes 5 and 6 (3.75 and 4mm) needles OR SIZE TO OBTAIN GAUGE
● Size G/6 (4.5mm) crochet hook
● Stitch markers

GAUGES
• 24 sts and 30 rows to 4"/10cm over k6, p2 rib using size 6 (4mm) needles.
• 22 sts and 30 rows to 4"/10cm over k2, p2 rib using size 5 (3.75mm) needles. FOR PERFECT FIT, TAKE TIME TO CHECK GAUGES.

Note
K1 garter selvage sts are worked on all seam edges and not figured into the finished measurements.

STITCH GLOSSARY
SSSK Sl 3 sts knitwise to RH needle without knitting and k3tog from this position.
SK2P Sl 1, k2tog, psso the k2tog.

BACK
(Note: Read before beg to knit.)
With larger needles, cast on 142 (150, 166) sts.
Row 1 (RS) K1 for selvage st, k2 (6, 6), [p2, k6] twice, p2 (first panel); [k6, p2] 4 (4, 5) times (right slant); [k6, p4] 3 times, k6 (center panel); [p2, k6] 4 (4, 5) times (left slant); p2, [k6, p2] twice, k2 (6, 6), k1 for selvage st (5th panel). Cont in rib as established for 1 row more.

Beg slant pat
Row 3 (RS) Rib 21 (25, 25) sts; SK2P, rib 29 (29, 37) sts, yo twice (right slant); rib 36 sts; yo twice, rib 29 (29, 37) sts, k3tog (left slant); rib 21 (25, 25) sts. Rep this row every 4th row for slant pat, working p2 on next WS row into double yo's. Work p2 into double yo's every 4th row for 2nd and 3rd set of eyelet holes and k2 into double yo's for 4th set of

eyelet holes (for continuity of k6, p2 pat). AT SAME TIME, when 22 rows or 3"/7.5cm are worked, beg side decs as foll:
Row 23 K3 (7, 7), p2, SK2P, work to center panel, [k6, p1, p2tog, p1] 3 times, k6; work to last 8 (12, 12) sts, k3tog, p2, k3 (7, 7). Cont to work slant pats, work side decs every 12th row 4 times more, every 8th row 3 times and AT SAME TIME, when piece measures 7½"/19cm from beg, work center panel dec as foll: in center panel, work [k6, p1, p2tog] 3 times, k6. After all decs are completed, there are 104 (112, 128) sts. Cont to work pat until there are 24 sets of eyelet holes. Work 1 row even. Piece measures approx 13"/33cm from beg. Change to smaller needles.

Beg yoke rib pat
Next row (RS) Work to 2 sts before 30 sts of center panel, pm, [p2, k2] 8 times, p2, pm, cont in established pat to end.
Next row (WS) Work to 2 sts before marker, place new marker, p2, [k2, p2] 9 times, pm, work in established pat to end. Cont to work in this way, displacing 2 sts from established pat and cont outwards in k2, p2 rib (placing new markers and removing old markers) until all sts are worked in k2, p2 rib. Work even until piece measures 17½ (18, 19)"/44.5 (45.5, 48)cm from beg.

Armhole shaping
Bind off 4 sts at beg of next 2 rows.
Next (dec) row (RS) K3, p2, sssk, work rib to last 8 sts, k3tog, p2, k3. Rep dec row every 2nd row once more, every 4th row 3 times, every 6th row 3 times

and AT SAME TIME, when armhole measures 3¼"/8.5cm, separate for V-neck as foll:

V-neck shaping
Next row (RS) Work to 2 center p sts, k1, join 2nd ball of yarn and k3, work rib to end. Cont to work k3 sts each side of V-neck and working both sides at once, work 1 row even.
Dec row 1 (RS) *First side* Work to last 7 sts, k2tog, p2, k3; *Second side* K3, p2, ssk, work to end. Cont armhole decs, rep dec row 1 for neck every 2nd row 6 (8, 10) times more. Work 1 row even.
Dec row 2 (RS) *First side* Work to last 8 sts, k3tog, p2, k3; *Second side* K3, p2, sssk. Rep dec row 2 for neck every 2nd row 4 (5, 7) times more—15 (15, 17) sts rem each side. Work even until armhole measures 7½ (8, 8½)"/19 (20.5, 21.5)cm.

Shoulder shaping
Bind off 5 sts from each shoulder edge 3 (3, 1) times, 6 sts 0 (0, 2) times.

FRONT
Work as for back to armhole.

Armhole shaping
Bind off 4 sts at beg of next 2 rows—96 (104, 120) sts.

Bodice dart shaping
Next row (RS) Rib 24 (24, 28) sts, insert RH needle into next 3 sts as for k3tog and sl to RH needle without knitting, k1, pass 2 of the sl sts one at a time over k st (2-st center dec), rib 40 (48, 56) sts, work 2-st center dec, rib 24 (24, 28) sts. Rep this row for center dec every 6th row 7 times more and AT SAME TIME, shape V-neck as on back when armhole measures 3¼"/8.5cm. When same length as back, shape shoulders for back.

LEFT SLEEVE
With smaller needles, cast on 42 (42, 46) sts.
Row 1 (RS) K2, *p2, k2; rep from * to end. Work even in k2, p2 rib for 11 rows more.
Row 13 (RS) Rib 28 (28, 32) sts, yo twice, rib 14 sts.
Row 14 (WS) Rib 14 sts, p2 into double yo, rib to end. Work 4 rows in rib as established.
Row 19 Rib 30 (30, 34) sts, yo twice, rib to end.
Row 20 Rib 14 sts, k2 into double yo, rib to end. Cont in this way to inc 2 sts by yo twice every 6th row 14 (16, 16) times more (working 2 more sts before inc and adding sts in alternating k2

then p2 ribs)—74 (78, 82) sts. Work even in rib until piece measures 16½ (17, 17)"/42 (43, 43)cm from beg.

Cap shaping
Bind off 4 sts at beg of next 2 rows. Bind off 2 sts at beg of next 4 rows. Dec 1 st each side every other row 10 (12, 14) times. Bind off 2 sts at beg of next 12 rows. Bind off 14 sts.

RIGHT SLEEVE
Work as for left sleeve for 12 rows.
Row 13 Rib 14 sts, yo twice, rib to end. Cont to work incs as on left sleeve (keeping first 14 sts constant throughout inc and having 2 more sts after double yo) and complete as for left sleeve.

FINISHING
Block pieces to measurements, pinning lower edge straight. Sew shoulder seams, side and sleeve seams. Set sleeves into armholes. With crochet hook, working from left to right, work an edge of backwards sc around neck (inserting hook into center of 2nd st from edge) as foll: *Work 1 sc, ch 1, skip 2 rows; rep from * around.

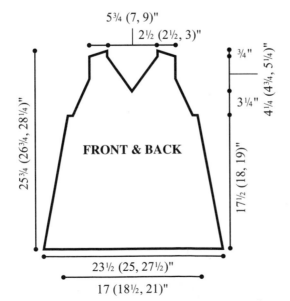

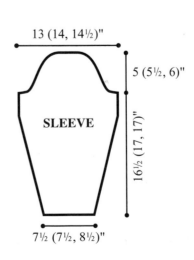

Summer Dress

Exquisite eyelet fashioning gives this
pretty lace and cable slip dress an
oh-so-feminine fit. Standard-fitting,
the A-line dress is knit in shiny gold
rayon for added luster and drape.
Shown in size 8. The Summer Dress
first appeared in the Spring/Summer
'96 issue of *Vogue Knitting*.

Mari Lynn Patrick

FOR EXPERT KNITTERS

SIZES
To fit sizes 6 (8, 10, 12). Directions are for smallest size with larger sizes in parentheses. If there is only one figure, it applies to all sizes.

KNITTED MEASUREMENTS
● Bust at underarm 30¾ (32½, 36¾)"/78 (82.5, 87.5, 93)cm.
● Length (above hem) 33¾ (33¾, 34, 34¼)"/85.5 (85.5, 86, 87)cm.

MATERIALS
Original Yarn
● 14 (14, 15, 16) 1¾oz/50g balls (each approx 77yd/69m) of Unger/JCA *Escape* (microfiber rayon 4) in #117 gold
Substitute Yarn
● 15 (15, 16, 17) 1¾oz/50g hanks (each approx 75yd/68m) of Lang/ Berroco *Glacé* (rayon 4) in #2441 gold
● One pair each sizes 7 and 8 (4.5 and 5mm) needles OR SIZE TO OBTAIN GAUGE
● Size 6 (4mm) circular needle, 16"/40cm long
● Cable needle (cn)
● Stitch holders and markers
● ½yd/.5m lining fabric (optional)
● 1yd/1m matching cord (optional)
Note
The original yarn used for this dress is no longer available. A comparable substitution has been made, which is available at the time of printing. Check gauge of substitute yarns very carefully before beginning.

Summer Dress

GAUGE
20 sts and 28 rows to 4"/10cm over St st using larger needles. FOR PERFECT FIT, TAKE TIME TO CHECK GAUGE.

STITCH GLOSSARY
3-st BC (RS rows) Sl 1 st to cn and hold to *back*, k2, k1 from cn.
3-st BC (WS rows) Sl 2 sts to cn and hold to *back*, p1, p2 from cn.
3-st FC (RS rows) Sl 2 sts to cn and hold to *front*, k1, k2 from cn.
3-st FC (WS rows) Sl 1 st to cn and hold to *front*, p2, p1, from cn.
SK2P Sl 1, k2tog, pass sl st over k2tog.
4-st BC Sl 1 st to cn and hold to *back*, k3, k1 from cn.
4-st FC Sl 3 sts to cn and hold to *front*, k1, k3 from cn.
6-st BC Sl 3 sts to cn and hold to *back*, k3, k3 from cn.

Eyelet Border (even number of sts)
Row 1 (RS) K1,*yo, k2tog; rep from*, end k1.
Row 2 Purl.
Eyelet Decrease #1 (over 14 sts)
Dec row (RS) K2tog, k2, k2tog, yo, k2, yo, SKP, k2, SKP (2sts dec'd).
Eyelet Decrease #2 (over 16 sts)
Dec row (RS) K3tog, k2, k2tog, yo, k2, yo, SKP, k2, SK2P (4 sts dec'd).

Note K1 st at beg and end of every row for garter st selvage sts. Do not count these sts when measuring.

BACK
With larger needles, cast on 168 (168, 168 176) sts. Work 2 rows St st. Work 2 rows eyelet border. Cont in St st until piece measures 4"/10cm from beg. Work 2 rows eyelet border.

Beg pats
Next row (RS) K6, p1, work 12 sts snake cable #1 beg with row 2, p1, k20 (20, 20, 22), place marker (pm), k12, pm, k20 (20, 20, 22), work 24 sts center

cable panel beg with row 2, k20 (20, 20, 22), pm, k12, pm, k20 (20, 20, 22), p1, work 12 sts snake cable #2 beg with row 2, p1, k6. Work in pat sts and St st as established for 3 more rows.
Next (Dec #1) row (RS) Work in pat to 1 st before first marker. *Place new marker. Work eyelet dec #1 over next 14 sts, removing old markers. Place new marker after last dec*. Work pat to 1st before next marker, rep between *'s once, work pat to end. Work 5 rows even. Rep last 6 rows 11 (12, 13, 12) times more—120 (116, 112, 124) sts.
Next (Dec #2) row (RS) Work pat to 2 sts before first marker. *Place new marker. Work eyelet dec #2 over next 16 sts, removing old markers. Place new marker after last dec *. Work pat to 2 sts before next marker, rep between *'s once, work pat to end. Work 5 rows even. Rep last 6 rows 5 (4, 3, 4) times more. Rep dec row #2 once more 64 (68, 72, 76) sts. Work 3 rows even. Remove markers. Piece measures approx 21¼"/54cm from beg. Change to smaller needles.

Bodice shaping
Work 2 rows eyelet border. Work in St st for 4 rows.
Next eyelet (inc) row (RS) K17 (18, 19, 20), *pm, k2, yo, k2, yo, k2, pm*, k18 (20, 22, 24) sts, rep between *'s once, k17 (18, 19, 20). Work 5 rows in St st.
Next row (RS) Knit, working sts between markers as foll: K3, yo, k2, yo, k3. Work 5 rows in St st.
Next row (RS) Knit, working sts between markers as foll: K4, yo, k2, yo, k4—76 (80, 84, 88) sts. Work 5 rows even, removing markers.

Top shaping
Next row (RS) With circular needle, k23, pm, k30 (34, 38, 42), pm, k23. Beg short rows as foll:

*Next row (WS) Work to 5 sts before marker, pm, turn.
Next row Sl 1, k to end*. Rep between *'s 3 times more. P across all sts on next row. Shape right side to correspond to left side, reversing RS and WS rows. Work 2 rows eyelet border across all sts. Bind off.

FRONT

Work as for back, but work dec #1 row a total of 16 (18, 19, 19) times, then dec #2 row a total of 3 (1, 0, 0) times—80 (88, 92, 100) sts. Work even until same number of rows as back to bodice. Change to smaller needles.

Bodice

Work 2 rows eyelet border. Work in St st for 4 rows.
Next eyelet row (RS) K 21 (23, 24, 26),

pm, k2tog, yo, k2, yo, SKP, pm, k26 (30, 32, 36), rep between *'s once, k21 (23, 24, 26). Rep eyelet row every 6th row 4 times more. P 1 row on WS.

Armhole shaping

Cont eyelet row every 6th row as established, bind off 4 (4, 5, 5) sts at beg of next 2 rows, 3 (3, 3, 4) sts at beg of next 2 rows.
Next dec row (RS) K4, yo, SK2P, work to last 7 sts, k3tog, yo, k4. Rep dec row every other row 6 (10, 10, 12) times more—52 (52, 54, 56) sts. Work even until armhole measures 4 (4, 4¼, 4½)"/10 (10, 10.5, 11.5)cm.

Neck shaping

With circular needle, work short row shaping as for top shaping of back,

marking center 18 (18, 20, 22) sts and leaving 3 sts unworked each side of neck a total of 5 times. Work 2 rows eyelet border across all sts. Bind off.

FINISHING

Block pieces lightly. With RS facing and circular needle, pick up and k 54 (54, 56, 60) sts evenly along front neck. P 2 rows. K 1 row. Bind off loosely. Work lower hem edges in same way, picking up 1 st in each cast-on st. Sew side seams.

Straps

With circular needle, cast on 42 sts, then pick up and k sts evenly along right armhole, across back and along left armhole, cast on 42 sts. P 2 rows. K 1 row. Bind off loosely. Line bodice and reinforce straps if desired with cord.

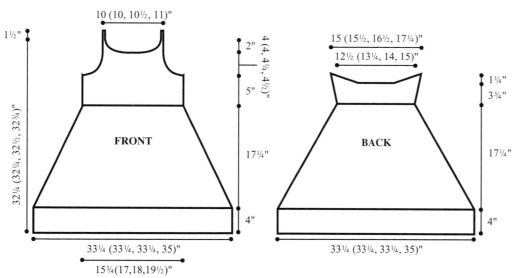

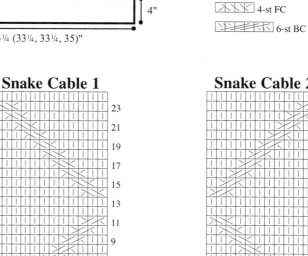

Stitch Key

	K on RS, p on WS
	3-st BC
	3-st FC

Stitch Key

	K on RS, p on WS
	P on RS, k on WS
	4-st BC
	4-st FC
	6-st BC

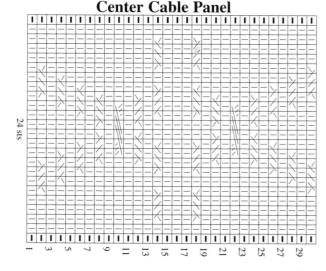

Center Cable Panel

24 sts

Snake Cable 1

12 sts

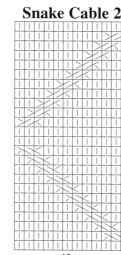

Snake Cable 2

12 sts

M a r i   L y n n   P a t r i c k

Knit to fit! This beautiful hand-knit suit jacket was adapted from a classic *Vogue Sewing* pattern. The full-fashioned tailored jacket is knit in waffle stitch and features a bias collar with self-tie and corded crochet trim. Shown in size 10. The Tailored Jacket first appeared in the Spring/Summer '97 issue of *Vogue Knitting*.

Tailored Jacket

FOR EXPERT KNITTERS

SIZES
To fit size 8 (10, 12, 14, 16, 18) OR Body Bust sizes 31½ (32½, 34, 36, 38, 40)". Directions are for smallest size with larger sizes in parentheses. If there is only one figure, it applies to all sizes.

KNITTED MEASUREMENTS
● Bust at underarm (buttoned) 37 (38, 39½, 42, 44, 46)"/94 (96.5, 100.5, 106.5, 117)cm.
● Hip 42 (43, 44, 46, 48, 50)"/106.5 (109, 112, 117, 122, 127)cm.
● Length 25¼ (25½, 25½, 26, 26¼, 26½)"/64 (65, 65, 66, 66.5, 67.5)cm.
● Sleeve width at upper arm 14¾ (14¾, 14¾, 15, 15, 15½)"/37.5 (37.5, 37.5, 38, 38, 39.5)cm.

MATERIALS
● 14 (14, 15, 16, 16, 17) 1¾oz/50g skeins (each approx 95yd/86m) of Classic Elite Yarns *Tapestry* (wool/mohair 4) in #2284 orange (MC)
● 5 (5, 6, 6, 6, 6) 1¾oz/50g skeins (each approx 143yd/129m) of Classic Elite Yarns *Tapestry 2-ply* (wool/mohair 3) in #6784 orange (L)
● One pair each sizes 4 and 7 (3.5 and 4.5mm) needles OR SIZE TO OBTAIN GAUGE
● Stitch markers
● Size E (3.5mm) crochet hook
● Tapestry needle
● Five 1"/25mm buttons

GAUGE
22 sts and 30 rows to 4"/10cm over pat st using size 7 (4.5mm) needles. FOR A PERFECT FIT, TAKE TIME TO CHECK GAUGE.

STITCH GLOSSARY
Pattern Stitch (uneven # of sts)
Row 1 (RS) P1, *k1, p1, rep from * to end.
Row 2 K1, *p1, k1, rep from * to end.
Rows 3 and 4 Knit. Rep rows 1-4 for pat st.
Note: All of the foll full-fashioned incs and decs are worked on pat row 2. Be sure to retain pat st while shaping.

FF dec 2 P3tog.
FF inc 2 Insert LH needle from back to front in st 1 row below st just worked and p1, k1 into front lp of this st.
Beg dec-1 K1, p1, k2tog.
End dec-1 (In last 4 sts) K2tog, p1, k1.
Beg inc-1p K1, p1, p1 and k1 into next st.
Beg inc-1k K1, p1, k1 and p1 into next st.
End inc-1p (In last 3 sts) k1 and p1 into next st, p1, k1.
End inc-1k (In last 3 sts) p1 and k1 into next st, p1, k1.

RIGHT BACK
With larger needles and MC, cast on 49 (49, 51, 53, 55, 57) sts. Work in pat st for 21 rows.
FF Dec row (WS) Work 19 sts, place marker (pm), FF dec-2, work to last 4 sts, End dec-1. Cont in pat rep FF dec-2 after marker every 12th row 4 times more and End dec-1 every 8th row 7 times more—31 (31, 33, 35, 37, 39) sts. Work even until piece measures 11"/28cm from beg, end with pat row 1.
FF Inc row (WS) Work 19 sts, work FF inc-2, work to last 3 sts, work End inc-1p. Cont in pat as established, inc by working FF inc-2 after marker every 12th row 3 times more and working End inc-1 k then End inc-1 p incs every alternate 8th and 12th rows a total of 4 times more—44 (44, 46, 48, 50, 52) sts. Work even until piece

measures 16¾ (17, 17, 17¼, 17½, 17½)"/42.5 (43, 43, 44, 44.5, 44.5)cm from beg, end pat row 4 (2, 2, 4, 2, 2).

Armhole shaping
Next row (RS) Bind off 1 st, work to end. Work 1 row even. Rep last 2 rows 2 (2, 2, 4, 4, 4) times more — 41 (41, 43, 43, 45, 47) sts. Work even until armhole measures 7½ (7½, 7½, 7¾, 7¾, 8)"/19 (19, 19, 19.5, 19.5, 20.5)cm, end with a RS row.

Neck shaping
Next row (WS) Bind off 10 sts, work to end. Cont to shape neck by binding off 2 sts from neck edge 4 times and AT SAME TIME, when armhole measures 8 (8, 8, 8¼, 8¼, 8½)"/20.5(20.5, 20.5, 21, 21, 21.5)cm, shape shoulder by binding off 5 sts 3 (3, 5, 5, 3, 1) times and 4 (4, 0, 0, 6, 6) sts 2 (2, 0, 0, 2, 4) times.

LEFT BACK
Work to correspond to right back reversing all shaping (pm at 19 sts from center) and working Beg dec's instead of End dec's.

Right side panel
With larger needles and MC, cast on 29 (31, 31, 33, 35, 37) sts. Work in pat st for 9 rows.
Next row (WS) Beg dec-1, work to end. Cont to work Beg dec-1 every 12th row 5 times more and End dec-1 on the 22nd row of pat st once, then every 16th row 3 times — 19 (21, 21, 23, 25, 27) sts. Work even for 11 rows.
Next row (WS) Work Beg inc-1p, work to end. Rep Beg inc every 8th row 3 times more, working alternate Beg inc-1k and Beg inc-1p sts into pat st, work even on 23 (25, 25, 27, 29, 31) sts until piece

measures 14¾ (15, 15, 15¼, 15½, 15½)"/37.5 (38, 38, 39, 39.5, 39.5)cm from beg, end with a WS row.

Underarm shaping
Next row (RS) Work 10 (11, 11, 12, 13, 14) sts, join 2nd ball of yarn and bind off 4 sts, work to end. Working both sides at once, bind off from center edge every other row as foll: Right Side—bind off 2 sts 3 (4, 4, 5, 6, 7) times and 1 st 4 (3, 3, 2, 1, 0) times, and left side—bind off 2 sts 2 (3, 3, 4, 5, 6) times and 1 st 5 (4, 4, 3, 2, 1) times.

Left side panel
Work to correspond to right side panel reversing all shaping including underarm left and right side shaping.

RIGHT FRONT
With larger needles and MC, cast on 59 (59, 61, 63, 65, 67) sts. Work in pat st for 21 rows.
FF Dec row (WS) Beg dec-1, work 17 (17, 19, 19, 21, 21) more sts and pm, FF dec-2, work to end. Cont to work decs same as for back AT SAME TIME, work 5 buttonholes, the first one at 5 (5¼, 5¼, 5¾, 6, 6¼)"/12.5 (13.5, 13.5, 14.5, 15, 16)cm from lower edge, the other 4 at 3¼"/ 8.25cm intervals as foll:
Buttonhole row (RS) Work 5 sts, bind off 4 sts for buttonhole, work to end. On next row, cast on 4 sts over bound-off sts. After all dec's there are 41 (41, 43, 45, 47, 49) sts. Work even until piece measures 11"/28cm from beg, end with pat row 1.
Next row (WS) Work Beg inc-1 p, work to marker, work FF inc-2, work to end. Cont to alternate Beg inc-1 k and Beg inc-1p every 8th row 5 times more and work FF inc-2 every 12th row twice more—53 (53, 55, 57, 59, 61) sts. Work even until piece measures same length as back to armhole, end with a RS row.

Armhole shaping
Next row (WS) Bind off 1 st (armhole), work to end. Work 1 row even. Rep last 2 rows 3 (3, 3, 5, 5, 5) times more—49 (49, 51, 51, 53, 55) sts. Work even until center front measures 19 (19¼, 19¼, 19¾, 20, 20¼)"/48 (49, 49, 50, 51, 51.5)cm, end with a WS row.

Neck shaping

Next row (RS) Bind off 15 sts (neck edge), work to end. Cont to dec 1 st at neck edge every other row twice, every 4th row 9 times and AT SAME TIME, when armhole measures 6½ (6½, 6½, 6¾, 6¾, 7)"/16.5 (16.5, 16.5, 17, 17, 18)cm, shape shoulder as for back.

LEFT FRONT

Work as for right front omitting buttonholes and reversing all shaping being sure to pm at same distance from side seam.

SLEEVES

With larger needles and MC, cast on 49 (49, 49, 51, 51, 53) sts. Work in pat st for 9 rows. Work Beg inc-1p and End inc-1p on next row and cont to alternate k and p incs every alternate 4th and 8th rows a total of 15 times more—81 (81, 81, 83, 83, 85) sts. Work even until piece measures 15¾ (16, 16½, 16½, 17, 17)"/40 (40.5, 42, 42, 43, 43)cm from beg.

Cap shaping

Bind off 4 sts at beg of next 2 rows. Bind off 2 sts at beg of next 4 rows. Dec 1 st each side (not full-fashioned dec's) every other row 16 (16, 16, 17, 17, 18) times. Bind off 2 sts at beg of next 10 rows. Bind off rem 13 sts.

COLLAR

(Note: Collar is knit on the bias beg at one corner and ending at the opposite corner.) With smaller needles and L, cast on 1 st. K1.

Row 1 (WS) K1 in front, back and front of st—3 sts.

Row 2 K1, p1, k1.

Row 3 K1 and p1 in first st, rib to last st, p1 and k1 in last st—5 sts.

Row 4 Knit.

Row 5 K2 sts in first st, k to last st, k2 sts in last st.

Row 6 *K1, p1, rep from * end K1. Rep rows 3-6 until there are 49 sts on needle and one angled edge measures 5½"/14cm.

Next row (WS) K2 tog, work to last st, inc 1 st in last st. Work 1 row even. Cont in this way until long edge of collar measures 51"/29.5cm.

Next row (WS) K2tog, pat to last 2 sts, k2tog. Work 1 row even. Cont to rep last 2 rows until 3 sts rem. Sl 1, k2tog, psso. Fasten off.

FINISHING

Do not press jacket pieces. Sew and seam all pieces with L.

Facings

With RS facing, smaller needles and L, pick up and k 106 (108, 108, 110, 112, 114) sts evenly along left front center edge (approx 3 sts for every 4 rows). K1 row on WS for turning ridge then work in St st for 2¾"/7cm or until facing fits across straight edge at neck. Bind off. Work right front facing in same way, working 5 buttonholes on 9th row as foll:

Row 9 (WS) P5, [join another ball of yarn and work 19 sts] 5 times only working rem sts after last joining. Work sections separately for 3 more rows. Then rejoin and work with one ball until 2¾"/7cm from beg. Press facings and sew to WS. For sleeve cuff facing, pick up and k 48 (48, 48, 50, 50, 52) sts along lower edge of sleeve and work in same way for ¾"/2cm. Bind off. Press and sew. Sew back and shoulder seams. Pick up and k 126 sts around neck and work neck facing in same way for ¾"/2cm. Press and sew. Sew side panels to back. Sew fronts to side panels. Beg and end at center front facings, pick up and k lower edge sts evenly and work facing for 2¾"/7cm. Press and sew. Lay garment flat aligning front and back at lower edge to locate underarms. Line up sleeve seam at underarm and pin sleeve cap around armhole. Sew sleeve into armhole. Fold collar in half at long edge and centering at back neck, pin open edges around neck up to front panels. Carefully pin ends of tie correcting bias. Sew inside edge of collar to WS of neck so that seam falls to inside. Sew outside edge of collar to RS of neck so that seam falls to inside. With crochet hook and L, work backwards sc around free ends of tie to close. Press collar and tie ends to correct bias. With crochet hook and L, work 1 backwards sc in each st of turning ridge of fronts, lower and sleeve facings. Press seams lightly. Finish buttonholes through both thicknesses using blanket stitch. Sew on buttons.

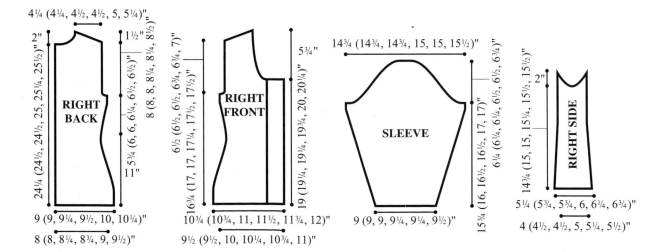

Wrapped Pullover

Irresistibly stylish, this surplice wrap jacket has a ribbed-to-fit waist, shawl collar, and set-in sleeves. It's standard-fitting with a mohair bouclé bodice that creates a fabulous faux-fur effect. Shown in size Medium. The Wrapped Pullover first appeared in the Winter '95/96 of *Vogue Knitting*.

MARI LYNN PATRICK

Wrapped Pullover

FOR EXPERIENCED KNITTERS

SIZES
To fit Small (Medium, Large, X-Large). Directions are for smallest size with larger size in parentheses. If there is only one figure, it applies to all sizes.

KNITTED MEASUREMENTS
● Bust at underarm (wrapped) 36 (38, 40, 42)"/91.5 (96.5, 101.5, 106.5)cm.
● Length 22 (22, 22½, 23)"/38 (38, 39.5, 40.5)cm.
● Sleeve width at upper arm 12½ (12½, 13, 14)"/32 (32, 33, 35.5)cm.

MATERIALS
Original Yarn
● 15 (15, 16, 16) 1½oz/40g balls (each approx 90yd/81m) of Classic Elite Yarns *Sharon* (mohair/wool/nylon 4) in #2506 grey (MC)
● 5 1¾oz/50g skeins (each approx 95yd/86m) of Classic Elite Yarns *Tapestry* (wool/mohair 4) in #2213 black (CC)
Substitute Yarn
● 13 (13, 14, 14) 1¾oz/50g balls (each approx 105yd/95m) of K1C2, LLC *Bon Bon* (mohair/wool/nylon 4) in #5111 Bavarian creme handpaint (MC)
● 5 1¾oz/50g skeins (each approx

95yd/86m) of Classic Elite Yarns *Tapestry* (wool/mohair 4) in #2213 black (CC)
● One pair each sizes 6 and 9 (4 and 5.5mm) needles OR SIZE TO OBTAIN GAUGE
● Size 6 (4mm) circular needle, 36"/90cm long
● Stitch markers
Note
The original yarns used for this sweater are no longer available. Comparable substitutions have been made, which are available at the time of printing. Check gauge of substitute yarns very carefully before beginning.

GAUGE
14 sts and 18 rows to 4"/10cm over St st using double strand of MC and size 9 (5.5mm) needles. FOR PERFECT FIT, TAKE TIME TO CHECK GAUGE.

BACK
Beg above ribbing, with larger needles and double strand of MC, cast on 63 (67, 70, 74) sts. Work in St st for 5"/12.5cm, end with a WS row.

Armhole shaping
Bind off 3 (3, 4, 4) sts at beg of next 2 rows. Dec 1 st each side every other row 3 (4, 4, 5) times—51 (53, 54, 56) sts. Work even until armhole measures 8½ (8½, 9, 9½)"/21.5 (21.5, 23, 24)cm, end with a WS row.

Shoulder shaping
Bind off 5 sts at beg of next 6 (4, 4, 2) rows, 6 sts at beg of next 0 (2, 2, 4) rows. Bind off rem 21 (21, 22, 22) sts for back neck.

LEFT FRONT
Beg above ribbing, with larger needles and double strand of MC, cast on 52 (54, 56, 58) sts. Work in St st for 5"/12.5cm, end with a WS row.

Armhole shaping
Bind off 3 (3, 4, 4) sts at beg of next row (armhole edge). Dec 1 st at armhole edge every other row 3 (4, 4, 5) times—46 (47, 48, 49) sts. P 1 row on WS.

Neck shaping
Next row (RS) K17 (18, 18, 19), k2tog (neck dec), place marker, k 27 (27, 28, 28). Rep dec for neck 2 sts before marker every 8th row 3 times more—42 (43, 44, 45) sts. Work even until same length as back to shoulder.

Shoulder shaping
Bind off 5 sts from shoulder edge 3 (2, 2, 1) times, 6 sts 0 (1, 1, 2) times, k to end on rem 27 (27, 28, 28) sts.

Collar shaping
Work short rows as foll:
*Short row 1 (WS)** P18 (18, 19, 19), turn.
Short row 2 Sl 1, K17 (17, 18, 18).
Short row 3 P21 (21, 22, 22), turn.
Short row 4 Sl 1, k20 (20, 21, 21), turn.
Working on all 27 (27, 28, 28) sts, purl 1 row, k 1 row*. Rep between *'s 6 times more, ONLY omit last k row on last rep. Bind off knitwise.

RIGHT FRONT
Work to correspond to left front reversing all shaping and beg collar short row shaping on first k row after shoulder shaping as foll:

Short row 1 (RS) K18 (18, 19, 19), turn. Cont to shape as for left collar, working k instead of p on short rows.

SLEEVES
Beg above cuff, with larger needles and double strand of MC, cast on 26 (26, 28, 29) sts. Work in St st inc 1 st each side every 10th row 2 (2, 2, 1) times, every 6th row 7 (7, 7, 9) times—44 (44, 46, 49) sts. Work even until piece measures 16"/40.5cm from beg, end with a WS row.

Cap shaping
Bind off 3 (3, 4, 4) sts at beg of next 2 rows. Dec 1 st each side every row 4 (4, 2, 2) times, every other row 10 (10, 12, 13) times—10 (10, 10, 11) sts. Bind off 3 sts at beg of next 2 rows. Bind off rem 4 (4, 4, 5) sts.

FINISHING
CUFFS
With larger needles and double strand of MC, pick up and k30 (30, 32, 33) sts along lower edge of sleeve. P 1 row, k 1 row, p 1 row.

Next row (RS) Knit, inc 4 sts evenly—34 (34, 36, 37) sts. Cont in St st until cuff measures 3½"/9cm. Bind off loosely. Steam pieces lightly. Sew shoulder seams. Sew collar to back neck. Sew back collar seam. Sew in sleeves. Sew side and sleeve seams, sewing cuff seam from RS for cuff turnback.

WAIST RIBBING
With RS facing, circular needle and CC, pick up and k around lower edge of body as foll: 79 (82, 85, 88) sts from left front, 93 (99, 105, 111) sts from back 79 (82, 85, 88) sts from right front—251 (263, 275, 287) sts.
Row 1 (WS) K1 (selvage st), *p3, k3; rep from *, end p3, k1 (selvage st). Work in k3, p3 rib for 3"/7.5cm, end with a RS row.

Separate for slits
Next row (WS) Rib 7 sts (first slit), join 2nd ball of yarn, rib 60 sts, (second slit), join 3rd ball of yarn, rib 30 (30, 36, 36) sts, (third slit), join 4th ball of yarn, rib to end. Cont to work slits by working with separate balls of yarn for

4 more rows.
Next row (RS) Rejoin slits by working all sts in rib with 1 ball of yarn. Cont in rib until waist ribbing measures 7"/18cm. Bind off in rib.

TIES
Long tie With smaller needles and CC, cast on 12 sts.
Row 1 (RS) K1, *p1, k1; rep from *, end k2 instead of k1.
Row 2 K1, *p1, k1; rep from *, end k2 instead of k1. Rep rows 1 and 2 until tie measures 38"/96.5cm, slightly stretched. Bind off in rib.
Short tie Work as for long tie for 19"/48cm. Bind off in rib. Sew long tie to edge of left front waist rib to correspond to slit. Sew short tie on top of long tie.
To wrap jacket: Right front is wrapped over left front. Pull long tie through right back (third) slit, around outside back waist and through right front edge (first) slit. Pull short tie through other right front (second) slit, adjust and tie at center front.

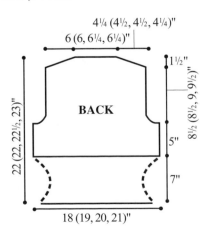

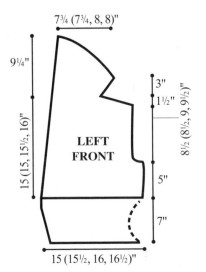

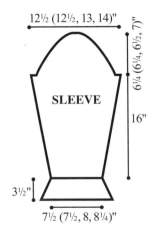

The understated chic of a lacy little shawl—this triangular eyelet and stockinette stitch shawl is given a modern twist when wrapped at the waist. The fine cashmere-blend yarn lends irresistible softness and drape. The Cashmere Shawl first appeared in the Fall '89 issue of *Vogue Knitting*.

Cashmere Shawl

FOR EXPERIENCED KNITTERS

SIZES
One size fits all.

KNITTED MEASUREMENTS
● Width across top edge 80"/20.3cm.
● Length from top edge to point 28"/71cm.

MATERIALS
Original Yarn
● 13¾oz/20g balls (each approx 110yd/100m) of Schaffhauser/Skacel Imports *Cashmere Bijou* (cashmere/wool 1) in #43 grey
Substitute Yarn
● 10⅞oz/25g balls (each approx 145yd/132m) of K1C2, LLC *Richesse et Soie* (cashmere/silk 1) in #9918 grey
● Sizes 2 and 3 (2.75 and 3.25mm) circular needles, 29"/80cm long OR SIZE TO OBTAIN GAUGE
● Stitch markers

Note
The original yarn used for this shawl is no longer available. A comparable substitution has been made, which is available at the time of printing. Check gauge of substitute yarns very carefully before beginning.

GAUGE
31 sts and 40 rows to 4"/10cm over St st using size 3 (3.25mm) needles. FOR PERFECT FIT, TAKE TIME TO CHECK GAUGE.

STITCH GLOSSARY
Eyelet St (multiple of 2 sts)
Row 1 (WS) Knit.
Row 2 (RS) K2, *yo, ssk; rep from *, end k2.
Row 3 Knit.

Note
To make counting easier, place markers at 50 or 100 st intervals while casting on. Stitch count must be accurate to ensure correct placement of lace st panels.

SHAWL
Beg at top edge with smaller circular needle, cast on 596 sts, placing markers as noted. Work back and forth as with straight needles as foll:
Rows 1, 3, 5 and 7 Knit.
Rows 2, 4, 6 and 8 K2tog, k to last 2 sts, ssk. Change to larger circular needle. Work next 95 dec rows and pats as foll:
Dec row 1 (WS) K2, p2tog, work to last 4 sts, p2tog tbl, k2.
Dec row 2 K2, ssk, work to last 4 sts, k2tog, k2. Rep dec rows 1 and 2, AT SAME TIME, work as foll: P 1 row, k 1 row, work 3 rows in eyelet st, 11 rows in St st, 27 rows in lace chart, 11 rows in St st, 3 rows in eyelet st, 9 rows in St st, 16 rows in lace chart, 10 rows in St st, 3 rows in eyelet st—398 sts. Work 176 rows in St st, cont dec as foll: *Work dec rows 1 and 2 on next 7 rows.
Next row (WS) K2, p3tog, work to last 5 sts, p3tog tbl, k2. Rep from * until 20 sts rem. Work dec rows 1 and 2 on next 6 rows—8 sts rem.
Next row (RS) K2, ssk, k2tog, k2.
Next row K2tog, p2tog tbl, k2tog.
Next row Skp.
Next row K2tog. Fasten off.

FINISHING
Block by pinning shawl on WS to large flat surface. Using a wet towel and steam iron, steam carefully.

Stitch Key

☐ or ☐ K on RS, p on WS

☐ P on RS, k on WS

☐ Yarn over

☐ or ☐ K2tog on RS, p2tog on WS

☐ or ☐ Ssk on RS, p2tog tbl on WS

☐ P3tog

☐ Sl 1, p2tog, psso

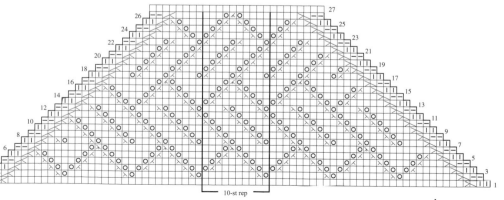

10-st rep

Michele Rose

Michele Rose was already an established designer in the garment industry when she visited the *Vogue Knitting* booth at a yarn show and met with editor Margery Winter. "I was still living in New York at the time, and I was interested in designing for the handknitting industry, because that was my first love," she recalls. "I came with an abundance of designs. Coming from the garment industry, I am used to designing large volumes of work—it was not a big deal for me to come with fifty designs. I don't think they are used to that, at least not in my experience."

Since then, Michele's work has appeared frequently on *Vogue Knitting's* magazine pages, to the delight of readers and editors alike. "Designing creative handknit sweaters for magazines is my love—getting to see them in a professionally done photograph," she says. "I was doing it really for the fun of it, and for the print, to have that on your bookshelf. It was a fun way to get to try nice handknitting yarns and to do complicated stitches that you might not be able to afford to produce commercially."

Michele first learned how to knit when she was only six years old. She remembers being inspired by one of her favorite books from childhood. "I have a bunch of books that were mine from when I was a little girl. One of the books is about a doll who knit this muffler for her teddy bear friend," she recalls. "And I can vividly remember that's what started me wanting to learn how to knit, because I wanted to knit a muffler just like this doll did. I came across this book again reading to my children and I was thinking, wow, this book launched my career, unbeknownest to me."

While her mother may have taught her the actual knit stitches, to Michele her mother's greatest gift was in guiding her to trust her

creative intuition. "My mother was an every-now-and-then knitter, it just came naturally to her. She came from Holland and learned to knit as a small girl. It's a different culture there, just part of what you learn growing up," she relates. "I think that's why designing came naturally to me, because I learned that way—not by reading instructions in books, but just by casting on and feeling it."

Michele also recognizes her father's influence on her career: "My father was an architect. I used to work summertimes in his office and learned a lot of technical-type drawing and writing. To me it's very similar to designing a garment—you are building something. When I approach a design, I use both that intuitive side and, when it comes to writing a pattern and creating the charts and graphs, that building-plan side. The combination of both backgrounds makes a perfect mix."

Even though she maintained her creative interests, Michele didn't really knit much again until she was a student at Yale. She veered off her original intention to study architecture, instead majoring in fine arts and economics. Meanwhile, in the background, knitting was increasingly becoming an all-consuming hobby. "I just enjoyed doing it," she says. "I worked in a yarn shop and started out knitting patterns from books, then quickly evolved to just making up my own things, making patterns."

She published her first design in 1983, while still a sophomore in college. After graduation, Michele gathered up her fashion sketches and swatches and headed to New York City. "I was of course very naive about the whole thing," she confesses. "I blindly went and knocked on doors. I put together a portfolio and hired somebody to take pictures of

"Using the computer as a creative tool is kind of like working on a canvas. I really love combining the different colors and patterns."

a bunch of sweaters that I had knitted and got a friend to model them." Eventually, Michele found an entry-level job with a sportswear firm and worked her way up from there.

After years of city life, Michele and her husband, Matt Orne, decided to leave Manhattan and move to Camden, Maine. She convinced her employer at the time to allow her to continue working from her new location, which, thanks to high-tech computers and overnight express, she's been doing ever since. "From the success of the last experience, the next one evolved," she says. "And in that time period the growth of the computer and the internet completely transformed my job."

Nowadays, Michele is the design director for a firm that provides handknit garments to American department stores and retail chains. From the comfort of her quaint New England village, she designs hundreds of sweaters a year, thousands of which are then hand knit, piece by piece, by women in China, then taken to a factory, sewn together and finished before eventually being sent back to the U.S.

Michele credits the computer for playing a role in the development of her colorwork patterns, which have become her trademark in the knitting industry. "Using the computer as a tool...it greatly facilitates that. It is kind of like a canvas," she says. "I really love combining different colors and patterns. From a creative standpoint, it is more painterly." While she enjoys *designing* the multi-colored knitting, she prefers *knitting* solid, multitextured cables. "However you look at it," she admits, "I seem to prefer more complicated things."

When designing for knitting magazines and yarn companies, Michele takes a more traditional approach. This is when she can have some fun and indulge her creative side, without worrying about cost and consumer demands. "When I do handknit things, I try to do a piece or a swatch or something. I won't do it beforehand on a graph—it evolves as I'm working on it," she explains. "When I'm working on a computer, it's easy to get carried away designing with a billion different colors. You can wind up with something too complicated for people to knit. If I design like that for the garment industry, the Chinese knitters will knit them, they are so skilled...but Americans and other handknitters are knitting for pleasure. They are not going to want to buy twenty-six different kinds of yarn." Michele's respect and admiration for the women who knit her pieces for the garment industry is apparent. "Here, you go to the mall and buy a sweater for fifty or one hundred dollars and you don't realize that someone actually knit that, on two needles," she exclaims.

Today, with a full-time career and a young family to take care of, Michele doesn't always have the time to do all of the things she would like. Asked about her plans for the future, she mentions possibly writing a few books, but admits she doesn't know when she will ever have the time. Someday, she says, she'd like to design and knit for creative satisfaction alone, without the concerns of finances and careers. But for now, she's enjoying the rewards of her spectacular career, and, thankfully, so are we.

Earthy taupes mix with red and cream in this cozy winter pullover patterned with Fair Isle snowflakes. It's oversized with raglan sleeves, ridged birdseye patterning, cabled edges, and face-framing turtleneck. For a finishing touch, add the Peruvian-style matching cap with earflaps and pompom. Shown in size Medium. The Fair Isle Pullover & Cap first appeared in the Winter '94/95 issue of *Vogue Knitting*.

Fair Isle Pullover & Cap

FOR EXPERIENCED KNITTERS

SIZES
To fit Small (Medium, Large). Directions are for smallest size with larger sizes in parentheses. If there is only one figure, it applies to all sizes.

FINISHED MEASUREMENTS
● Bust at underarm 44 (48, 52)"/112 (122, 132)cm.
● Length 28 (28½, 29)"/71 (72.5, 74)cm.
● Sleeve width at upper arm 19 (20, 21)"/48.5 (51, 53.5)cm.

MATERIALS
PULLOVER:
● 8 (8, 10) 3½oz/100g balls (each approx 220yd/200m) of Plymouth *Indiecita Alpaca Worsted 4-Ply Yarns* (alpaca 3) in #201 cream (MC)
● 3 balls in #208 taupe (A)
● 2 balls each in #2020 burgundy (B) and #206 dark camel (C)
● One pair each sizes 4 and 6 (3.5 and 4mm) needles OR SIZE TO OBTAIN GAUGE
● Size 4 (3.5mm) circular needle, 16"/40cm long

CAP:
● 1 ball each in #201 cream (MC), #208 taupe (A), #2020 burgundy (B) and #206 dark camel (C)
● Size 5 (3.75mm) double-pointed needles (dpn), OR SIZE TO OBTAIN GAUGE
● Size 5 (3.75mm) circular needle, 16"/40cm long
● Size D/3 (3mm) crochet hook

BOTH:
● Cable needle (cn) and stitch markers

GAUGE
24 sts and 30 rows to 4"/10cm over St st using size 6 (4mm) needles. FOR PERFECT FIT, TAKE TIME TO CHECK GAUGE.

STITCH GLOSSARY
2-st Front Cross Sl 1 to cable needle (cn), hold in *front* of work, k1; k1 from cn.
2-st Back Cross Sl 1 to cn, hold in *back* of work, k1; k1 from cn.
2-st Front Purl Cross Sl 1 to cn, hold to *front* of work, p1; k1 from cn.
2-st Back Purl Cross Sl 1 to cn, hold to *back* of work, k1; p1 from cn.
3-st Back Cross (3BC) Sl 2 to cn, hold to *back* of work, k1; k2 from cn.
6-st Front Cable Sl 3 to cable needle (cn), hold to *front* of work, k3; k3 from cn.

Boxed Cable Rib
(multiple of 10 sts plus 2 extra)
Rows 1 and 5 (RS) *P2, k3; rep from *, end p2.
Row 2 and all WS rows *K2, p3; rep from *, end k2.
Row 3 *P7, work 3BC; rep from *, end p2.
Row 7 *P2, work 3BC, p5; rep from *, end p2.
Row 8 Rep row 2. Rep rows 1-8 for boxed cable rib pat.

Garter Check (multiple of 4 sts)
Row 1 (RS) *K2B, k2A; rep from *.
Row 2 *P2A, k2B; rep from *.
Row 3 *K2MC, k2C; rep from *.
Row 4 *P2C, k2MC; rep from *.
Rows 5-6 Rep rows 1-2.
Rows 7-8 With A, knit.
Rows 9-10 With B, knit.

Ridged Birdseye (multiple of 8 sts)
Row 1 (RS) With MC, knit.
Row 2 With MC, purl.
Row 3 *K2MC, *k1C, k3MC; rep from *, end k1C, k1MC.
Rows 4-5 With MC, knit.
Row 6 With MC, purl.
Row 7 *K1C, k3MC; rep from *.
Row 8 With MC, knit. Rep rows 1-8 for ridged birdseye pat.

PULLOVER

BACK
With smaller needles and A, cast on 132 (142, 152) sts.
Preparation row *K2, p3; rep from *, end k2. Work in boxed cable rib pat for 3"/9cm, inc 0 (2, 4) sts on last row and end with a WS row—132 (144, 156) sts. Change to larger needles.
Beg chart #1: Row 1 (RS) Beg and end as indicated for chosen size, working 10-st rep 13 (14, 15) times. Work through chart row 20 as established. Work 10 rows in garter check pat.
Beg chart #2: Row 1 (RS) Beg and end as indicated for chosen size, working 16-st rep 8 (9, 9) times. Work through chart row 26 as established. With MC, k 2 rows. Work in ridged birdseye pat until piece measures 17"/43.5cm from beg, end with a WS row.

Raglan shaping
Cont in pat, bind off 5 (5, 6) sts at beg of next 6 rows—102 (114, 120) sts.
Beg cabled raglan: Next row (RS) With MC, k1, 6-st front cable, p1, pm, ssk, cont in pat to last 10 sts, with MC k2tog, pm, p1, 6-st front cable, k1.
Next row (WS) With MC, p7, k1, p1,

cont in pat to last 9 sts, with MC, p1, k1, p7. In same way, dec 1 st before and after markers each side every other row 28 (35, 38) times more, every 4th row 3 (0, 0) times. Bind off 38 (42, 42) sts.

FRONT
Work to correspond to back, working through raglan shaping until 44 (48, 48) sts rem. Bind off all sts.

LEFT SLEEVE
With smaller needles and A, cast on 52 (52, 62) sts.
Preparation row *K2, p3; rep from *, end k2. Work in boxed cable rib pat for 3"/9cm, inc 4 sts on last row and end with a WS row—56 (56, 66) sts. Change to larger needles. Work pats and incs (working incs into chart pat when possible) simultaneously as foll:
Beg chart #1: Row 1 (RS) With A, k1, m1, k2, pm, work 10-st rep 5 (5, 6) times, with A, k2, m1, k1. Work sts before and after markers in St st and work through chart row 20, AT SAME TIME, inc 1 st each side every 4th row 4 times and *for size small (med) only*, inc 2 sts on row 20—68 (68, 76) sts. Work 10 rows in garter check pat, inc on rows 3 and 7—72 (72, 80) sts.
Beg chart #2: Row 1 (RS) *For size small (med) only*, beg and end as indicated, working 16-st rep 4 times. *For size large*, work 16-st rep 5 times. Work through chart row 26, inc on row 3, then every 4th row 6 times—86 (86, 94) sts. With MC, k 2 rows. Work in ridged birdseye pat, AT SAME TIME, inc 1 st each side every 4th row 14 (18, 17) times—114 (122, 128) sts. Work even until piece measures 19½ (20, 20½)"/49.5 (51, 52)cm from beg, end with a WS row.

Raglan shaping
Bind off 5 sts at beg of next 6 rows—84 (92, 98) sts.
Next row (RS) With MC, k1, 6-st front

cable, p1, pm, ssk, cont in pat to last 10 sts, with MC, k2tog, pm, p1, 6-st front cable, k1. Working sts before and after markers as for back, dec 1 st each side every other row 28 (32, 35) times, end with last RS dec row—26 sts.
Next row (WS) Bind off 9 (9, 7) sts, cont in pat to end—17 sts. Bind off 2 sts at beg of next 2 WS rows, AT SAME TIME, dec 1 st at beg of next 4 RS rows. Bind off rem 9 sts.

RIGHT SLEEVE
Work to correspond to left sleeve, reversing shaping at top of sleeve.

FINISHING
Block pieces lightly. Sew underarm and raglan seams.

Highneck
With circular needle and MC, pick up 110 sts evenly around neck edge. Pm, join and work in boxed cable rib pat for 8"/20.5cm. Bind off all sts. Sew sleeve and side seams.

CAP

Notes
1 Change to dpn when necessary.
2 Work chart #2 in rnds by reading every row from right to left.

STITCH GLOSSARY
Garter Check Pat (over 14 sts)
Row 1 (RS) K3A, *k2B, k2A; rep from *, end k2B, k3A.
Row 2 K3A, *k2B, p2A; rep from *, end k2B, k3A.
Row 3 K3A; *k2A, k2MC; rep from *; end k5A.
Row 4 K3A, *p2A, K2MC; rep from *, end p2A, k3A. Rep rows 1-4 for garter check pat.

With circular needle and A, cast on 112 sts. *Being careful not to twist sts,* place marker (pm) and join. Work in circular garter st (k 1 rnd, p 1 rnd) as

foll: 4 rnds with A, 2 rnds with B, end at joining marker. Place separate marker on first rnd under joining marker for center back.
Beg chart #2: Rnd 1 Work 16-st rep 7 times. Work through chart rnd 28. With MC, k 2 rnds.
Next rnd *K1C, k3MC; rep from *. **With MC, p 1 rnd, then k 1 rnd.**
Dec rnd 1 With MC, *k2, k2tog; rep from *—84 sts.
Next rnd *K2MC, k1C; rep from *. Rep between *'s once.
Dec rnd 2 With MC, *k1, k2tog; rep from *—56 sts.
Next rnd *K1C, k1MC; rep from *. Rep between *'s once. Cont with MC only.
Dec rnd 3 *K2tog—28 sts. K 3 rnds.
Dec rnd 4 *K2tog; rep from *—14 sts. K 1 rnd.
Dec rnd 5 [k2tog] 7 times—7 sts.
Dec rnd 6 [Sl 1, k2tog, psso] twice, k1. Fasten off.

Earflaps
(Note: Work back and forth in rows on dpn.)
Right earflap With RS facing, dpn and A, beg 12 sts to right of center back and pick up and k20 sts. K 1 row. Work 6 rows in garter check pat.
Next row (RS) K2A, ssk, cont pat row 3 to last 4 sts, k2tog, k2A. In same way, dec 1 st each side every other row 5 times more—8 sts. With A, k2 rows. Bind off.
Left earflap Beg 12 sts to left of center back marker and work as for right earflap.

FINISHING
With MC, make pompom (see page 46—1½" pompom). Attach to top of cap.

Ties
With hook, join A to center of right earflap. Ch 40. Work 1 sc in 2nd ch from hook and in each ch across. Sl st to flap. Fasten off. Rep for 2nd flap. Block cap.

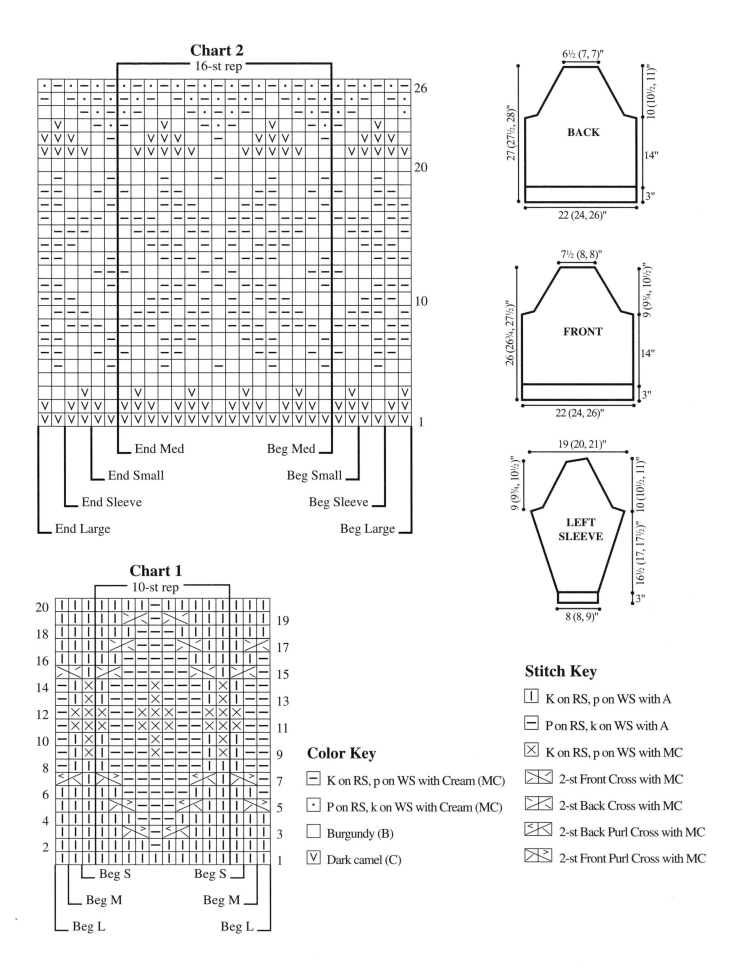

Chart 2

16-st rep

26

20

10

1

End Med | Beg Med
End Small | Beg Small
End Sleeve | Beg Sleeve
End Large | Beg Large

Chart 1

10-st rep

20
18
16
14
12
10
8
6
4
2

19
17
15
13
11
9
7
5
3
1

Beg S · Beg S
Beg M · Beg M
Beg L · Beg L

Color Key

— K on RS, p on WS with Cream (MC)

· P on RS, k on WS with Cream (MC)

☐ Burgundy (B)

V Dark camel (C)

Stitch Key

I K on RS, p on WS with A

— P on RS, k on WS with A

X K on RS, p on WS with MC

2-st Front Cross with MC

2-st Back Cross with MC

2-st Back Purl Cross with MC

2-st Front Purl Cross with MC

BACK

6½ (7, 7)"
27 (27½, 28)"
10 (10½, 11)"
14"
3"
22 (24, 26)"

FRONT

7½ (8, 8)"
26 (26¾, 27½)"
9 (9¾, 10½)"
14"
3"
22 (24, 26)"

LEFT SLEEVE

19 (20, 21)"
9 (9¾, 10½)"
10 (10½, 11)"
16½ (17, 17½)"
3"
8 (8, 9)"

With great color and shaping, this roomy V-neck cardigan will never go out of style. The pattern borrows from Native American traditions, while the color is pure Southwest. Peruvian-inspired charms, beads, and stones combined with whip-stitched edges provide the finishing touch. Shown in size Medium. The Western Jacket first appeared in the Fall '92 issue of *Vogue Knitting*.

Western Jacket

FOR EXPERIENCED KNITTERS

SIZES
To fit Small (Medium, Large). Directions are for smallest size with larger sizes in parentheses. If there is only one figure, it applies to all sizes.

KNITTED MEASUREMENTS
● Bust at underarm (buttoned) 39½ (44¼, 48½)"/100.5 (112.5, 123)cm.
● Length 26 (27, 28)"/66 (68.5, 71)cm.
● Sleeve width at upper arm 19 (20, 22)"/48.5 (51, 56)cm.

MATERIALS
● 4 3½oz/100g balls (each approx 127yd/118m) of Classic Elite Yarns *Montera* (llama/wool 5) each in #3858 red (A) and #3897 olive (C)
● 3 balls in #3827 eggplant (B)
● 2 balls in #3885 light rust (E)
● 1 ball each in #3839 taupe (D) and #3809 gold (F)
● One pair each sizes 5 and 6 (3.75 and 4mm) needles OR SIZE TO OBTAIN GAUGE
● Five 1"/25mm buttons
● 6 (6, 7)yd/5.5 (5.5, 6.4)m rawhide lacing (optional)
● Assorted charms (optional)
● Stitch markers and bobbins

Note
One of the original colors used in this sweater is no longer available. A comparable color substitution has been made, which is available at the time of printing.

GAUGE
20 sts and 25 rows to 4"/10cm over chart pat using size 6 (4mm) needles. FOR PERFECT FIT, TAKE TIME TO CHECK GAUGE.

Note
Use a separate ball or bobbin for front placket. When changing colors, twist yarns on WS to prevent holes.

BACK
With smaller needles and A, cast on 99 (111, 123) sts. Work in garter st for 10 rows (5 ridges on RS). Change to larger needles and St st.
Beg chart: Row 1 (RS) Beg with st 10, work through st 12, work 12-st rep of chart 8 (9, 10) times. Work even in pat as established until piece measures 25 (26, 27)"/63.5 (66, 68.5)cm from beg, end with a WS row.

Shoulder and neck shaping
Bind off 11 (13, 15) sts at beg of next 6 rows, AT SAME TIME, bind off center 23 sts for neck. Working both sides at once, bind off from each neck edge 3 sts once, 2 sts once.

LEFT FRONT
With smaller needles and A, cast on 51 (57, 63) sts. Work in garter st as for back. Change to larger needles.
Beg chart: Row 1 (RS) Beg with st 4 (10, 4), work through st 12, work 12-st rep 3 (4, 4) times, place marker (pm), k last 6 sts with A for placket. Cont to work in pat as established keeping 6 placket sts in garter st and A until piece measures 12 (13, 14)"/30.5 (33, 35.5)cm from beg, end with a WS row.

Neck shaping
Next row (RS) Work to last 8 sts, k2tog, work 6-st of placket (neck edge). Cont to work in pat dec 1 st at neck edge before 6-st placket every 4th row 13 times, then every 6th row 4 times—33 (39, 45) sts. When piece measures same length as back to shoulder, shape shoulder as for back—6 sts of placket rem. Cont to work 6-st placket for 3¼"/8cm more. Bind off. Place markers on placket for 5 buttons with first marker ¾"/2cm from lower edge and last marker at beg of neck shaping and 3 evenly between.

RIGHT FRONT
(Note: If desired, omit buttonhole in garter edge.) Cast on as for left front. Work 8 rows in garter st (4 ridges on RS).
Next row (RS) K2, bind off 2 sts, work to end. On next row, cast on 2 sts above bound-off sts.
Beg chart pat: Row 1 (RS) Work 6 sts in garter st with A for placket, pm, work 12-st rep of chart 3 (4, 4) times, then work sts 1-9 (1-3, 1-9). Complete as for left front reversing all shaping and working buttonholes opposite markers.

SLEEVES
With smaller needles and A, cast on 46 (50, 54) sts. Work in garter st for 8 rows (4 ridges on RS). Change to larger needles.
Beg chart: Row 1 (RS) Beg with st 2 (11, 7), work through st 12, work 12-st rep of chart 3 (4, 4) times. Cont in pat, AT SAME TIME, inc 1 st each side (working inc sts into chart pat) every other row 0 (0, 5) times, every 4th row 25 (25, 23) times—96 (100, 110) sts.

Work even until piece measures 18 (18½, 18½)"/45.5 (47, 47)cm from beg. Bind off.

FINISHING

Block pieces. Sew shoulder seams. Sew short ends of placket together. Sew placket along back neck. Place markers 9½ (10, 11)"/24 (25.5, 28)cm down from shoulders on front and back for armholes. Sew top of sleeves between markers. Sew side and sleeve seams. Sew on buttons. Whipstitch using 2 strands of B or rawhide around lower and front edges and sleeve cuffs. Following color photo for placement, sew on charms.

Stitch Key

⊡ With A, k on RS, p on WS

⊡ With A, p on RS, k on WS

+ With B, k on RS, p on WS

X With B, p on RS, k on WS

T With C, k on RS, p on WS

V With C, p on RS, k on WS

— With D, k on RS, p on WS

✳ With E, k on RS, p on WS

\ With F, k on RS, p on WS

/ With F, p on RS, k on WS

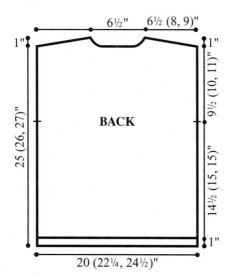

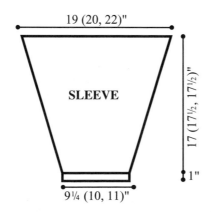

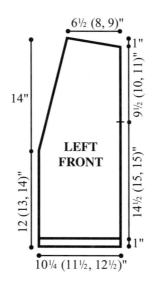

Patchwork Cardigan

A patchwork of heathered colors and embroidered florals gives this intarsia cardigan the spirited look of American folk art. The cardigan is oversized and boxy with drop shoulders and round neck. Shown in size Medium. The Patchwork Cardigan first appeared in the Fall '90 issue of *Vogue Knitting*.

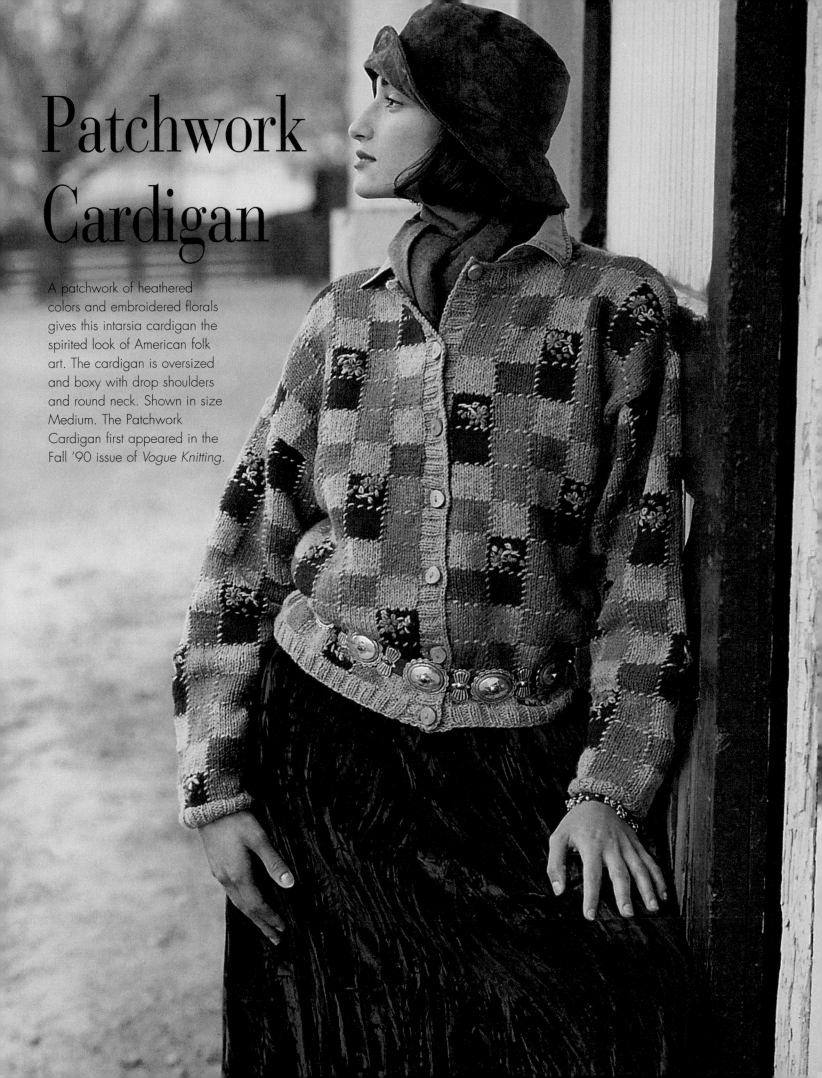

FOR EXPERIENCED KNITTERS

Patchwork Cardigan

SIZES
To fit Small (Medium, Large). Directions are for smallest size with larger sizes in parentheses. If there is only one figure, it applies to all sizes.

KNITTED MEASUREMENTS
● Bust at underarm (buttoned) 41½ (45¼, 48¼)"/104.5 (112.5, 121)cm.
● Length 22½ (22½, 24)"/56.5 (56.5, 60)cm.
● Sleeve width at upper arm 20 (20, 21)"/50 (50, 53)cm.

MATERIALS
Original Yarn
● 3 (3, 4) 1¾oz/50g balls (each approx 149yd/135m) of Crystal Palace/Jacques Fonty *Granit* (wool 4) in #388 grey/brown heather (C)
● 1 ball each in #392 celery (A), #387 rose heather (B), #390 brown (D), #391 mustard (E), #407 brick (F), #399 blue (G), #389 curry (H), #393 blue/green (I) and #401 light charcoal (J)
Substitute Yarn
● 3 (3, 4) 1¾oz/50g balls (each approx 137yd/123m) of GGH/Muench *Wollywasch* (wool 4) in #63 grey/brown heather (C)
● 1 ball each in #124 celery (A), #122 rose (B), #103 brown (D), #5 mustard (E), #53 brick (F), #94 blue (G),

#119 curry (H), #69 blue/green (I) and #64 light charcoal (J)
● One pair each sizes 5 and 7 (3.75 and 4.5mm) needles OR SIZE TO OBTAIN GAUGE
● Seven ¾"/20mm buttons
● Bobbins

Note
The original yarn used for this sweater is no longer available. A comparable substitution has been made, which is available at the time of printing. Check gauge of substitute yarns very carefully before beginning.

GAUGE
19 sts and 26 rows to 4"/10cm over St st and chart pat using size 7 (4.5mm) needles. FOR PERFECT FIT, TAKE TIME TO CHECK GAUGE.

Notes
1 Each square of chart equals 8 sts and 10 rows, unless otherwise stated in the instructions. Work chart in St st.
2 Use a separate bobbin for each block of color.
3 K first and last st of every row (matching colors) for selvage sts. Do not count these sts when measuring pieces.
4 End pieces with complete blocks, binding off in matching colors.

BACK
With smaller needles and C, cast on 98 (106, 114) sts. Work in k2, p2 rib for 1"/2.5cm. Change to larger needles. Work in St st as foll:
Beg chart: Row 1 (RS) K1 E (selvage st), work 40-st rep of chart twice, work first 16 (24, 32) sts once more, end with a D (C, B) square, k1 D (C, B) for selvage st. Cont in pat until piece measures 21½ (21½, 23)"/54 (54, 57.5)cm from beg.

Neck shaping
Next row (RS) Work 37 (40, 44) sts, join 2nd ball of yarn and bind off 24 (26, 26) sts, work to end. Working both sides at once, bind off from each neck edge 3 sts once, 2 sts once. Bind off rem 32 (35, 39) sts each side.

LEFT FRONT
With smaller needles and C, cast on 50 (54, 58) sts. Rib as for back. Change to larger needles.
Beg chart: Row 1 (RS) K1 B (C, C) for selvage st, k8 B (4C, 8C), beg with A (B, B) square, cont chart pat, end with a B square, k1 B (selvage st). Cont in pat until piece measures 19¾ (19¾, 21¼)"/49.5 (49.5, 53)cm from beg, end with a RS row.

Neck shaping
Next row (WS) Bind off 4 (5, 5) sts (neck edge), work to end. Cont to bind off from neck edge 3 sts twice, 2 sts twice, dec 1 st every other row 4 times. Bind off rem 32 (35, 39) sts.

RIGHT FRONT
Work to correspond to left front, working chart pat as foll:
Beg chart: Row 1 (RS) K1 A (selvage st), beg with A square, work chart pat to last 9 (5, 9) sts, work these sts with A (E, E). Complete as for left front, reversing neck shaping by dec at beg of RS rows.

SLEEVES
With smaller needles and C, cast on 42 sts. Work in k2, p2 rib for 1½ (1, 1)"/4 (2.5, 2.5)cm. Change to larger needles.
Beg chart: Row 1 (RS) K1 E (selvage st), work 40-st rep of chart once, k1 A (selvage st). Cont in pat, inc 1 st each side (working inc sts into pat inside of

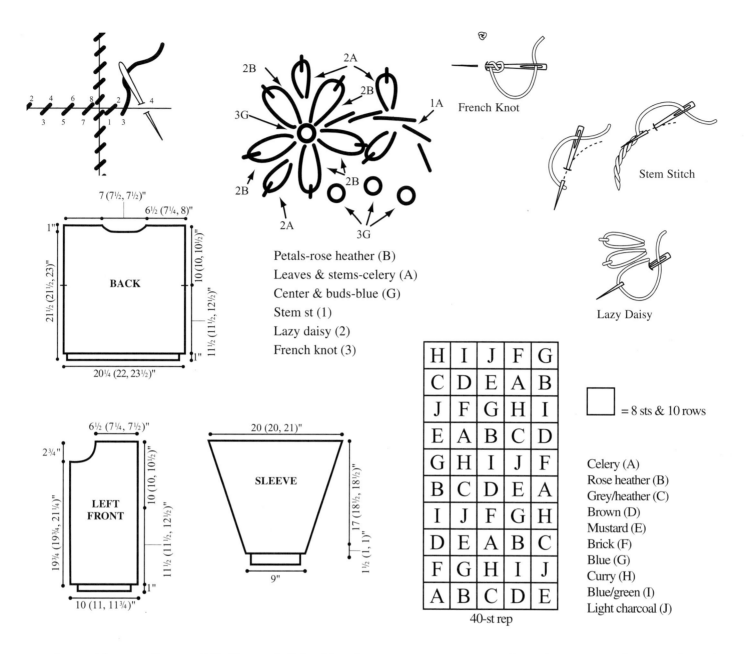

French Knot

Stem Stitch

Lazy Daisy

Petals-rose heather (B)
Leaves & stems-celery (A)
Center & buds-blue (G)
Stem st (1)
Lazy daisy (2)
French knot (3)

BACK

7 (7½, 7½)"
6½ (7¼, 8)"
1"
21½ (21½, 23)"
10 (10, 10½)"
11½ (11½, 12½)"
1"
20¼ (22, 23½)"

LEFT FRONT

6½ (7¼, 7½)"
2¾"
10 (10, 10½)"
19¾ (19¾, 21¼)"
11½ (11½, 12½)"
1"
10 (11, 11¾)"

SLEEVE

20 (20, 21)"
17 (18½, 18½)"
1½ (1, 1)"
9"

☐ = 8 sts & 10 rows

H	I	J	F	G
C	D	E	A	B
J	F	G	H	I
E	A	B	C	D
G	H	I	J	F
B	C	D	E	A
I	J	F	G	H
D	E	A	B	C
F	G	H	I	J
A	B	C	D	E

40-st rep

Celery (A)
Rose heather (B)
Grey/heather (C)
Brown (D)
Mustard (E)
Brick (F)
Blue (G)
Curry (H)
Blue/green (I)
Light charcoal (J)

selvage sts) every other row 5 (0, 3) times, every 4th row 23 (28, 27) times—98 (98, 102) sts. Work even until piece measures 18½ (19½, 19½)"/46.5 (48.5, 48.5)cm from beg. Bind off.

FINISHING
Block pieces.

Embroidery
With C, work overcast st around each square foll diagram. In each D square, embroider floral motif using chart and embroidery diagrams with random blossom placement.

Left front band
Sew shoulder seams. With RS facing, smaller needles and C, pick up and k118 (118, 126) sts along left front straight edge. Beg with a p2, work in k2, p2 rib for 1¼"/3cm. Bind off knitwise. Place markers on band for 6 buttons, with the first ¾"/2cm from lower edge, the last 3"/7.5cm below first neck dec and 4 others evenly between.

Right front band
Work to correspond to left front band, working buttonholes opposite markers by binding off 3 sts for each button-hole after ½"/1.5cm has been worked.

On next row, cast on 3 sts over bound-off sts.

Neckband
With RS facing, smaller needles and C, pick up and k94 (98, 98) sts around neck edge, including tops of front bands. Work in k2, p2 rib for ½"/1.5cm. Work a buttonhole 2 sts in from right front edge. Rib until band measures 1"/2.5cm. Bind off knitwise. Place markers 10 (10, 10½)"/25 (25, 26.5)cm down from shoulders on front and back. Sew top of sleeves between markers. Sew side and sleeve seams. Sew on buttons.

Icelandic yoke-shaping combines with bands of Fair Isle colorwork and corrugated ribbing to create this beautiful cable-patterned pullover. It's oversized for roomy comfort and easy layering. Shown in size Medium. The Fair Isle Pullover first appeared in the Fall '94 issue of *Vogue Knitting*.

Fair Isle Pullover

FOR INTERMEDIATE KNITTERS

SIZES
To fit Small (Medium, Large). Directions are for smallest size with larger sizes in parentheses. If there is only one figure, it applies to all sizes.

KNITTED MEASUREMENTS
● Bust at underarm 43 (47½, 51)"/109 (120.5, 129.5)cm.
● Length (including neck) 29 (30, 30)"/73.5 (76, 76)cm.
● Sleeve width at upper arm 16¼ (17½, 18½)"/41.5 (44.5, 47)cm.

MATERIALS
Original Yarn
● 4 (4, 5) 3½oz/100g balls (each approx 110yd/100m) of Reynolds *Lopi* (wool 5) in #0058 grey (E)
● 2 3½oz/100g balls (each approx 154yd/139m) of Reynolds *Naturgarn* (wool 5) in #153 taupe (MC)
● 1 ball in #118 navy (A)

● 1 3½oz/100g ball (each approx 170yd/153m) of Reynolds *Candide* (wool 5) in #1 cream (B)
● 2 3½oz/100g balls (each approx 110yd/100m) of Reynolds *Andean Alpaca Regal* (alpaca/wool 5) in #4 light beige (C)
● 1 ball in #2 light grey (D)
● 2 1¾oz/50g balls (each approx 66yd/59m) of Adrienne Vittadini *Gigi* (alpaca/wool 5) in #7638 charcoal grey (F)

Substitute Yarn
● 4 (4, 5) 3½oz/100g balls (each approx 110yd/100m) of Reynolds *Lopi* (wool 5) in #0058 grey (E)
● 4 1¾oz/50g balls (each approx 83yd/75m) of Reynolds *Contessa* (wool/angora/polyamid 5) in #84 camel (MC)
● 1 ball in #78 blue (A)
● 1 3½oz/100g ball (each approx 170yd/153m) of Reynolds *Candide*

(wool 5) in #1 cream (B)
● 2 3½oz/100g balls (each approx 110yd/100m) of Reynolds *Andean Alpaca Regal* (alpaca/wool 5) in #4 light beige (C)
● 2 balls in #3 charcoal grey (F)
● 1 ball in #2 light grey (D)
● One pair size 10½ (6.5mm) needles OR SIZE TO OBTAIN GAUGE
● One each size 10½ (6.5mm) circular needles, 16"/40cm and 29"/80cm long
● Size 8 (5mm) circular needle, 16"/40cm long
● Cable needle (cn)
● Stitch holders and markers

Note
Some of the original yarns used for this sweater are no longer available. Comparable substitutions have been made, which are available at the time of printing. Check gauge of substitute yarns very carefully before beginning.

GAUGE
14 sts and 16½ rows to 4"/10cm over St st using MC and size 10½ (6.5mm) needles. FOR PERFECT FIT, TAKE TIME TO CHECK GAUGE.

STITCH GLOSSARY
Make 3 K into front, back, front of st.
3-st Front Purl Cross Sl 2 to cn, hold to *front*, p1; k2 from cn.
3-st Back Purl Cross Sl 1 to cn, hold to *back*, k2; p1 from cn.
5-st Front Cross Sl 3 to cn, hold to *front*, k2; sl center st (first st on cn reading from left to right) back to LH needle and purl it; k2 from cn.

5-st Back Cross Sl 3 to cn, hold to *back*, k2, sl center st (first st on cn reading from left to right) back to LH needle and purl it; k2 from cn.

Note
Body and sleeves are worked separately, then joined into circularly knit yoke.

BACK
With straight needles and MC, cast on 75 (83, 89) sts. K 1 row.
Beg chart #1: Row 1 (RS) Beg with st 11 (1, 10), work to end of rep, work 12-st rep 7 (6, 8) times, end last rep with st 1 (11, 2). Work chart #1 through row 70.

Sl first and last 6 (6, 7) sts on st holders. Sl rem 63 (71, 75) sts to holder or spare needle.

FRONT
Work as for back.

SLEEVES
With straight needles and MC, cast on 31 (33, 35) sts. K 1 row.
Beg chart #1: Row 1 (RS) Beg with st 9 (8, 7) work to end of rep, work 12-st rep 3 times, end last rep with st 3 (4, 5). Work pat and incs simultaneously as foll: Work chart #1 as established through row 70, AT SAME TIME, beg

with row 11, inc 1 st each side (working inc sts into chart pat) every other row 0 (0, 2) times, every 4th row 11 (14, 13) times, every 6th row 2 (0, 0) times—57 (61, 65) sts. Sl first and last 6 (6, 7) sts on holders. Sl rem 45 (49, 51) sts on holder or spare needle.

YOKE

(Note: For size large only: On row 71, dec 2 sts across each sleeve, 4 sts across front, 4 sts across back—total of 12 decs.)

Joining row: Row 71 With RS facing and longer size 10½ (6.5mm) circular needle, work row 71 of chart #1 across 1 sleeve, front, 2nd sleeve, back—216 (240, 240) sts. Place marker and join. Work chart #1 in rnds as foll:

Rnd 72 Beg with st 2 (6, 6), work to end of rep, work 12-st rep 18 (20, 20) times, end last rep with st 1 (5, 5). Cont to work chart #1 as established in rnds through rnd 77. Cont with E only for rem of piece.

For size small only: Beg chart #2:
Rnd 1 Beg with st 10, work through st 18, work 18-st rep 12 times, end last rep with st 9.

For sizes medium (large) only: Beg chart #3: Rnd 1 Beg with st 11, work to end of rep, work 20-st rep 12 times, end last rep with st 10.

For all sizes: Cont to work charts as established through rnd 34 (39, 39) changing to shorter 10½ (6.5mm) circular needle when necessary—72 sts.

Highneck
Change to size 8 (5mm) circular needle. Rep rnd 39 (k2, p1 rib) until piece measures 12 (13, 13)"/30.5 (33, 33)cm from joining row yoke. Bind off loosely in pat.

FINISHING
Graft underarm sts to body sts. Sew side and sleeve seams.

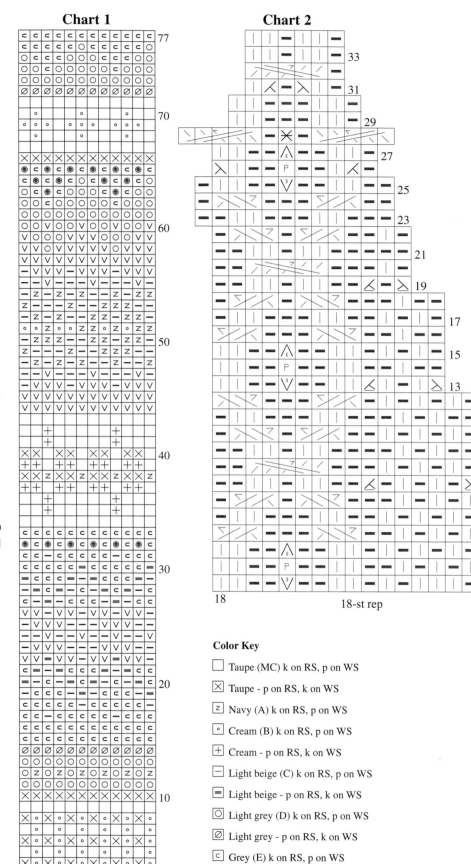

Chart 1

12-st rep

Chart 2

18-st rep

Color Key

☐ Taupe (MC) k on RS, p on WS

☒ Taupe - p on RS, k on WS

z Navy (A) k on RS, p on WS

∘ Cream (B) k on RS, p on WS

+ Cream - p on RS, k on WS

— Light beige (C) k on RS, p on WS

▬ Light beige - p on RS, k on WS

○ Light grey (D) k on RS, p on WS

⊘ Light grey - p on RS, k on WS

c Grey (E) k on RS, p on WS

◉ Grey - p on RS, k on WS

∨ Charcoal grey (F) k on RS, p on WS

Chart 3

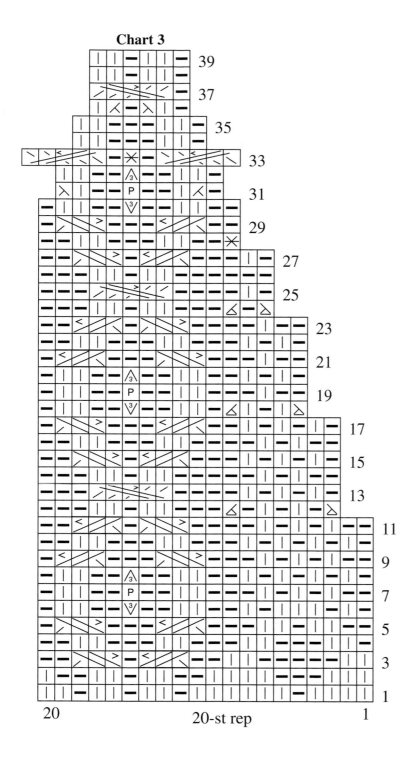

20   20-st rep   1

Stitch Key

☐ K on RS, p on WS

— P on RS, k on WS

⟍ Ssk

⟋ K2tog

◿ P2tog tbl

◺ P2tog

⊠ Sl 1, p2tog, psso

∨ Make 3

△ P3tog

P P 3 sts

3-st Front Purl Cross

3-st Back Purl Cross

5-st Front Cross

5-st Back Cross

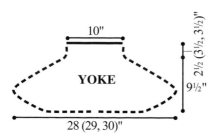

10"

YOKE

2½ (3½, 3½)"

9½"

28 (29, 30)"

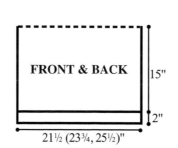

FRONT & BACK

15"

2"

21½ (23¾, 25½)"

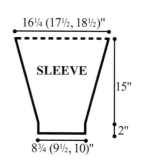

16¼ (17½, 18½)"

SLEEVE

15"

2"

8¾ (9½, 10)"

Elizabeth Zimmermann
Meg Swansen

It's no surprise, when speaking with America's best handknit designers, to hear the name Elizabeth Zimmermann come up again and again. Not only was Elizabeth the source of countless techniques, but she was also an accomplished writer who communicated her passion and love of the craft in her numerous books and articles. In her warm and friendly style, Elizabeth invited people everywhere to pick up their needles and fearlessly explore all that knitting had to offer.

Elizabeth Zimmermann's relationship with *Vogue Knitting* dated back to 1958, when she met with the editors for the first time to show them a few of her designs. While interested in the garments, the editors were also intrigued by the natural unbleached wool that was used to knit some of the sweaters. When her sweater was published, Elizabeth was listed as the source of the unique yarn. That brief mention eventually led to the founding of Elizabeth's mail-order knitting-supply business, Schoolhouse Press, which is headed today by her equally gifted daughter, Meg Swansen.

Meg first joined her mother's business in 1965, and for more than two decades she and Elizabeth wrote and worked as a team. In 1988, Meg took the lead in writing articles for *Vogue Knitting*, and eventually began publishing under her own name after Elizabeth fully retired in 1989.

Like her mother, Meg was taught to knit as a child and took to it almost immediately. "We all learned to knit, my

brother and sister as well, but I'm the only one it really grabbed by the nape of the neck," she says. "It appealed to me." Still, Meg didn't knit much during her school years, finding that most of her knitting needs were already being met by her mother. It wasn't until after her marriage in 1964 to composer Chris Swansen that Meg started knitting professionally. She opened a yarn shop in Pennsylvania, then joined her mother's mail-order business after moving to upstate New York. In the early seventies, after their children were born, the Swansens moved to Wisconsin to be closer to Elizabeth and the rest of the family. "It was nice moving out here," she says, "because then my mother and I were in daily communication about the business and designing and knitting in general."

With a mother and business partner as dynamic and dedicated as Elizabeth Zimmermann, Meg had no choice but to know and speak her own mind. "We didn't always agree," she explains. "I rebelled because I was brought up by a rebellious woman. Elizabeth never took anything at face value, and that's what she taught me: When presented with a new bit of information, the first thing to do is to question it! I was never placid about doing what I was told or accepting what I was told was the way things were."

That uncompromising approach to life is evidenced in Meg's knitting: "I knit exactly what I want," she confesses.

"I'm sure I am influenced by things I see, but to this day, I am practically helpless when it comes to following instructions for a specific design in a magazine. I'm practically incapable of knitting from standard instructions. Anyone who has read any of the *Wool Gatherings* [a biannual publication of original knitting patterns] or any designs I have written on my own will see that I have an unconventional method of constructing a garment and putting a sweater together. I like to present options. 'Knitter's choice' is my feeling—then everyone gets to do what they want."

In her books and magazine articles, Meg, like her mother, depends on the knitter to use their own brain, and provides a minimum of hand-holding: "Elizabeth would give the general garment construction and perhaps the pattern she used, but you had to work it out for yourself and, of course, I've maintained that, because I don't know how to do it any other way! I think I present a bit more in the way of instructions, but not much more," she says.

Housed in an old schoolhouse Elizabeth bought at auction in the early 1970s, Schoolhouse Press has expanded over the years from a mail-order business into a knitting book and video publisher. "After *Knitter's Almanac* (Dover), my mother's second book, was published, we wanted to do a combination video series and book, and we couldn't find any publisher who was interested," she explains. "So we did it ourselves, and that was *The Knitting Workshop* book and the television series, which was shown on PBS public television. That's how we kind of backed into publishing and video production, because we couldn't find anyone else to do it."

Today, in addition to *Wool Gathering*, Schoolhouse Press publishes books by a number of well-known knitting writers, with nineteen titles currently in print. "Producing books is absolutely thrilling," Meg says. "I'm quite unprofessional at it. When I do a book from scratch, I don't follow the standard mode, because basically it's just me and the author. I don't have a staff of editors, proofreaders, and graphic designers. My main concern is that the information is presented clearly, so the knitter can understand what's going on. Our publications are kind of humble."

Meg is characteristically open-minded when discussing her plans for the future. "I have never been a goal-oriented person," she admits. "I enjoy knitting, I enjoy writing, and I find publishing books very exciting. I just hope I can keep doing it and die with my needles in my hand!" Asked if she sees the family legacy being passed on to another generation, she replies that while her daughter and son are both knitters, they are absorbed in other careers. "On the other hand, I now have a granddaughter, Cecelia, and who knows, we might skip a generation! She's fascinated when I knit, she gets hypnotized," and, as a proud grandmother she adds, "she's the light of my life, she's wonderful!" And with such a family behind her, who could expect otherwise?

The very first Aran pattern commercially published in the United States, this historic sweater first appeared in the *Vogue Pattern Book* in 1958. The editors listed Elizabeth Zimmermann as the source of the rare, natural unbleached wool from which the sweater was knit. As a result, orders and inquiries came flooding in, and the mail-order knitting-supply business which is now Schoolhouse Press was born. Shown in size Small, the First American Aran was reprinted in the Winter '98/99 issue of *Vogue Knitting* as a 40th anniversary celebration.

First American Aran

FOR EXPERIENCED KNITTERS

SIZES
To fit Small (Medium, Large). Directions are for smallest size with larger sizes in parentheses. If there is only one figure, it applies to all sizes.

KNITTED MEASUREMENTS
● Bust 38 (41, 45)"/96.5 (104, 114)cm.
● Length 26½"/67cm.
● Upper arm 14 (15½, 16¾)"/35.5 (39.5, 42.5)cm.

MATERIALS
● 6 (6, 7) 4oz/113g balls (each approx 272yd/248m) of Briggs Little/Schoolhouse Press *Regal 2 Ply* (wool 3) in washed white
● One pair each sizes 5 and 6 (3.75 and 4mm) needles OR SIZE TO OBTAIN GAUGE
● Cable needle (cn)
● Stitch holders

GAUGES
• 22 sts and 30 rows to 4"/10cm over St st using size 6 (4mm) needles.
• 25 sts to 4"/10cm over all pats using size 6 (4mm) needles.
FOR PERFECT FIT, TAKE TIME TO CHECK GAUGES.

STITCH GLOSSARY
2-St RC Sk 1 st, wyib insert needle into 2nd st as to p and hold on needle, k the skipped st, drop both sts from LH needle.
2-St LC Sk 1 st, k the 2nd st from the back and hold on needle, sl the skipped st as to p, drop both sts from LH needle.
4-st RC Sl 3 sts to cn and hold to *back*, k1, k3 from cn.
4-st LC Sl 1 st to cn and hold to *front*, k3, k1 from cn.

BACK
With smaller needles, cast on 115 (131, 147) sts. Beg with a WS row, work chart 1 for 23 rows, inc 3 (dec 3, dec 7) sts evenly across last row—118 (128, 140) sts. Change to larger needles.

Beg pats
Reading row 1 of charts from left to right, work as foll:
Next row (WS) P2 (7, 2), [work sts 11-1 of chart 2] 1 (1, 2) times, *14 sts chart 3, sts 25-1 of chart 2*; rep between *'s once more, 14 sts chart 3, [sts 25-15 of chart 2] 1 (1, 2) times, p2 (7, 2). Cont in pats as established, keeping first and last 2 (7, 2) sts in St st, until piece measures 16 (15½, 15)"/40.5 (39, 38)cm from beg.

Armhole shaping
Bind off 6 (6, 7) sts at beg of next 2 rows. Dec 1 st each side on next row, then every other row 5 (6, 5) times more—94 (102, 114) sts. Work even until armhole measures 9½ (10, 10½)"/24 (25.5, 26.5)cm.

Shoulder shaping
Bind off 7 (8, 9) sts at beg of next 4 (6, 2) rows, 8 (9, 10) sts at beg of next 4 (2, 6) rows. Place rem 34 (36, 36) sts on a holder for back neck.

FRONT
Work as for back until armhole measures 8 (8½, 9)"/20 (21.5, 22.5)cm, end with a WS row.

Neck shaping
Next row (RS) Work 37 (40, 46) sts, join 2nd ball of yarn and place center 20 (22, 22) sts on a holder, work to end. Working both sides at once, dec 1 st at each neck edge every other row 7 times. When same length as back to shoulder, shape shoulders as for back.

SLEEVES
With smaller needles, cast on 51 sts. Beg with a WS row, work chart 1 for 23 rows, inc 24 sts evenly across last row—75 sts. Change to larger needles.

Beg pats
Reading row 1 of charts from left to right, work as foll:
Next row (WS) Work sts 11-1 of chart 2, 14 sts chart 3, sts 25-1 of chart 2, 14 sts chart 3, sts 25-15 of chart 2. Cont in pats as established, inc 1 st each side (working inc sts into St st) every 20th (12th, 8th) row 6 (10, 5) times, every 10th row 0 (0, 8) times—87 (95, 101) sts. Work even until piece measures 20"/50.5cm from beg, end with a WS row.

Cap shaping
Bind off 6 (6, 7) sts at beg of next 2

rows. Dec 1 st each side on next row, then every other row 18 (20, 22) times more, bind off 3 sts at beg of next 8 rows. Bind off rem 13 (17, 17) sts.

FINISHING
Block pieces to measurements.

Collar
With RS facing and smaller needles, k 34 (36, 36) sts from back neck holder, inc 17 (15, 15) sts—51 sts. Work 23 rows of chart 1. P next row on WS for turning ridge. Work in k1, p1 rib until same length as first half of collar. Bind off loosely in rib. With RS facing and smaller needles, pick up and k 51 sts evenly along front neck, including sts from holder. Work same as back collar. Sew shoulder and collar seams. Fold collar in half to WS at turning ridge and sew in place. Set in sleeves. Sew side and sleeve seams.

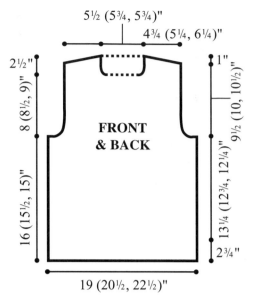

FRONT & BACK

5½ (5¾, 5¾)"
4¾ (5¼, 6¼)"
2½"
1"
8 (8½, 9)"
16 (15½, 15)"
9½ (10, 10½)"
13¼ (12¾, 12¼)"
2¾"
19 (20½, 22½)"

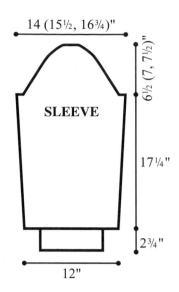

SLEEVE

14 (15½, 16¾)"
6½ (7, 7½)"
17¼"
2¾"
12"

Chart 2

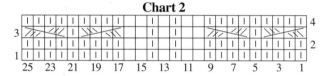

25 23 21 19 17 15 13 11 9 7 5 3 1

Chart 1

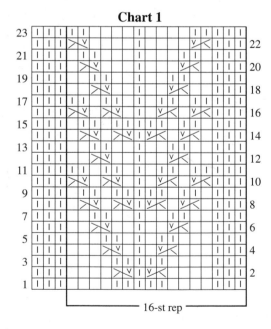

16-st rep

Chart 3

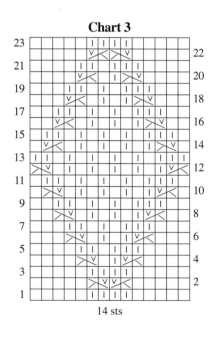

14 sts

Stitch Key

| K on RS, p on WS

☐ P on RS, k on WS

2-st RC

2-st LC

4-st RC

4-st LC

Twisted-Stitch Cap

At first glance, Bavarian Twisted Stitch resembles Aran knitting, but closer inspection reveals a single, significant difference: there are no plain knit stitches, just twisted knit, purl, traveling stitches, and sometimes cables. Meg Swansen has provided different twisted-stitch methods to choose from: decide which one works best for you! The Twisted-Stitch Cap first appeared in the Fall '99 issue of *Vogue Knitting*.

Twisted-Stitch Cap

FOR EXPERIENCED KNITTERS

The origins of Bavarian twisted stitch are somewhat of a mystery. Its earliest documented appearance dates from the late 18th century when it was used in the handknit stockings worn by German and Austrian men. A close cousin of Aran knitting, this intricate technique is prized for its wonderfully sculpted appearance.

To highlight the lovely shapes and make the final fabric look as if it were "carved" in yarn, you need to knit firmly with a wool that has been tightly spun and plied—it will make the twisted designs pop out of the purl background most beautifully.

I have picked out three Bavarian twisted stitch patterns from the books available on the subject and will arrange them around my cap, separated by groups of P1, K1tbl, P1, K1tbl, P1 (represented by an X on the diagram). I have opted for no border on the blue hat; the yellow begins with a small band of ribbing. You may also begin with garter-stitch. I have named the three patterns #1 (16 sts wide), #2 (7 sts wide), and #3 (12 sts wide) and the in-between groups I will call X (5 sts wide).—*Meg Swansen*

MATERIALS
● 1 3½oz/100g ball (each approx 245yd/233m) of Wendy/Berroco, Inc. *Guernsey Wool* in #674 blue or 1 3½oz/100g ball (each aprox 210 yd/199m) of Schoolhouse Press *Canadian Québécoise* in yellow
● Size 4 to 6 (3.5 to 4mm) circular needle,16" (40.5cm) long

Cast on 142 sts. Establish patterns according to the charts shown. Continue for about 7"/17.5cm.

SHAPE TOP
I decided to continue the patterns to the bitter end and use the Xs as decrease points. Since the Xs are not evenly spaced from each other, I was very interested to see what would happen. On the blue version, I decided to swirl to the left by working the 2nd K1tbl (of the X group) together with the purl that followed it (SSK). If you want to lean right, work the first K1tbl together with the purl that precedes it (K2tog). If you want to go straight, as in the yellow cap, work a dec at either side of the Xs on every 4th round.

*So, decrease 1 stitch at each of the 8 Xs, then work one round plain, maintaining continuity of patterns. Repeat from * until you have about half the stitches remaining, then speed up the decrease by working it every round down to practically nothing (switching to double-pointed needles when necessary). Draw the working wool through the remaining few stitches and finish

off. See how the widely spaced decreases consumed the close-together ones? Isn't it lovely?

Block the hat to suit your taste.

BAVARIAN TWISTED-STITCH CLINIC
There are four different methods of working each twisted-traveling-stitch situation. Practice each one and check the results against the ease of execution—then make your decision. Every time I say "knit" it is understood that I mean knit into the back of the stitch.

RIGHT TWIST K OVER P (2-ST RPT)
A. Leave the 2 stitches on the L needle and work them out of order: go between the stitches and K into 2nd stitch. Bring wool to front and P the 1st stitch. Slip them both off the L needle. Next are 3 variations of reversing the position of the sts on L needle.
B. Take the 2 sts off the L needle and pick them up again in reverse order (with the K in front) and work.
C. Transfer both sts to R needle. With L needle grab the P from behind and slide both sts off R needle letting the K fall free for a moment. Pick up the K. Replace both sts onto L needle and work.
D. Leave sts on L needle. Grab K from front and slide both sts off L needle letting P fall free for a moment. Pick it up (from behind) onto L needle. Insert L needle into K stitch on R needle and work.

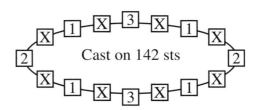

Cast on 142 sts

RIGHT TWIST K OVER K (2-ST RT)

Work as above, substituting a K for the P stitch.

LEFT TWIST K OVER P (2-ST LPT)

A. Work sts out of order on L needle (a mean feat, this one)—from behind. Insert R needle between the 2 sts. Grab the near side of the P st and yank it to the back. Purl into it (with help from the L needle), then K first stitch.

B. Take the 2 sts off the L needle and pick them up again in reverse order–ducking under the working wool when picking up the P st—and work.

C. Transfer both sts to R needle. With L needle grab K from in front and slide both sts off R needle, letting the P fall free for a moment. Pick up the P from behind (and under working wool) with R needle. Put on L needle and work.

D. Leave sts on L needle. From under the working wool, grab P from behind and slip both sts off L needle. Pick up K with L needle. Slip P to L needle and work the sts.

LEFT TWIST K OVER K (2-ST LT)

As above substituting a K for the P stitch. A is not such a bear; and in B, C and D there is no need to duck under working wool.

RIGHT TWIST K2B OVER P (3-ST RC)

B, C and D as in the first method—with the addition of a second K stitch. (A is not worth the effort.)

LEFT TWIST K2B OVER P

A, B, C and D as in the second method—with the addition of a second K stitch.

I prefer method C in all cases, as, for me, there is the least distortion of stitches.

Pattern 2

7 sts

Pattern 1

16 sts

Pattern 3

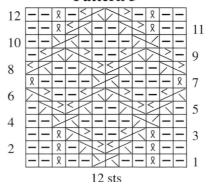

12 sts

Only Elizabeth Zimmermann, with her passion, enthusiasm, and incredible talent, could rise to the challenge of incorporating the universal principle of the Moebius ring—a ring with one surface and one edge—into a knitted garment. Woven seamlessly in garter stitch, the ring can be worn as a scarf, hood, or combination of both. The Moebius Ring first appeared in the Holiday '87 issue of *Vogue Knitting*.

The Moebius Ring

VERY EASY VERY VOGUE

Some years ago at a knitting workshop in the Twin Cities, a voice piped up asking if I had any opinion on the Moebius Ring. I admitted ignorance, and the questioner proceeded to perform a piece of sheer magic: she showed us a long strip of paper (a yard long by 2 inches wide), gave it half a twist and taped the ends firmly together. All right, we said, so what? All right, she said, which is the inside and which the outside of this paper circle? She placed her finger on the "front," and without removing it from that surface, traced the entire circle, inside and out, and lo! The front and the back were the same...try it and see. She showed us that the right-hand edge of the piece of paper (or the left-hand one if you prefer) was the only edge it had. We were struck practically speechless; this demonstration had all the earmarks of a miracle.

We were told that this ring was the discovery of an 18th-century German mathematician/topologist, August Ferdinand Moebius. The theory has been advanced that its principle embodies the riddle of the universe, and this certainly makes sense to me, ignorant of science as I am. However, I am not ignorant of knitting, and my second thought was—why not knit one?

Since I produce nearly all my knitting on circular needles, I could not resist casting stitches onto a round needle, then "join being careful to twist." Alas, this does not work as it gives the knitting a 360-degree spiral when only a 180-degree turn is required. Try again.

With a #10 (6mm) needle, I cast on some stitches in 2-ply Icelandic wool and knitted straight for about 55 inches (140cm), gave it half a twist (180 degrees), wove the beginning to the end, and produced—wonders—the Moebius Ring.

To knit your own Moebius Ring you have several texture-stitches to choose from. Be sure you select a reversible one (as both sides of the ring will show at the same time), and consider the ease with which the stitch will weave to itself. We have made them in garter stitch, mistake stitch, lace, seed stitch, and ribbing. It is garter stitch I recommend as it is simple to knit and can be woven perfectly. A beginner can make a strip of garter stitch, twist it, connect the ends, and produce the Riddle of the Universe, for a very first project.

The selvage (singular!) when completed, looks a bit lonesome. You may border it with I-cord, either built-in or applied in a contrasting color; I offer directions for both.

This is the warmest imaginable piece of headgear. Put it around your head as a scarf; the twist will lie nice and flat under your coat. Or, allow the twist to twist and pull the resulting loop over your head for a combination scarf/hat.
—*Elizabeth Zimmermann*

THE ENDLESS SEAMLESS ONE-SURFACED ONE-EDGED SCARF/HAT

MATERIALS
● 3 9oz/100g wheels of Schoolhouse Press *Unspun Icelandic Wool*
● 1 wheel contrasting color for trim (optional)
● Size 8-10 (5 to 6mm) needle OR SIZE TO OBTAIN GAUGE.

Note For once gauge is not critical.

Cast on about 8-10"/20.5 to 25.5cm worth of stitches. Use invisible cast on, or be prepared to pick out regular casting on to facilitate weaving when finished. Work back and forth in all knit.

BUILT-IN I-CORD BORDER
*K to last 3 sts, wool forward (wyif), slip 3 purlwise, turn. Repeat from *.

At about 50-55"/127 to 140cm, pull out the invisible casting on (or unpick regular casting on) to reveal a row of stitches. Give one end of the piece half a turn and weave.

To heighten the mysterious appearance of the ring, you may want to edge it in a contrasting color with applied I-cord. In that case, omit the purlwise slipped stitches. Slip each first stitch and knit each last stitch. When piece is finished and woven, with a smaller double-pointed needle, pick up one stitch for each ridge (about 12 at a time). At right-hand edge of double-pointed needle, cast on 3 sts. *K2, slip 1, k1 picked-up stitch, psso. Replace the 3 sts onto left-hand needle and repeat from *. This makes a spectacular selvage and you arrive back where you started— yes! only one edge! Weave the 3 I-cord stitches to each other. That's it.

Above directions were previously published in Elizabeth Zimmermann's Wool Gathering *and are reprinted by permission of Schoolhouse Press.*

Tomten, meaning "elf" in Swedish, is the name Elizabeth chose for this adorable hooded baby's jacket. Its size is determined by the total width factor, so you can knit it in a wide variety of yarns. Here it's knit in heather grey Shetland wool with bright red trim to emphasize the Nordic flavor. Shown in size 12 months. The Tomten Jacket first appeared in the Spring/Summer '88 issue of *Vogue Knitting*.

The Tomten Jacket

FOR INTERMEDIATE KNITTERS

There are few knitting pleasures greater than that of knitting for babies. First, one knits love into every stitch; and second, the projects are small and finished quickly. Is it not possible that wool was made for babies? Why not start right off with it, and let them automatically adjust themselves to wool's warmth and comfort. Wool wears so beautifully that the finished sweater or blanket may become a cherished and beloved family garment.

Which reminds me of the Tomten jacket, now over 50 years old, which was worn by our three children and is still a treasure. It was knitted up in a soft grey worsted-weight wool at a gauge of four stitches to one inch. Grey is a practical color, and so becoming to babies. I much prefer muted heather shades to the standard pink, powder blue, and yellow. The lovely Shetland colors—silver, moon, beige, and lovat, the last being an indescribable soft grey/green, originally achieved with lichen dyes, which is the color of the Scottish hills on a misty day—these are colors for a baby.

Back to the Tomten: There is practically no shaping except for the sleeves and the back of the hood. Or you may eliminate the hood entirely in favor of a neck border or a collar. Pockets may be worked as you knit, or added when the jacket is completed. (This versatile jacket may be knitted with the sleeves tied over the hands by a drawstring, obviating the need for mittens, and may then grow with the child.)

By the way, "Tomten" is Swedish for "a little elf," who is also kept warm by a pointed hood on his jacket. The following is a *modular* pattern, which can be used for any weight yarn. All operations in the construction of this sweater are fractions of the number of cast-on stitches, which should optimally be divisible by 8.—*Elizabeth Zimmermann*

SIZES
Sample is 10-12 month size. Note: All measurements are given in inches only. By varying wool thicknesses and needle size this pattern can fit from baby to slender adult.

MATERIALS
● 4 4oz/112g skeins of Briggs Little/Schoolhouse Press *Canadian Regal* in soft grey
● One pair size 7 to 8 (4.5 to 5mm) needles or SIZE TO OBTAIN GAUGE

GAUGE
10 sts and 32 rows to 4"/10cm (or 4 sts and 8 rows to 1"/2.5cm) over garter stitch using size 7 to 8 (4.5 to 5mm) needles.

Cast on sufficient stitches (X) for lower edge. We cast on 96 sts to equal 24"/61cm.

Knit (every row for garter st) to wanted length, taking into account a deep armhole. Our sample measures 6" or 48 rows (24 ridges). We also inserted pockets after 3"/7.5cm as follows: Make two pocket linings with single strand by casting on 20 sts. Work 2"/5cm in stockinette stitch. Place sts on a holder. To join pockets, work as follows:

Next Row (RS) K5, bind off 20 sts, k to last 25 sts, bind off 20 sts, k to end.
Next Row K5, k across sts on one holder, k to next bind-off, k across sts on 2nd holder, k to end.

At desired length to underarm, knit ⅛ of X (12 sts), bind off ¼ of X (24 sts), knit ¼ X, bind off ¼ of X. Knit on the remaining ⅛ (12 sts) only until there are twice as many ridges as there are stitches. Therefore, ⅛ of 96 = 12 sts, and 12 times 2 = 24 ridges (48 rows). After these rows have been worked, place stitches on a holder. Work the same number of ridges on the other two sections.

Continue on all (48) stitches, increasing (for hood) 2 stitches at center-back every 2nd row 8 times. The number of increase pairs is equal to ½ of X.

At 24 ridges (¼ X), knit to the center of the piece and weave the stitches together.

Pick up and knit 1 stitch for each ridge (note: we picked up with CC and worked 1 row then changed to MC) along sides of the armholes which is ¼ of X (24 sts) along each side and knit ⅛ of X (12) ridges for sleeves.

Decrease 2 stitches at center every 3rd ridge until ¼ of X (24) stitches remain.

Bind off, and sew sleeve seam. Zipper, if you must, and when baby is quite young, knit a soft hood lining and

sew it in. A twisted cord can be threaded between it and the hood proper so
the hood can be snugged around the
infant's face. We worked I-cord edging
around the front and pocket edges.

*Directions for the Tomten Jacket and
I-cord edging are from Elizabeth
Zimmermann's book, KNITTING
WORKSHOP. Reproduced by permis-
sion of Schoolhouse Press.*

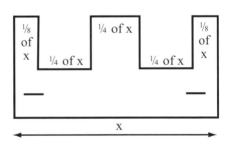

This afghan is snug, soft, and eminently comforting, with the neutral undyed wool shades fitting well into any color scheme. The finished fabric is totally reversible, and, when worked in different directions, creates a fascinating play of light and shadow. If desired, you can alter the size of the finished blanket by adding to, or subtracting from, the base number of stitches. The Garter-Stitch Blanket first appeared in the Winter '94/95 issue of *Vogue Knitting*.

Garter-Stitch Blanket

VERY EASY VERY VOGUE

SIZE
Approximately 42"x 64"/106cm x 162cm figured on a base number of 24 sts and 24 ridges.

MATERIALS
- 5 4oz/112g skeins of Bartlett Yarns *Sheepsdown* (wool) in pale grey (A)
- 11 skeins in medium grey (B)
- 1oz/28g of a finer, more firmly spun matching wool for sewing up.
- Size 10½ and 15 (6.5 to 10mm) circular needle, 24"/60cm long
- Blunt sewing needle

GAUGE
2¼-2½ sts to 1"/2.5cm.

Notes
2 rows = 1 ridge. Slip all first stitches purlwise wyif (or: slip first stitch knitwise, p last st) for a handsome braided selvage. Splice in each new skein of wool to obviate the need to darn in ends; on a reversible item such as this, there is nowhere to hide. If the diagonal line of holes bothers you, you may employ the wrapping technique of short rows at each turn to eliminate them.

PIECE A (make 2)
With color A, cast on 24 sts (base number). Work 24 ridges (48 rows). Turn corner as follows:
K23, turn, work back (just leave the 24th st on the needle).
K22, turn, work back.
K21, turn, work back.
K20, turn, work back, until only

2 sts remain.
K2, turn, work back.
K3, turn, work back.
K4, turn, work back.
K5, turn, work back, picking up the orphan stitches, one at a time, until all 24 sts have been knitted.
Work 24 ridges. Bind off loosely.

PIECE B (make 2)
With color B, cast on 24 sts. Work 24 ridges. Turn corner (as above), work 48 ridges (96 rows), turn corner in the same direction, working 48 ridges, turn corner in the same direction, work 24 ridges. Bind off loosely.

FINISHING
With a blunt sewing needle, assemble the four pieces neatly with the finer more firmly spun matching wool (twisted together with the Sheepsdown if you like; retwist every 5 to 10 sts). Consistency is the watchword as you unite ridge to ridge: there is no right or wrong; just stick to whatever part of the selvage you decide to sew into.

You may want to wash and block the blanket before adding the border. This will allow the fabric to settle into its final dimensions.

I-CORD EDGING
With a smaller-size needle, pick up 1 st for each ridge along the outer selvage (work about 20 sts at a time). On the blanket-size needle, with color A, cast on 2 sts, and immediately transfer them to the pick-up needle. *K1, slip 1, yo, k1 (picked up st), pass 2 threads over (being the 2nd cord st and the yo). Replace 2 sts to lefthand needle, and repeat from*. (If your edging is the same color as the blanket, you may eliminate the yo.) To turn the corner, you need a bit of extra fabric to swing around the point: work to corner stitch (k2 cord sts and replace them to lefthand needle; attach cord to corner stitch as usual. K2, replace to lefthand needle). Continue on to next corner. When you arrive back where you started, unite (weave or sew) the last cord sts to the first.

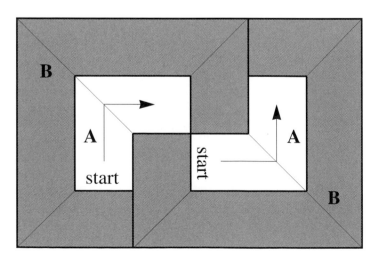

Here's a baby cardigan with an abundance of virtues: It knits up quickly—without much yarn, and it offers you a chance to test new patterns. The Best Baby Sweater first appeared in the Fall '90 issue of *Vogue Knitting*.

Best Baby Sweater

FOR INTERMEDIATE KNITTERS

This baby sweater will grow with the newborn infant, male or female, for a surprising number of months—yea, even years. Starting at the neck in the softest Shetland wool, you work the jacket back and forth in garter stitch until the yoke increases are completed. The rest of the body and sleeves are worked straight, with no concern for shaping within the pattern, and permit you to introduce your favorite texture or lace design.

The front borders are kept in garter stitch, and buttonholes are inserted as you work your way to the lower edge. Finish off the body and sleeves by repeating the initial garter stitch of the yoke, and all that remains is a brief spurt of sleeve sewing and the application of the buttons.

So, there it is. That didn't take long, did it?—*Elizabeth Zimmermann and Meg Swansen*

GAUGE
Approximately 5½ sts to 1"/2.5cm.

STITCH GLOSSARY
Gull Pattern (multiple of 7 sts)
Row 1 and all wrong side rows Purl.
Row 2 *K1, k2tog, yo, k1, yo, ssk, k1; repeat from * to end.
Row 4 *K2tog, yo, k3, yo, ssk; rep from * to end. Repeat rows 1-4.

Note
Work buttonholes one stitch in from one front edge by yo, k2tog and placing them as follows: The first one after 1 ridge (2 rows) and the others about every 8th ridge (16 rows).

Cast on 50 sts and work in garter stitch (knit every row). Work 4 ridges (8 rows).
Next (inc) row K4, *k2, m1; rep from * to last 4 sts, k4—71 sts.

Work 4 ridges. Rep inc row, end k5 instead of k4—102 sts. Work 4 ridges. Rep inc row, omitting 1 inc—148 sts. Change to pat, keeping first and last 4 sts in garter stitch and continuing buttonholes as described. At 4½"/11.5cm, work 25 sts and place them on a holder for the left front. Work back and forth in pat on the next 28 sts (plus 7 sts cast on at each end of them; 42 sts in all for the sleeve) for about 3"/7.5cm, ending with 1"/2.5cm of garter stitch. Work 42 sts and place them on a holder for the back. Rep for 2nd sleeve. Work last 25 sts for right front. Work in pat on rem 92 sts (fronts and back) knitting up 4 X 7 sts at the cast-on sleeve sts (120 sts in all), and cont with pat and border for 5"/12.5cm, or to desired length. Dec 10% (k8, k2tog across) and finish with 1"/2.5cm of garter stitch. Bind off loosely in purl on right side. Sew sleeve seams.

Resources

Write to the yarn companies listed below for yarn purchasing and mail-order information.

BARTLETT YARNS
PO Box 36
Water Street
Harmony, ME 04942

BARUFFA
distributed by Lane Borgosesia
PO Box 217
Colorado Springs, CO 80903

BERROCO, INC.
PO Box 367
14 Elmdale Road
Uxbridge, MA 01569

BRIGGS LITTLE
distributed by Schoolhouse Press
6899 Cary Bluff
Pittsville, WI 54466

CLASSIC ELITE YARNS
300A Jackson Street, #5
Lowell, MA 01852

DALE OF NORWAY, INC.
N16 W23390 Stoneridge Drive
Suite A
Waukesha, WI 53188

FILATURA DI CROSA
distributed by
Tahki/Stacy Charles, Inc.
1059 Manhattan Ave.
Brooklyn, NY 11222

GGH
distributed by Muench Yarns
285 Bel Marin Keys Blvd. Unit J
Novato, CA 94949

JCA
35 Scales Lane
Townsend, MA 01469

JUDI & CO.
18 Gallatin Drive
Dix Hills, NY 11746

K1C2, LLC
2220 Eastman Ave, #105
Ventura, CA 93003

LANG
distributed by Berroco, Inc.
PO Box 367
14 Elmdale Road
Uxbridge, MA 01569

LANE BORGOSESIA U.S.A.
PO Box 217
Colorado Springs, CO 80903

MUENCH YARNS
285 Bel Marin Keys Blvd. Unit J
Novato, CA 94949

NATURALLY
distributed by S. R. Kertzer, Ltd.
105A Winges Road
Woodbridge, ON L4L 6C2
Canada

PATON®
PO Box 40
Listowel, ON N4W 3H3
Canada

PLYMOUTH YARN
PO Box 28
Bristol, PA 19007

REYNOLDS
distributed by JCA
35 Scales Lane
Townsend, MA 01469

ROWAN
distributed by Westminster Fibers
5 Northern Blvd.
Amherst, NH 03031
UK: Green Lane Mill
Holmfirth
West Yorkshire HD7 1RW

SCHAFFHAUSER
distributed by Skacel Collection
PO Box 88110
Seattle, WA 98138-2110

SCHOOLHOUSE PRESS
6899 Cary Bluff
Pittsville, WI 54466

SKACEL COLLECTION
PO Box 88110
Seattle, WA 98138-2110
UK: Spring Mill House
Baildon, Shipley
West Yorkshire BD17 6AD

S.R. KERTZER, LTD.
105A Winges Road
Woodbridge, ON L4L 6C2
Canada

TAHKI•STACY CHARLES,INC.
1059 Manhattan Ave.
Brooklyn, NY 11222

TRENDSETTER YARNS
16742 Stagg St.
Suite 104
Van Nuys, CA 91406

WENDY
distributed by Berroco, Inc.
PO Box 367
14 Elmdale Road
Uxbridge, MA 01569

WESTMINSTER FIBERS
5 Northern Blvd.
Amherst, NH 03031

Vogue Knitting
161 Avenue of the Americas
New York, NY 10013-1252
Fax 212-620-2731
www.vogueknitting.com

In UK and Europe:
Vogue Knitting
New Lane
Havant Hants PO9 2ND, England
Tel 01705 486221
Fax 01705 492769

We have made every effort to ensure the accuracy of the contents of this publication. We are not responsible for any human or typographical errors.

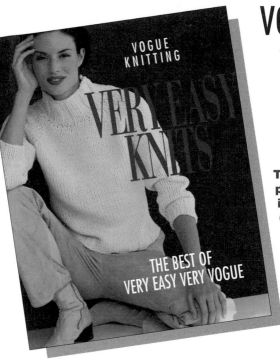
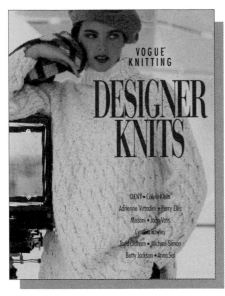

ACKNOWLEDGEMENTS

There are many people who contributed to the making of this book. In particular, and most importantly, we would like to thank the previous editors of *Vogue Knitting* magazine, including Polly Roberts, Marilyn F. Cooperman, Lola Ehrlich, Margaret C. Korn, Meredith Gray Harris, Sonja Bjorklund Dagress, Nancy J. Thomas, Margery Winter, Carla S. Scott, and Gay Bryant, for their vision and impeccable design selections. We would also like to extend our warmest appreciation and gratitude to all of the dedicated and knowledgeable *Vogue Knitting* staff members, past and present, for their skill and countless hours of hard work in bringing the best of knitting to their readers. Special thanks also goes to the tireless knitters and contributing technical experts, without whom the magazine would not be possible.

PHOTO CREDITS

Paul Amato (pages 45, 85, 97, 101, 113, 148 and front cover), Richard Bailey (page 25), Jeffrey Barone (page 13), Courtesy of D. Newton (page 93), Patrick Demarchelier (page 107), Jack Deutsch (pages 155, 157), Robert Diadul (page 33), Arthur Elgort (page 95), Bob Frame (pages 41, 135), Tim Geaney (page 39), Torkil Gudnason (page 124), Barry Hollywood (page 47 and above), Barbara Hunt (page 11), Jim Jordan (page 73), Neil Kirk (page 69), Brian Kraus (pages 111, 119), Francois Lamy (page 63), Frances Milon (page 103), Rudy Molacek (pages 129, 139), Bob Murray (page 153), Kristin Nicholas (page 90), Dewey Nicks (pages 19, 133), Dick Nystrom (pages 57, 78), Leslie O'Shaughnessy (page 61), Clifford Pearson (page 29), Jose Picayo (page 55), Laurie Nicholas Rabe (page 77), Peter Sakas (page 151), Schoolhouse Press (page 143), Peggy Sirota (pages 35, 65), Alberto Tolot (page 23), Robert Trachtenberg (pages 87, 115, 121), Nick Vaccaro (pages 51, 145), Amy Wilton (page 127).